Special Forces
Brothers in Arms

Special Forces Brothers in Arms

Eoin and Ambrose McGonigal: War in the SAS and SBS

Patric McGonigal

Pen & Sword
MILITARY

First published in Great Britain in 2022 by
Pen & Sword Military
An imprint of
Pen & Sword Books Ltd
Yorkshire – Philadelphia

ISBN 978 1 39908 219 8

Typeset by Mac Style
Printed and bound in the UK by CPI Group (UK) Ltd,
Croydon, CR0 4YY.

Pen & Sword Books Limited incorporates the imprints of Atlas,
Archaeology, Aviation, Discovery, Family History, Fiction, History,
Maritime, Military, Military Classics, Politics, Select, Transport,
True Crime, Air World, Frontline Publishing, Leo Cooper, Remember
When, Seaforth Publishing, The Praetorian Press, Wharncliffe
Local History, Wharncliffe Transport, Wharncliffe True Crime
and White Owl.

For a complete list of Pen & Sword titles please contact

PEN & SWORD BOOKS LIMITED
47 Church Street, Barnsley, South Yorkshire, S70 2AS, England
E-mail: enquiries@pen-and-sword.co.uk
Website: www.pen-and-sword.co.uk

Or

PEN AND SWORD BOOKS
1950 Lawrence Rd, Havertown, PA 19083, USA
E-mail: Uspen-and-sword@casematepublishers.com
Website: www.penandswordbooks.com

Pct. Lt. Eoin Christopher McGonigal [97290]: Royal Ulster Rifles; Cameronians (Scottish Rifles); 11 (Scottish) Commando; 'L' Detachment SAS Brigade. (*Image © National Museums Scotland*)

'The way we are living,
timorous or bold,
will have been our life.'

Seamus Heaney

Contents

Acknowledgements ix
Foreword: Lord Ashcroft x
Introduction: Judge Christopher Ian McGonigal xii
Maps xvi
Heroes xvii
Vows xviii

Chapter 1   Brothers   1

Chapter 2   'A Certain Piquancy': 'A Declaration of War on the Irish Nation'   3

Chapter 3   Malone Road, Belfast   9

Chapter 4   Leaders of Boys   18

Chapter 5   Brothers in Law   23

Chapter 6   Leaders of Men: 'Oh, that's for me'   27

Chapter 7   The Royal Ulster Rifles: 'wild young men'   33

Chapter 8   11 (Scottish) Commando in Arran   42

Chapter 9   Landour Spirit: 'I'll shoot you, Blair'   58

Chapter 10   Longing for a show: 'the best trained, disciplined and soldier-like unit of the whole lot'   65

Chapter 11   Egypt–Cyprus: 'C Battalion of Layforce'   76

Chapter 12   Litani River, Syria: Commando Assault 9 June 1941   79

Chapter 13   Aftermath: 'my silver cigarette case'   92

Chapter 14   Blair v Keyes: 'a truculent Irishman'   99

Chapter 15   'Blooded'   104

Chapter 16   'L' Detachment SAS Brigade: a new breed of dervishes   108

Chapter 17   The Final Four Months with a 'band of vagabonds'   117

Chapter 18   Kabrit: 'Stirling's Rest Camp'   122

Chapter 19   Parachute Training: 'nice and soft in the sand'   134

Chapter 20   A Monstrous Scheme: 'desert marching is not meant
            for Irishmen!'   144

Chapter 21   The First (and Last) Parachute Mission: Operation
            Squatter   149

Chapter 22   'Eoin has not yet come back'   183

Chapter 23   Subsequent Missions   192

Chapter 24   The VC: 'a signal act of valour'   196

Chapter 25   Ambrose   201

Chapter 26   Raiding across the Channel: a 'bare-knuckled
            fighting opponent'   205

Chapter 27   Sark   210

Chapter 28   'Hiltforce'   219

Chapter 29   The SBS: 'urgently required for operations in
            Yugoslavia'   223

Chapter 30   Into the Balkans: 'an aggressive, independent
            Irishman'   226

Chapter 31   Croatia – Unie, Cherso, Lussino, Istria: 'Kill the
            f——ing lot of them'   232

Chapter 32   King Farouk and the Charismatic Company
            Commander   241

Chapter 33   Eoin: 'A Huge Character of a Guy'   244

Chapter 34   An Unknown Soldier   257

Chapter 35   Ambrose after Demob: 'The Black Prince'   261

Chapter 36   The First Death Sentence since the Troubles Began   265

Chapter 37   McElhone: 'shot in the back'   268

Chapter 38   'A Torturer's Charter'   271

Chapter 39   'A lawyer, a judge, a soldier and a gentleman'   274

Chapter 40   Brothers and Brothers in Arms   278

Chapter 41   The Brothers – final notes   281

Chapter 42   Heroes   284

Chapter 43   Commando   287

Appendices   290
Bibliography and Sources   336
Index   339

Acknowledgements

Thank you to Tami, Malin and Kaze, my parents and sister for their support and encouragement. And to Christopher McGonigal, Anne, Luke and Emma Charleton, David McGonigal, Jayne McGonigal, Mary-Patricia Smith, Richard and Miranda Hungerford, Peter Forbes, David McCallion (of the unique and outstanding *War Years Remembered* museum), the Fergusons (for permitting access to Blair Mayne's *War Chest*), Alan Orton and Michael McRitchie for the multiple invaluable insights, the Rt Hon Sir Donnell Deeny, Robin Wells, Lorie Randall (née Lorna Welch), Robert and Jan Carson, Kathryn Baird (daughter of Sir Robert 'Beezer' Porter) and David Truesdale. To Martin Dillon, Gavin Mortimer, Michael Asher, Hamish Ross, Damien Lewis, John Lewes, Richard Doherty, Saul David and Gil Boyd – thank you for taking the time to respond to my mostly random requests for information. To the team at Pen & Sword – Henry, George and Matt, thank you for your patience.

Foreword

Lord Ashcroft

My passion for bravery dates back well over half a century to when my father Eric, then a young Army officer, told me about his exploits on Sword Beach, Normandy, during the D-Day landings of 6 June 1944. In more recent years, I have done everything in my powers to champion gallantry through my medal collections, my books, my media work and my lecturing. I believe those who have risked, or even given, their lives for their country, their monarch, their comrades or wider freedoms must *never* be forgotten.

I am particularly pleased when others take up the 'cause' of highlighting the courage of remarkable individuals, particularly when those men (or women) are linked to them by family ties. I was therefore both delighted and honoured when Patric McGonigal asked me to pen the Foreword to his book, *Special Forces Brothers in Arms. Eoin and Ambrose McGonigal: War in the SAS and SBS*.

It was last year (2021) that I first become aware of the courage shown by the McGonigal brothers, particularly Eoin. This was because I researched a major magazine article and short film on the life of Lieutenant Colonel Blair 'Paddy' Mayne DSO & 3 Bars, in which I concluded he was seemingly the bravest man *never* to have been awarded the VC. I discovered that Eoin McGonigal and Mayne, despite being on different sides of the religious divide, were firm friends while serving in the SAS during the Second World War. Furthermore, Mayne and Ambrose McGonigal were well known to each other too.

Patric McGonigal's book does more than simply champion the valour of two soldiers who were, as the subtitle of the book suggests, very much brothers in arms. It tells the story of their entire lives, first growing up in a country, as is Ireland's wont, that meant life was rarely, if ever, straightforward. Ambrose and Eoin McGonigal were born in pre-partition Ireland in 1917 and 1920 respectively. As the unrest in the country grew, their Catholic father John, one of no fewer than seventeen siblings, decided to move his young family from Dublin to his home city of Belfast. When war broke out in September 1939, both brothers had seemed destined to follow their father – and indeed their elder brother Richard, too – into a law career. Instead, they both joined the Royal Ulster Rifles in Ballymena, Count Antrim.

Both men went on to serve with distinction in the newly-formed Special Forces, Eoin with the SAS and Ambrose with the SBS – initially the Special Boat Section and, later, the Special Boat Squadron. Both men showed outstanding bravery in battle but had very different fates – Eoin dying on an early SAS mission in North Africa codenamed Operation Squatter, in late 1941, and Ambrose surviving the war and twice being decorated with the Military Cross (known as an MC & Bar) for his gallantry.

I congratulate Patric McGonigal for delivering a diligently-researched work that is beautifully illustrated with family photographs and other striking images from yesteryear. This is a real labour of love in which the author tells a wonderful story of two courageous brothers and I have no hesitation in commending this book to one and all.

Lord Ashcroft KCMG, PC is an international businessman, philanthropist, author and pollster. For more information on his work, visit www.lordashcroft. com. Follow him on Twitter and Facebook: @LordAshcroft. To view his bravery website, visit: www.lordashcroftonbravery.com.

Introduction

Judge Christopher Ian McGonigal

'My Irish Cousins'

In a reference to the activities of Jellicoe's SBS (the then SAS offshoot), Simon Wingfield Digby, Conservative MP for West Dorset, stood up in the Commons in 1944 and challenged the Prime Minister: 'Is it true, Prime Minister, that there is a body of men out in the Aegean islands, fighting under the Union flag, that are nothing short of being a band of murderous, renegade cut-throats?'

Sir Winston Churchill replied, 'If you do not take your seat and keep quiet, I will send you out to join them!'

While Eoin may have been with the SAS, and later Ambrose may have been with the SBS in the Aegean in 1944 (and involved in a hand-to-hand fighting incident resulting in thirty-seven German casualties), I would defy anyone who tried to describe my Irish cousins as renegades!

Having grown up in England as the son of an Irish-born father whose extended family remained, for the most part, firmly established in Ireland, I have for a long time been fascinated by our family's Irish background and in particular, the stories that surrounded the McGonigal brothers, Ambrose and Eoin.

In times of extreme turmoil, both in Ireland and abroad, little transpired as one might expect in any conventional sense, and the Irish branch of our family seemed to personify this in taking entirely independent, unconventional paths.

The McGonigals did not seem to tie themselves to any particular tradition. The available records reveal a family history starting off in Inishowen Peninsula in Donegal, the most northerly point of the island of Ireland. The location sets the tone for the spirit of the county – independent, untamed and exciting, three quarters of its border framed by the Atlantic Ocean. As Patric explains, the family embraced this environment with stories of priests and smugglers (or 'gentlemen farmers' and traders) eventually giving way to soldiers and lawyers.

Their grandfather was the first to move from Inishowen to Belfast and there he married into a well-known Church of Ireland family – the percentage of such marriages at the time was tiny, less than 1 per cent, reflecting the deeply embedded historical challenges faced by such unions. However, in the McGonigal family they were not unusual. The absence of any partisan approach to life and an ability to straddle both traditions was important given the environment – two of the brothers' aunts and the families of two of their uncles were raised as Protestants. Several of the uncles became lawyers, but there were also seven unmarried and formidable aunts hovering, omnipresent – their father had decreed that none of his daughters should become engaged or get married until all their older sisters had got married. One was a nurse in South Africa in the Boer War and was awarded a Red Cross medal – she became engaged, but her fiancé died, and she blocked her younger sisters (although it may also have been due to a lack of available suitors following the Great War). Another, cousin 'Dorrie', went on to manage the family solicitor business in Belfast despite being neither legally trained nor qualified. Dorrie lived in a gas-lit home and wore dark Victorian dress throughout her life with high necks and skirts down to her

A sombre-looking sisterly gathering!

ankles. She supported many charities and was awarded the MBE for her work as secretary to Naval and Army charities during the two world wars.

There is much more that might be written, but suffice it to say, it was from this family background that we saw Ambrose and Eoin take their lead. They were unconventional and adventurous men; leaders, soldiers and lawyers (in Eoin's case, an aspiring lawyer). Educated in the newly independent Ireland but raised as Catholics in a Northern Ireland which had been designed in 1921 to ensure that a comfortable majority of its population was religiously Protestant and politically Unionist, politics and religion were inextricably entwined. Yet the brothers had no hesitation in choosing to join the British Army and in doing so, choosing to join new units that were formed to carry out unconventional warfare. This was not simply a case of bored and naïve young men opting for an overseas adventure or giving in to public expectation. While some distant examples existed, there was no real blueprint for the British special forces at the time – those who volunteered would be guinea pigs. They would be risking their lives on high-risk operations of an unknown but assuredly 'hazardous' nature and taking the opportunity to make the most of their individual skills and talents.

I have some understanding of this. Just as Ambrose and Eoin joined up in the 1939–45 war, earlier McGonigals joined the army in 1914–18. One – the brothers' first cousin, my father, Harold McGonigal – was raised a Catholic in Westport, in the West of Ireland and later commissioned into the Leinster Regiment. He was posted to the 1st Battalion, part of General Allenby's force which cleared the Turks out of Palestine, and in the process was awarded the Military Cross for bravery. However, apart from the occasional holiday, it marked the beginning of his exile from Ireland. And, if anything, the period was marked by even more confusion in Ireland than when the brothers enlisted just 20 years later.

The IRA's Easter Rising of 1916 in Dublin, though doomed to failure, underlined the deep division and damage that such rifts can produce. Approximately 82 Irish rebel forces and 143 British soldiers and police (of whom 38 were Irish) were killed, and 2,200 civilians and rebels as well as 400 British soldiers and policemen were wounded. Britain's call to arms against Germany only highlighted these tensions – my father was in Dublin on leave from Sandhurst, and perhaps a little naively, his proud mother wanted to show off her soldier son in his Officer Cadet uniform. They walked into St Stephen's Green on Easter Monday and were greeted by rifle shots, quickly forcing them to take refuge in the nearby Stephen's Green Club … Ireland was my father's home, but he would soon leave and after 16 years spent overseas on service, including in Lucknow, India and Shanghaiguan (where he met my mother, working as a governess to the new CO's daughter at the time), he eventually retired back to Hampshire in England. In July 1939, he was recalled to the colours to take command of the East Yorkshire Regimental Depot in Beverley. We never discussed his reasons for not returning to Ireland but I suspect oscillating feelings towards Irish officers in the British Army played their part and would have put him 'beyond the pale' for many – whether swathed in civvies or an officer's uniform.

My father used to joke that, for the Irish, rules were made so that they could broken. He may have left Ireland but was always proud of his country and in particular, his Irish cousins. Although it is spelled differently, I am named after Eoin and it is a link of which I am similarly proud. The McGonigal family was unconventional and the brothers excelled in this regard. Ambrose lived an extraordinary life, not only in terms of his time at war with the Commando and SBS but also in his post-army career in Belfast as the senior Catholic judge during the worst of the Troubles. It seemed that conflict was never far from his life, and he was always working to make up for the life that his younger brother was unable to experience in full. As one of only two officers from an Irish regiment to join the Commando and the youngest of the 'original' five SAS officers, I have no doubt that Eoin would have gone on to achieve even more extraordinary things had he survived. This book is a great personal endeavour and the remembrance of two independent, bold and fearless Irish brothers.

Now retired, His Honour Judge Christopher McGonigal, the former senior partner of international law firm Clifford Chance LLP's contentious business area, was the first solicitor to be appointed a Circuit Mercantile Judge when chosen to lead the then newly established Mercantile Court Lists on the North Eastern Circuit in 1997.

Maps

1. Isle of Arran   51
2. Middle East   79
3. Litani River   83
4. The Western Desert   125

Heroes

In part, we define our ideals and ambitions in life through our heroes, and those ideals help to define us. Our heroes tend to symbolize the characteristics to which we would like to aspire. And to remember who you are or want to be, you will sometimes look to your heroes. This is all the more so when they are family.

Vows

Belfast, 19 December 1941

'Ambrose?'

'Yes mother, I am a little occupied … can it wait? I must get to the church or my bride will kill me!'

'He's not coming back.'

And with that a young man went on to make two vows that day.

Chapter 1

Brothers

Ambrose and Eoin McGonigal were born in Ireland in 1917 and 1920 respectively, at a time of great unrest both in pre-Partition Ireland and in the world. They started life at 18 Herbert Street, Dublin but soon moved north when their father decided to return to his home town of Belfast with his family in 1922. This came just after the War of Independence, the Partition of the island of Ireland under the Government of Ireland Act of 1920 and the birth of the Irish Free State in 1922.

At the time, their father, John McGonigal KC was on his way to becoming one of the most senior barristers in Ireland. John had been called to the Bar in 1892 and although based in the Four Courts in Dublin, Ireland's main judicial building, he practised on the North East circuit. He was a prominent figure at the Chancery Bar (dealing with property disputes, bankruptcies, the administration of wills, probate and trusts) and a lecturer at the Honorable Society of King's Inns in Dublin – the country's principal institution for aspiring lawyers. In short, at the time of the establishment of

John McGonigal KC.

the Supreme Court of Judicature of Northern Ireland in 1921, John was in his prime as a counsel and involved in some of the leading cases of the day.

As such, the decision to leave Dublin to establish a practice at the new Northern Irish Bar was not an entirely obvious step, and John would not have taken it without some reservations. It was not considered a particularly commercial or 'career-enhancing' move; indeed, when the new Northern Irish 'courts' opened on 26 October 1921, only seven silks (KCs) and fourteen junior barristers were present. They gathered under the chairmanship of the Attorney General of Northern Ireland, who appointed a committee to recreate the physical conditions and facilities that barristers enjoyed in Dublin. However, it would take time to establish a viable presence, and it was not until 1933 that new law courts and a dedicated Bar library were finally constructed. An inaugural photo shows John amongst those present, as the Father of the Northern Irish Bar and the only Catholic member at that time. The number of permanently practising members of the new Northern Irish Bar then grew to about sixty and remained at that level all the way through to the early 1970s.

Having grown up as one of seventeen (!) siblings and gone to primary school in Belfast (St Malachy's College, the then leading Roman Catholic school), John had friends and deep family roots in Ulster. This extended to both sides of the ethno-religious divide in the North – the 'mixed' marriage of his mother (Church of Ireland) and father was one of fewer than 1 per cent of all marriages in Ireland. A statute of George II was enacted in 1745 to discourage Protestants from marrying Catholics; it annulled all marriages celebrated by any 'Popish Priest … between Protestant and Papist'. This was supplemented, just four years later, by a further Act making any 'Popish Priest who celebrates any marriage between a protestant and a papist … guilty of a felony, even though the marriage be null and void'. Nevertheless, setting a pattern whereby the McGonigals who followed tended to eschew any unwarranted partisan path in life, John's father Michael had married Catherine Mack in a registry office in Belfast in 1854; she was the daughter of a well-known Church of Ireland family of drapers. Two of the couple's seventeen offspring would go on to marry Church of Ireland wives, and two daughters would be raised in the Church of Ireland tradition like their mother. Michael and Catherine died the same year, 1894, but Catherine was buried separately from Michael and her deceased children, in a Protestant graveyard. So John knew the territory – it would be a return to familiar ground, and the creation of the new courts allowed him to move his family back home and take an active role in supporting the development of the new Bar against the background of a changing political and religious climate in the newly demarcated Six Counties of Northern Ireland.

Chapter 2

'A Certain Piquancy': 'A Declaration of War on the Irish Nation'

Being a Catholic in increasingly sensitive times politically meant that the decision to swap Dublin for Belfast could not be taken lightly – in some Nationalist circles, the possibility of being appointed to the bench in the North by accepting a commission from the King would create much division. John recognized there would be complications he could not control, and perhaps predictably some challenges did emerge.

John became the chief crown prosecutor for Belfast and in time was elected the 'Father' of the Northern Irish Bar. As a KC he was engaged in several of Northern Ireland's biggest cases, an outstanding one of which was the Workman Clark Debenture case, as well as another highly publicized case in which he acted as lead counsel for the Spanish government in connection with various Spanish ships anchored at Belfast and Derry docks. However, he was also repeatedly passed over for appointment as a judge despite public expectation to the contrary. On 5 February 1921, the *Irish Times* reported on various proposals made by Northern Ireland's government after Partition:

> One of the first acts of the new regime will be the setting up of the judiciary for the area. It will consist of two courts – High Court and Appeal Court – and be manned by five judges – the Lord Chief Justice and four judges. Mr Denis Henry K.C. is expected to be the Lord Chief Justice, and the other justices will probably be Mr Justice Moore, Mr T.W. Brown K.C., Mr J.W. Andrews K.C. and Mr J. McGonigal K.C.

Instead, John was controversially appointed to a less senior county court position in Tyrone in 1939. As the first Catholic judge appointed in the North following Partition, (apart from the first Chief Justice – who although a Catholic was not a nationalist and in fact, prior to his appointment, was an Ulster Unionist MP) it was considered a significant appointment, but it had come a full eighteen years after the *Irish Times* article appeared. It was widely believed that religion in particular, as well as an earlier public stance taken against conscription, had played a part against him. Indeed, many years later, when speculation circulated surrounding the possible appointment of his son

John McGonigal KC.

John McGonigal's fob.

Ambrose as a High Court Judge in Northern Ireland, an article in the *Irish Times* of 24 February 1968 noted:

> Mr McGonigal's name has a certain piquancy because his father, Mr John McGonigal, K.C., who went to Belfast at the time of the Treaty as Public Prosecutor, was passed time and again when High Court judgeships became available, and late in life he was given a county court judgeship, a meagre return for his services.

However, things were slow to change and even as late as 1969, only six of the sixty-eight senior judicial appointments that were made were of Catholic lawyers. Still, life on the island of Ireland – in both a political and social sense – has always been complicated. The ongoing debate over borders and Brexit continues the tradition today, and 100 years ago, with Ireland on the path to independence and caught between two world wars, things were no less entangled. This was especially the case for John, for whom contrasting traditions and loyalties presented some difficult decisions. A few years previously, he had taken a public stand against the introduction of compulsory military service in Ireland. In early 1918, as the British Army was finding itself dangerously short of troops on the desperately attritional Western Front, the British Government had sought to extend conscription to Ireland with Parliament at Westminster passing the Military Service Act on 16 April 1918. In response, the Catholic hierarchy of Ireland issued a Declaration:

Taking our stand on Ireland's separate and distinct nationhood, and affirming the principle of liberty that the Governments of nations derive their just powers from the consent of the governed, we deny the right of the British Government, or any external authority, to impose compulsory service in Ireland against the clearly expressed will of the Irish people.

The passing of the Conscription Bill by the British House of Commons must be regarded as a declaration of war on the Irish nation. The alternative to accepting it, as such, is to surrender our liberties and to acknowledge ourselves slaves. It is in direct violation of the rights of small nationalities to self-determination, which even the Prime Minister of England – now prepared to employ naked militarism to force his Act upon Ireland – himself officially announced as an essential condition for peace at the Peace Congress. The attempt to enforce it will be an unwarrantable aggression, which we call upon all Irishmen to resist by the most effective means at their disposal.

With widespread support for this view amongst Irish Catholics resulting in a one-day general strike on 23 April 1918 in railways, docks, factories, mills, theatres, shipyards and so on, John was one of just seventeen (out of eighty-six) King's Counsel to sign a document approving and adopting the Declaration. As a Crown Prosecutor, it cannot have done his career prospects much good, but he had no regrets in putting his name to it, and his decision to do so perhaps tells us something of the source of the independent nature of his two young sons – he was no stranger to controversy if it meant doing what he believed to be right.

ANTI-CONSCRIPTION PLEDGE.

The following is a copy of the Pledge:—

" Denying the right of the British Government to enforce Compulsory Service in this Country *we pledge ourselves solemnly to one another to resist Conscription* by the most effective means at our disposal."

The pledge taken at the church door of every parish in 1918.

It is clear from the language of the following report on the KCs' adoption of the Declaration (written in response to a negative commentary by the *Irish Times*) that tensions were running high:

Since when did the *Irish Times* consider that a man's opinions were entitled to less consideration because he prosecuted criminals on

behalf of the Crown? If Mr [McGonigal] be willing to sacrifice …
£500 [about €33,000 today] per year for conscience sake, I should have
thought that gave added weight to the principles [he stands] for. None
of my senior brethren stood to lose anything by conscription … If your
masters win in this struggle, then the signatories have thrown away
the fairest hope of wealth and dignity that ever blossomed before the
eyes of Irish barristers. If Serjeant Sullivan and his colleagues remained
silent, no man could blame them. Life is a poor thing at first and the
man who would face death with a laugh might well blanch from the
prospect of penury and perhaps worse. The seniors have risked their
lives, in common with their younger countrymen, for the sake for their
country, and that risk would never have threatened them if they had
not voluntarily have assumed it. They have risked more than life, and
Ireland will not forget it. Those who called our profession place-hunters
and hirelings will be the first to regret that they allowed a patriotic zeal
to obscure judgment and charity.

J.F. Meagher … At Sessions, Mallow, April 25, 1918

Sir Edward Carson (centre) and John McGonigal KC (on Carson's right).

Ultimately, the Act was never put into effect, and nobody was conscripted.
However, the saga helped galvanize support for the Nationalists and
influenced events leading up to the Irish War of Independence, which in
turn culminated in the Anglo-Irish Treaty and the ensuing 11-month-long
Irish Civil War of 1922/3. Indeed, for John and his fellow members of the
Law Library in Dublin, the complicated questions of loyalty and allegiance
were brought to their door when on 30 June 1922 the Four Courts building
was destroyed in a massive explosion during the 'Battle of Dublin' – the
start of the Irish Civil War between the Irish Republican Army and the pro-
Treaty Free State forces, which in many cases saw former comrades turned
rival combatants.

The 'Catholics of Derry'

John's independent ways extended also to how he went about his work. Having made the move north, and although a proud Ulsterman, a pride he instilled in his two youngest sons, John found himself having to tread a delicate line as one of the few Catholics in a role as prominent as that of the Senior Crown Prosecutor for Belfast (a position he held from 1917 to 1938). This included his accepting the brief to act as leading counsel for the Nationalists at the 'Wards Inquiry' in Derry in October 1936.

> Derry was the crucible of the civil rights movement … the town in which a Nationalist majority was denied control of local government by a particularly flagrant gerrymander of the electoral boundaries … The … Unionists wanted to reduce the numbers elected to the Corporation from 40 to 24 and to rearrange the wards in such a way as to secure a return of 16 Unionists and 8 Nationalists … the 16 Unionist members would come from 7,536 Unionist voters while the 8 Nationalist members would come from 9,409 nationalist voters. An inquiry was set up and met between the 7 and 9 October 1936.

John is reported in the *Londonderry Sentinel* on 10 October 1936 as having presented the case for the 'Catholics of Derry' – he is quoted, referring to the boundary line between the North and South Wards, as saying: 'It conforms to nothing. As a geographical line it is absurd. This scheme is to prevent the Catholics getting a majority. They have a majority of 27,000 to 18,000 Protestants, but they are only able to get one-third of the representation.'

A report on the Inquiry noted:

> It appears that the case put forward by the Nationalists was well thought-out and close to perfect, whereas the Unionist case was littered with errors. The *Irish News* reported how 'their intelligent and straightforward answering was in striking contrast to the shallow fallacies and evasions which came from the mouths of the Unionist witnesses'… the inspector in charge of the inquiry had little choice but to recommend the rejection of the scheme. This high-profile rejection briefly put the Ministry of Home Affairs in a rather embarrassing position.

As a result, the government was forced to step in, reducing the number of councillors to twenty, nevertheless

> In 1936 the city was divided into three local government electoral wards, two of which elected eight councillors whilst the third ward

elected four. In the North and Waterside wards nearly eight thousand Unionist electors sent twelve representatives to the council, while the huge South ward returned eight Nationalist councillors on a poll of over ten thousand. Unionist control of local government was resented because it represented minority control and the resentment was kept alive by accusations of discrimination in the allocation of council jobs and housing.

John may have been successful in the Wards Inquiry, but Nationalist concerns over the disparity in representation were far from resolved.

Chapter 3

Malone Road, Belfast

What was made of these events and their father's role in such a controversial case by Ambrose and Eoin is not known, but they were both then of an age that these matters would have been of interest – Ambrose had just started at university and Eoin was in his final two years at school.

Politics aside, life for Ambrose and Eoin at the family home in Malone Road, Belfast was generally happy. The family was well off, but there were still plenty of daily chores for the children. There were none of the modern electrical conveniences taken for granted today such as fridges, freezers, dishwashers, washing machines or vacuum cleaners. Food was stored in a larder and clothes were washed on a scrubbing board and dried in a hand-operated mangle. The streets were lit by gas, turned on at dusk by a man with a long, lighted pole. Transport in the city was by electric tram, and milk, bread and coal were delivered by horse and cart.

The brothers' home at 47 Malone Road was a substantial, seven-bedroom property with internal bathrooms and WCs, a large double dining room, a mistress's pantry, scullery and general pantry, as well as a large yard with coalhouse and store. Notably, they also had electric light and a 'Tayco' boiler

Malone Road, Belfast shortly before the McGonigal family's arrival.

Eoin and Ambrose, Ballygally Beach, Larne.

in the kitchen – considerable luxuries at the time, given that electricity in the home and the installation of boilers only became widespread in Britain in the 1930s. Holidays from boarding school in the South were usually spent roaming the coast or the hills, in the nearby seaside town of Ballygally or across in Inishowen, County Donegal, the family's ancestral home.

Ballygally.

There was one elder brother, Richard, known as 'Dick'. He was fifteen years older than Ambrose, and by the time the two younger boys were in secondary school, Dick had already become one of the leading young lawyers at the Irish Bar.

Richard (Dick) McGonigal.

Dick practised in Dublin and on the North West court circuit of Ireland and regularly represented the interests of the Irish government and major corporations in the notable cases of the day (particularly in constitutional matters such as the famous water fluoridation challenge).

Dick was also well-known for his interest in the arts and amassed an enviable collection of jade as well as numerous paintings by the young Jack Yeats (brother of W.B. Yeats), spotted by Dick as an up-and-coming artist. Several of the paintings owned by Dick are now in the National Gallery of Ireland, and one of them is said to have been a portrait of Dick: 'About to Write a Letter' (see below). Dick possessed a Regency-style green swallowtail fancy dress coat and is thought to have posed for a preparatory sketch by Yeats at home.

Dick had the reputation of being a gregarious character. He would host drinks evenings at home during the Horse Show week at the RDS and lunches at Jemmet's in Dublin with an eclectic crowd, including the Waddingtons, the well-known art dealers and Dublin agents for Yeats.

After Partition, when John and the rest of the family moved north, Dick remained in Dublin, eventually becoming Treasurer of the Honorable Society of King's Inns (a role which at that time carried responsibility for the

Jack Yeats, *About to Write a Letter*.

running of the Inns), the 'Father' of the Irish Bar and Ireland's first judge on the European Court of Human Rights in Strasbourg.

The brothers had four sisters. Of these only the eldest, Ina, did not marry and remained at home until after the war. The other three all married Army officers and left home while Ambrose and Eoin were still at school. Peggy,

Richard McGonigal SC sitting at the ECHR.

the second oldest sister, married Charleton Lochinvar Gordon-Steward, an officer in the West Yorkshire Regiment and moved to South Dorset. Cattie, the third sister, married Lieutenant Colonel Humphrey Stacpoole, also of the West Yorkshire Regiment, and also lived in Dorset, but later in Wimbledon. The youngest of the four, Letty, married Colonel Robert John Heyworth ('Jack') Carson OBE of 1 RUR and at that time lived in Antrim, later moving to Kent, where the couple ran a fruit farm.

Cattie McGonigal and her young brothers, Ambrose and Eoin.

With a gap of nine years between Eoin and Letty, the youngest sister, Eoin was very much the baby and doted upon as the youngest of the 'new' McGonigal family. He was named after his father, 'Eoin' being an Irish form of John, although through a family quirk, always pronounced 'Ian' – and he was adored by all. Ambrose, while he always had a wild side to him, was the more serious of the two brothers. From a young age, with Dick long since grown up and living in Dublin, Ambrose appeared to feel a sense of responsibility as the eldest son in the house. Eoin on the other hand was very much the carefree young boy, always quick with a wry comment and a smile, and always getting into trouble. He is often seen in photos with his mother Margaret holding his hand – perhaps a response to her almost losing Eoin when he nearly managed to impale himself on the railings outside the family home as a youngster.

The boys' mother, Margaret Mary ('Dolly') Davoren, was a formidable character. She was born in Dublin, and her father, Richard ('Birdy') Davoren, a solicitor, was a major shareholder in and Chairman of the Dublin Distillers Co Ltd in 1911 – Ireland's largest whiskey enterprise at the time (then valued at IR£650,000 – about €45m today). Unfortunately, it all came crashing down (along with the rest of the Irish whiskey industry) as a result of the rise of the Irish Free State and the ensuing trade war with England as well as prohibition in the US, Ireland's other main market. This was a sore point within the family as much of Margaret's personal wealth was spent paying off the resulting debts – the upshot being that the couple eventually went their separate ways. Indeed, the McGonigals' relationship with alcohol

Eoin McGonigal.

has sometimes been a little troublesome – one of John's cousins from North Donegal was imprisoned in 1925 for being in possession of *poitín* (illegal farm/home-produced alcohol normally made from potatoes); he had been caught with it hidden under a baby in its cot! In fact, in the late nineteenth century it was not uncommon to find so-called 'gentlemen farmers' of flax along parts of the north Donegal coast supplementing their income with the export/smuggling of yarn, linen and alcohol. *A History of Moville* by the Rt Revd Henry Montgomery (1847–1932) records:

> There were adventurous spirits in those days in this far-away spot. I mention no names, but two of the inhabitants of Stroove were yarn merchants. A great deal of flax was grown and spun and woven, and the linen conveyed to market on slipes [sleds] – there were no wheeled vehicles. I think Coleraine must have been their market. But they had other ventures. Vessels brought to Malin Head and Inishowen silks, satins and velvets which escaped the Revenue Officers, and were deposited in a house in Shrove, which is no longer in existence. In one of the rooms of the house there was a bed, and when you removed it a trap door, well concealed, was uncovered: this led to a commodious cellar with shelves all round the walls. An old friend tells me that, when a child, she often descended into that cellar, but was told to make no allusion to it.

On this, all that should be said is that John's grandfather and great-grandfather were both well-established 'gentlemen farmers' from Shrove, Inishowen – just down along the coast from Malin Head. They lived in an area where the land

Richard ('Birdy') Davoren.

Ina Davoren (née Nugent).

was described as 'of inferior quality' and 'in a backward state', yet they managed to have several sons educated at the reputable Greencastle School (where they were taught Latin), pay premiums to masters to teach them to qualify for trades or professions, and support lifestyles appropriate for gentlemen. This included putting one son through King's Inns in 1824 at a time when any person who wished to 'act as a pleader' in any of the King's Courts had to have resided and studied at one of the Inns of Court in London – a requirement which remained in place until 1885 and did not come cheaply. One can assume, however, that the budding lawyer from Shrove would at least have been well dressed!

Margaret and John McGonigal.

As for Richard Davoren, when he wasn't overseeing the collapse of his whiskey empire, he was one of John McGonigal's instructing solicitors when John was still based in Dublin, and this may well have paved the way for John's introduction to Margaret. Margaret's mother, Ina Davoren (née Nugent), was considered an austere, severe woman whose father was said to have been disappointed at the arrival of a daughter and so had her educated as a boy and taught Latin.

Although formidable herself, Margaret could not have been more unlike Ina. Severe she was not, and in comparison with John's more serious persona and slightly distant and formal relationship with the boys, Margaret was known to be great fun, enjoyed singing and worked hard to write and stay in communication when both were away – whether at boarding school, university or in the army. She is described as having been quite unfussy; she would not interfere with decisions made by her children and kept an open house where their friends were always welcome. She also had an interest in Japanese and Chinese art, with a collection of netsuke and snuff bottles which she would mischievously explain to her children and young family friends as 'tear bottles' for crying Chinese ladies.

During the war, when it became difficult to find provisions in the North, Margaret used to hide various goods under her long coat and skirt when travelling up to Belfast from Dublin on the train. On arriving in Belfast she would march through customs saying, 'Young man, over there – those are my suitcases.' No one would dare challenge her. In contrast, the more detached John was known to come home and, seeing the two brothers sometimes wonder out loud, 'Who are those two boys in my front garden?' Nobody was sure whether it was said in jest.

As for his daughters, even though they were much older, John worried about them when they went out dancing late in the evening, so Margaret would sometimes creep out of bed and turn the clocks back an hour or so while he was asleep.

The brothers with their sister, Letty.

Chapter 4

Leaders of Boys

Despite the McGonigal family's ties to Ulster, Ambrose and Eoin both attended schools in the South. They started off as primary boarders at Dominicans in Cabra, Dublin. However, this was not a happy experience for them – they both hated it and attempted several 'escapes'. As a result, they were both then sent to attend senior school at Clongowes Wood College in County Kildare – a far happier experience. Clongowes is a Catholic boarding school that has been described as the 'Eton of Ireland', having produced a disproportionately high number of Ireland's lawyers and CEOs (or as one McGonigal wife once put it, in slightly more prosaic fashion, 'only the cream of Ireland – sons who were rich and thick'). Ambrose attended from 1930 to 1936 and Eoin from 1931 to 1938 – Eoin hated Cabra so much that his parents managed to get him into Clongowes a year earlier than planned.

Ambrose and Eoin both did well academically and both excelled at sports – they were the archetypal all-rounders and popular leaders at school. A love of sport ran in the family; their grandfather Michael was a founder

Clongowes Wood College.

A TRIBUTE TO THE MEMBERS OF THIS CLUB WHO SERVED
IN THE SECOND WORLD WAR 1939-1945 AND IN HONOURED MEMORY
OF THE 28 WHO GAVE THEIR LIVES FOR THEIR KING AND COUNTRY

K.D.ADAMS	P.G.E.IRELAND	F.W.McMURRAY	D.E.REAY
R.ALEXANDER	G.B.S.JACKSON	G.A.MAGINNIS	C.N.REAY
S.D.CORRY	D.LOUDEN	R.H.MARTIN	H.D.ROBINSON
J.G.M.ERSKINE	W.T.McCALLA	T.D.MAYNE	J.F.SMELLIE
D.H.FREELAND	R.H.S.McCONNELL	R.N.MORGAN	G.L.STEED
S.N.GRAY	J.T.M.McFADDEN	W.W.PHILLIPS	J.G.STEWART
W.J.HURST	E.McGONIGAL	H.M.POLLOCK	S.F.STEWART

THEY PLAYED THE GAME

Memorial once housed at the North of Ireland Cricket and Football Club on Ormeau Road, Belfast. (*N.I. War Memorial Museum*)

member of the famous North of Ireland Cricket (and later Rugby Football) Club (the 'North') at Ormeau Road (founded in 1859 and now called Belfast Harlequins following a merger with Collegians in 1999). It was located off Malone Road in South Belfast, and Ambrose and Eoin were members. John was also a keen sportsman in his younger years – he especially enjoyed cricket but was also a keen golfer and county-level tennis player.

The brothers inherited their father's love of sport and were very competitive. Being a little older, Ambrose always led the way, with Eoin striving to match and outdo him. This was quite a challenge for both boys; whereas Ambrose was tall for his age, strong and aggressive, Eoin was slighter in stature but fast and particularly competitive.

Both captained the school cricket teams for their respective years and both played in back row positions for the school's rugby 'firsts' teams during their years there, including their respective senior cup teams. In fact, Ambrose, who was also a keen boxer at school, played for the Clongowes senior cup

Ambrose – front, 4th right, standing below the first step but as tall as those around him!

rugby team in the schools national finals at the home of Irish rugby, Lansdowne Road, on 2 April 1936. In the same year he also won an interprovincial rugby cap for Leinster against Ulster at Ravenhill, Belfast on 25 March.

The school annual described Ambrose as a 'good, and at times, almost a brilliant third row forward.' Faint praise perhaps, but as they say, even though 'almost' never won the race, he did at least make it to Lansdowne Road!

Eoin never made it to the senior rugby cup finals, but unlike Ambrose he

Ambrose, top middle.

did captain the senior cup team and won three interprovincial rugby caps for Leinster as well as one for Leinster in cricket, when he played against Ulster at Cliftonville in Belfast on 4 July 1938. In fact, there wasn't too much that Eoin didn't excel in at Clongowes, since he also played for the school tennis team.

However, rugby was Eoin's real passion and as captain of the school team, the 1936 school annual noted that 'his keenness both in practice and in matches did much to encourage and inspire the rest of the team. As a leader, he directed the forwards well and was always at the forefront of the attack.'

hoto]   THE HOUSE XV.   [Keogh Bros
Standing : R. Thompson, E. O'Malley, W. O'Meara, B. Devane, O. Lochrin, F. O'Meara.
Seated : J. Leonard, A. McGonigal, A. Devane, D. Kent (Capt.), A. Comyn, D. Fleury, L. McMonagle.
On Ground : M. Ahearne, E. White.

Eoin, Captain of House XV with Leinster and CWC caps.

In his final year, as captain of the senior rugby cup team, taking penalties and playing lock, it was noted in the school annual that 'among the forwards, E. McGonigal was the best. As a tribute to him let us say that all the other forwards deserve the highest praise.'

Eoin was also an opening batsman, wicketkeeper and captain of the school cricket team. As noted in the school annual, he was 'above Lower Line standard in batting. He has two invaluable qualities – steadiness, and the patience to wait for the bad balls. When they come,

Eoin, for CWC and Leinster cricket.

he seldom misses them, with the result that he gets plenty of runs … He has a quick eye, good hands and an abundance of courage.'

And in the following year's annual: 'The batting was our strong point, and E. McGonigal, perhaps, was the best bat. He hits hard and keeps the ball always on the ground. His off and on drives are his most powerful strokes … As a wicket keeper also he deserves much praise.'

Academically, with records only retained from the 1936 Annual, Ambrose is recorded as having won house prizes at Christmas in Latin, English and French, while Eoin won a house prize in Latin. In his Leaving Certificate exams Ambrose achieved honours in English, Latin, History, Geography and Mathematics, while Eoin achieved honours in his Intermediate Certificate exams in English, Greek, Latin, French, History, Geography and Mathematics.

Ambrose and Eoin were also both appointed 'leaders' of the Clongowes Debating Society. In 1936, as leader in support of the motion 'That War is at times necessary for National Development', Ambrose was described as speaking 'unfalteringly for the Government and seemed to leave little doubt in the minds of his hearers'. And on the influence of cinema '[Ambrose] made a fine speech; he showed how the cinema often changes the plots of books, destroying their dignity in order to get sensation, and often their whole theme to satisfy the masses' – a concern that, coincidentally in the case of the SAS 'originals', is sometimes now levelled at the makers of historical, military-related dramas.

Similarly, in a debate reported in the *Leinster Leader* in 1936 which celebrated the Society's centenary and involved past pupils who were past debate gold medallists, it was reported that 'Ambrose McGonigal, in the best-delivered speech of the boys, vigorously attacked the pretensions of the Anglo-Irish literature to be really Irish at all.'

In turn, two years later, Eoin was noted for being 'very good at repartee' and won the President of the Union's Prize for impromptu speaking in his final year. Eoin was a larger than life personality, and a typical quote from the school annuals reads: 'Our deputy from Belfast, E. McGonigal, was as usual in good form and provided us with a speech which effectively combined humour and reason. He, of course, is one of our veteran debaters, and with such a reputation, that an excellent speech can almost be taken for granted.'

In an earlier edition, when debating the motion 'That the greatest glory of a nation is its literature', it was reported of Eoin that he 'in a warlike speech agreed' with the sentiment that 'Men are stirred by love of country, as no other motive, save religion, can move them, and they gladly sacrifice their lives that the spirit of their country may live' – a sentiment which might be said to have foreshadowed what in his case later became all too real a prospect. Eoin concluded the motion by saying that 'the sword … must triumph over the pen if nations are to be truly free, and that 'Cuchulainn defending his native Ulster 'against his enemies the men of Ireland' was a picture to stir the blood of patriots.' (Cuchulainn was a mythological Irish hero who defended Ulster single-handedly against armies from Connaught.)

Chapter 5

Brothers in Law

After leaving Clongowes, Ambrose went on to attend Queen's University, Belfast where, in his own words, he spent 'two inglorious years' studying for an arts degree before changing course and enrolling at King's Inns in Dublin (where his father had been a lecturer from 1910 to 1938) with the aim of becoming a barrister.

At the same time, in autumn 1938, Eoin enrolled at Trinity College, Dublin to study law. This was a similar route to that already taken by their elder brother Dick, save that although Dick also attended university in Dublin (obtaining a master's degree in science before going on to study at King's Inns), he graduated from University College Dublin (UCD). As a Catholic born in Dublin, Eoin was not in theory permitted to attend Trinity and so should probably have followed Dick's path to UCD. In response to the imposition of restrictions on membership of Trinity whereby professorships, scholarships and fellowships were reserved for Protestants, the Catholic hierarchy in Ireland banned Irish Catholics from attending Trinity for 99 years – only removing the ban in 1970. Eoin did not have dispensation from the Irish church to study law at Trinity but enrolled instead, on the basis of his family's address in Belfast, as a British Catholic – an option not available to Dick at the time he left school. Eoin never gave any indication of being particularly religious, and having been born a British subject, the question of nationality would have been mostly a question of practicality; Eoin always saw himself (as did Ambrose) as an Ulsterman first and foremost.

For whatever reason, whether a lack of imagination, the existence of an established network, the intellectual challenge or a sense of independence and duty, the McGonigal family was steeped in the law and had produced several advocates and attorneys (solicitors) who had passed through the doors of King's Inns. The brothers' grandfather Michael McGonigal a prominent businessman and property owner from Inishowen, County Donegal, was a Justice of the Peace in County Antrim at a time when such a role was viewed as carrying considerable local prestige. Michael's uncle and younger brother both attended King's Inns, and more than one son qualified through King's Inns to practise law. In fact, Richard and Ambrose were the

The Honorable Society of King's Inns, Dublin.

fourth generation of McGonigals in succession to study law at King's Inns, following in the steps of relations practising on both sides of the border since their great-great-uncle David McGonigal first entered King's Inns in 1824. The line continues unbroken today, almost 200 years later, with Ambrose's son, Eoin McGonigal SC, who qualified from King's Inns and was called to the Bar in 1971.

In fact, the family could not have started much earlier given that after the Williamite-Jacobite wars of the 1690s, Catholics were effectively excluded from the legal profession by the Penal Laws. This exclusion lasted until the Catholic Relief Act of 1792, when they were allowed to practise at the outer Bar.

In the mid-twentieth century a career at the Bar in Ireland was seen in a quite different light to today. It was considered an honourable profession, and the pursuit of financial reward was not a primary motivation for training as a barrister (or even a realistic one in Ireland for much of the time). Instead, most young lawyers were drawn to a life as independent journeymen advocates, very much adhering to the 'cab-rank rule' – taking on whatever work came through their door, regardless of their clients' character, reputation, cause, guilt or innocence. A great many barristers were idealists, attracted to the role of representing those who were unable to represent themselves. This carried over into political life, and the fact that many barristers in those days were actively engaged in Ireland's fight for independence – whether on the side of the Ulster Unionists, such as Edward Carson, or the Home Rulers, such as Daniel O'Connell and later Padraig Pearse. The website of the Law Library of Ireland explains:

The major changes in the Irish legal system in the first half of the twentieth century merely reflected the dramatic changes taking place politically. First, many people embraced a more radical nationalism after the Easter Rising of 1916, culminating in independence. In 1921 the country was partitioned with the creation of the state of Northern Ireland. Both events had a major impact on the law and were heavily influenced by lawyers.

The failure to secure Home Rule before the outbreak of the First World War led to attempts to obtain independence through other means. The Easter Rising of 1916, which was organised by Patrick [Padraig] Pearse, marked the beginning of a radical new phase in Irish nationalism. The execution of the leaders brought about a dramatic shift in public opinion and in the general election of 1918 the Sinn Féin party won a majority of the Irish seats. They refused to go to Westminster and instead set up their own parliament in Dublin – the Dáil – declaring independence from Britain in January 1919. This led to a bitter conflict, the Irish War of Independence, which ended in December 1921 with the signing of the Anglo-Irish Treaty that established the Irish Free State.

'The Hungry Tree' in the grounds of King's Inns.

The Irish Bar was also divided by partition, with the creation of a separate Bar for Northern Ireland. Barristers had to choose in which jurisdiction they would practise. The King's Inns provided books for the use of the members who practised in the North. To this day close relations are maintained with the Bar of Northern Ireland.

The Bar in Ireland has changed considerably over the past 200 years, with perhaps the most significant change being the dramatic increase in the number of people qualifying as barristers. From a figure of just 330 members registered in 1920 (not all of whom would have been active), there are now approximately 2,300 practising barristers – the increase being attributed as much to financial ambition as anything else, since the practice of law is now perceived to be a lucrative career. This is despite it having gradually become more and more difficult for junior barristers to survive beyond even their first year or two in practice. On 10 June 2021, the chair of the Council of the Bar of Ireland was reported as saying, 'While there is a perception that the barrister's profession is one that is highly remunerated, the fact is that junior barristers appearing in the district court in criminal matters are paid €25 for an appearance, that is often their only fee earned in a day.' Nevertheless, other areas of the law are more lucrative, and the Bar is now invariably seen by the public as a profession of expensively hired guns (working solely for their clients' interests to the exclusion of any wider duties owed to the courts, third parties or the public interest), as opposed to having any connection with those who picked up guns to fight for freedom, whether Ireland's or that of the Allied nations in the two world wars.

Coincidentally, the shift in public perception of barristers was due in no small part to the sensationalist reporting of fees paid those involved in various tribunals of inquiry established to address a succession of political controversies, principally beginning with the 'Beef Tribunal' in the early 1990s, in which Ambrose's son Eoin acted on behalf of the Tribunal.

As it was, the McGonigal brothers only managed to complete a year's legal study before war intervened.

Chapter 6

Leaders of Men: 'Oh, that's for me'

Despite being born into a Catholic family, educated in the recently liberated, neutral Republic and enjoying good career prospects in the law, Ambrose and Eoin both joined the Royal Ulster Rifles in Ballymena at the outbreak of war.

This presented difficult questions for their parents – while proud that their sons had not hesitated to volunteer, Margaret and John both understood only too well the harsh realities of young men going off to war; many of those who went (like Margaret's own brother, who was killed in the Great War) would not return. As for John, he had opposed forced enlistment for Ireland during the First World War partly so that young Irishmen like Ambrose and Eoin would have a choice. As their father he was concerned for them personally, but he understood their desire as proud Ulstermen to sign up and fight. He also recognized there was little point trying to talk them out of it. Having lived through the Great War and experienced at first hand the impact of civil unrest in Ireland, he knew there was very little romance involved in war of any type; it was primarily a creature of politics and fed upon the imagination and zeal of youth. Eoin was determined to play his part against the Nazis, and Ambrose was never going to let his younger brother enlist alone. John had worked hard to try to protect them from having to make such a choice, but like so many fathers (and mothers) of the day he stood aside to let them find their own way.

The brothers lived in a politically charged environment and so, as with other Irish volunteers, their personal motivations could not have been straightforward. They were British subjects by birth but educated in the newly created, semi-independent Irish Free State where, at least initially, many people still viewed any enemy of England as a friend of Ireland (with some in the Irish Republican movement even choosing to side with the Third Reich, in the belief this might eventually lead to a united Ireland). It should be remembered that on 29 December 1937, the Irish Free State came to an end – the Oath of Allegiance to the King was abolished and a new Constitution came into force: the state formally became 'Ireland' and entirely independent. The poet Francis Ledwidge, who was to die in preparation for the Third Battle of Ypres in 1917, perhaps best exemplifies the fluctuating Irish nationalist sentiment towards war and relations with Britain: 'I joined the British Army because she stood between Ireland and an enemy common to our civilization, and I would not have her say that she defended us while we did nothing at home but pass resolutions.' However, after the leaders of the 1916 Easter Rising – including his friend and literary mentor Thomas MacDonagh – were executed during his military leave, he is reported by Lord Dunsany to have said, 'If someone were to tell me now that the Germans were coming in over our back wall, I wouldn't lift a finger to stop them. They could come!'

Nevertheless, as the situation became clearer, a significant number of Irishmen (estimated conservatively to have been at least 50–70,000 from the Republic and 35–40,000 from Northern Ireland) eventually recognized the urgent threat presented by Hitler and volunteered to join the Allied forces throughout the course of the war. Theirs was a vital contribution, and as Rudyard Kipling, who lost his son, Lieutenant John Kipling of the Irish Guards, in the First World War, famously noted:

> Head to the storm as they faced it before!
> For where there are Irish there's bound to be fighting,
> And when there's no fighting it's Ireland no more.

Those who did enlist also included 4,983 members of the Irish Defence Forces who had to risk being prosecuted as deserters to do so. Indeed, on 8 August 1945 the Irish Government issued what is commonly referred to as the 'Starvation Order' – essentially, a list of all those former members of the Irish Defence Forces who had joined the Allies. The Order meant that those whose names were listed lost their pension rights and unemployment benefits, and were barred from holding any government or public sector jobs – marked confidential, the list was circulated to all civil service departments and state-run services such as post offices, the health service, state-owned bus, rail, air and shipping companies, etc. It made finding employment very difficult and resulted in great hardship for those affected. Eventually, an amnesty was provided to over 7,000 soldiers by the Irish Government, but not until 2013 (the figure including both those who had been affected by the Starvation Order and those who had been court-martialled prior to the Order).

So whether this was a case of young men naively looking for adventure, or reflected a sense of disappointment and frustration at Ireland's failure to take up the moral fight against Nazism, there is no simple answer. The more prosaic and perhaps accurate answer is that many were just looking for a job.

As for Eoin and Ambrose, they were not the first McGonigals to go to war, and perhaps the example set by members of their own family in defending what in the broader sense was their country may have been the more relevant factor. In addition to their three uncles who were all officers in the British Army, the exploits of their much older first cousin, Captain Robert McGonigal of the Royal Garrison Artillery, read like something straight from Hollywood. Robert, who also qualified in the law and later worked in the family's practice in Belfast (David McGonigal & Sons), was awarded a Military Cross and Bar during the First World War. The first was awarded in 1916 at St Eloi for an act of the type which has formed the basis of scenes from films like *Saving Private Ryan*:

> For conspicuous gallantry… when owing to a faulty charge, a bomb fired from a trench mortar fell in our own trench a yard or two from the gun, [Robert McGonigal] dashed in, picked up the bomb and flung it over the parapet. The fuse was burning and timed for about 5 seconds. His pluck and presence of mind saved the lives of many men.

Then in 1918, Robert was awarded a bar to his Military Cross

> For conspicuous gallantry and devotion to duty. When in command of two sections he fought his guns until the enemy were in close proximity on three sides. One gun was destroyed by enemy shell fire, and the remainder rendered useless by the detachment. Though badly wounded in the leg, he directed the retirement of his men, and then insisted on being carried to the battery commander to explain the situation.

Robert's brother David, a Belfast solicitor turned sports editor in Cape Town, wrote home in 1938, possibly reflecting similarly held views in the family when commenting:

> There is a doubtful feeling that the word of Hitler is not to be trusted, and that this move against the Czechs is but the prelude to further efforts to gain Rumania and Jugoslavia. It is all very upsetting, for there can be no doubt whatsoever that Hitler has never given the world any idea that he is really the man of peace that he proclaims himself to be … The cruel thing about the whole business is, that while alleged Statesmen and mere politicians plot and plan the poor old world is steadily moving towards another period of slaughter, in which countless lives are to be sacrificed simply to satisfy the ill-judged vanity of two dictatorial puppets [Hitler and Mussolini] … It is all too tragic for words, and it looks as if it will be far more tragic before it is all over. If

ever a couple of bullets would help towards the settling of the world it is now – one in Berlin and the other in Rome. (Appendix J).

The brothers' aunt, Catherine (Kathy) McGonigal, was awarded both the Red Cross Award and a South African Medal for 'bravery on the field of battle' as a Nursing Sister in the Irish Hospital in South Africa in 1900 during the Second Boer War. And another aunt, Margaret (Dorrie) McGonigal, having been recognized in 1918 by the War Office for coming 'to the notice of the Secretary of State for War for valuable services rendered in connection with the establishment and maintenance of societies for the benefit of the Naval and Military Forces', was later awarded the MBE.

Various other cousins had also served in the armed forces, including Major Harold McGonigal of the 1st Bn. Leinster Regiment. Harold was twice Mentioned in Despatches and won a Military Cross during the First World War in Palestine. On a later occasion, in August 1921, when sent to defend the Malappuram garrison in Kerala, India, his platoon was charged by hundreds of rebel Moplahs. Harold was described as having been involved in an intense action, 'doing deadly execution with his revolver' while being fired on from all sides at close range.

In fact, Ambrose was named after his mother's brother, Lieutenant Ambrose J.S. Davoren, who died on 18 July 1917 near Ypres in France – just four months before Ambrose was born. Ambrose J.S. also attended Clongowes before going on to study for the Bar at King's Inns. He was a good friend of John McGonigal and the two used to play tennis together. Two of Margaret's sisters, May and Carmen, joined the VAD (Voluntary Aid Detachment) and drove ambulances in France during the Great War. Carmen later had occasion to drive Winston Churchill in London, and was awarded an OBE for her service with the VAD. (She returned her medal in disgust when the Beatles were awarded MBEs in 1965!)

So even in their own family there was plenty to inspire impressionable young men. Equally, this meant that they should not have been under any romantic illusions about the nobility of battle. Or perhaps, like many others, they were simply looking for a change; some adventure and an opportunity to leave a then troubled and inward-looking Ireland. Many thought the war would not last long, and if they didn't get going, it would all be over and they would have missed their chance.

Young, inexperienced men often act without any great thought or the ideals that we might in retrospect like to ascribe to their actions. Tom Barry, a future leader in the IRA who enlisted in the Royal Field Artillery at Cork and became a soldier in the British Army, recalled:

In June, in my seventeenth year, I had decided to see what this Great War was like. I cannot plead I went on the advice of John Redmond or any other politician, that if we fought for the British we would secure Home Rule for Ireland, nor can I say I understood what Home Rule meant. I was not influenced by the lurid appeal to fight to save Belgium or small nations. I knew nothing about nations, large or small. I went to the war for no other reason than that I wanted to see what war was like, to get a gun, to see new countries and to feel a grown man. Above all I went because I knew no Irish history and had no national consciousness.

Steven O'Connor in *Irish Officers in the British Forces, 1922–1945* writes:

There were many reasons why Irish officers decided that the Second World War was their war. This fateful decision changed their lives irrevocably and their accounts illustrate the complexity of ordinary people living through extraordinary times. Among the officers a few were idealistic, some were patriotic, some were naïve, almost all were very young. Their decision to volunteer sometimes derived from a romanticised understanding of what war was like, while for others it came after long consideration of the possible consequences. In short, there was a wide mixture of motives among Irish officers who went to war ranging from loyalty, peer pressure, family tradition and idealism to attractive career prospects, the fear of missing all the excitement and the appeal of travel. Officers such as Sydney Watson and Brian Inglis had attended British public schools and knew friends and relatives who were joining up or were enduring the 'Blitz'. In such families it was common to regard men of military age who stayed in neutral Ireland as 'white feathers' or cowards. For example, Watson believed 'if he did not join up with his British friends and relations, he would be committing the most heinous sin against the ethos of prewar public schools by 'letting the side down'. Other officers were swept into the British forces on the tantalising prospect of adventure in distant lands. In 1941 Majella, a nurse from Kildare, joined the Queen Alexandra's Imperial Military Nursing Service in which she held rank equivalent to an army lieutenant. Majella expected the war to be over in a year: she was eager 'to get into it before it ended'. As a young person during the war, she explained, 'the only thing you're thinking about is where you're going to go and all the excitement that goes with it.' When she was posted to India instead of France as expected, 'that was a surprise, but of course more excitement.' In her perception of the war as offering opportunities for adventure Majella was not exceptional. Other Irish recruits contrasted the prospects for adventure in the war with the boredom of civilian life in Ireland. Arthur Smith joined the RAF in 1943: 'Dublin was a very boring, small place then, you know, I was itching to get away.'

Whatever the thinking, there were certainly many reasons why the brothers did not need to volunteer. There was obviously far less pressure in Ireland than in England to 'do your bit for King and country'. And while there are some indications from early writings and letters, we do not really know what inspired them. Of the two, Ambrose was much more the realist, while Eoin had a strong idealistic streak. Looking back at how they pushed each other at school, a decision by one may well have stimulated the other. They did not enlist on the same day, but that may have been simply a question of location and opportunity. As at school, Ambrose led the way in joining the RUR the day before Eoin; but as ever, Eoin was not to be outdone and quickly stole a march as their time with the army progressed. Still, they were both fast out of the blocks, off to prepare for war and experience the world beyond the confines of Ireland. Interestingly, after the war and after he had become a judge, an old colleague of Ambrose recalled him explaining in typically laconic fashion that when it came to his decision to enlist, 'I had been bumbling along; was at a bit of a loose end when war came along and so thought, "Oh, that's for me" and signed up.' So much for grandiose thoughts of patriotism, taking up the moral fight against the Nazis or defending the honour of small nations. Ambrose apparently just had nothing better to do at the time!

Chapter 7

The Royal Ulster Rifles: 'wild young men'

Although it had been clear for some time that events in Europe were leading towards war, it was a war for which Britain was mostly unprepared. With the inexorable rise of Germany, the budget for the British Army was increased significantly from 1938 onwards to help fund the introduction of a rapid recruitment programme, but it was still an all-volunteer force at this point with inbuilt inefficiencies resulting in the misallocation of men with professional skills or trades. The Secretary of State for War, Leslie Hore-Belisha, attempted to address some of these problems by seeking permission to introduce conscription in 1938 but was rebuffed by Britain's then Prime Minister, Neville Chamberlain, whose government was pursuing a policy of appeasement and who would not agree to increased defence spending. Nevertheless, by early 1939, with Hitler's flouting of the Munich Agreement (through the further occupation of Czechoslovakia), Hore-Belisha was finally allowed to introduce a form of conscription with the Military Training Act of 27 April 1939. This required all men aged twenty and twenty-one to undergo six months military training, and it was extended on the declaration of war to include all fit men between the ages of eighteen and forty-one. Conscription was also gradually brought in, starting in October 1939 and applying to all fit men between twenty and twenty-three, and this age group was widened as the war continued.

Ambrose and Eoin neither waited for nor needed the new legislation to inform their decision to volunteer. Throughout this period, like most men of fighting age, Ambrose and Eoin had discussed the prospect of war and whether and when to get involved. Between Ambrose leaving school in 1936 and Eoin leaving two years later, Hitler's forces had entered the Rhineland, annexed Austria and occupied part of Czechoslovakia. Churchill described the policy of appeasement and the agreement to allow Germany to occupy Czechoslovakia as 'an unmitigated disaster'. And so it proved. For young men like Ambrose and Eoin, war seemed inescapable – and if it was going to happen, they needed to be ready.

In March 1939 Germany occupied the remainder of Czechoslovakia and on 1 September 1939 unleashed 'blitzkrieg' on Poland. On 3 September

1939 Neville Chamberlain finally announced that Britain (and France) were at war with Germany. Just three days later, on 6 September 1939, Ambrose enlisted with the TA (Royal Ulster Rifles, or RUR) cadet battalion, and on the following day Eoin was posted to the RUR's Infantry Training Centre (ITC) and commissioned as a junior officer. Having followed events closely over the previous two years, both were ready to act quickly; at university they had both been members of part-time army reserve units – Ambrose with the QUB Training Corps and Eoin with the Territorial Army (TA), the 5th LAA Regiment RA. The TA did not exist in Northern Ireland at that time, so the part-time units in the Province formed part of the Supplementary Reserve (SR) and were numbered in sequence after the Regulars.

After enlisting with the RUR cadet battalion, Ambrose moved to the 165 Officer Cadet Training Unit at Dunbar, East Lothian, Scotland on 15 September 1939. The course lasted four months, after which he was commissioned into the RUR on 12 January 1940.

On exactly the same day, John and Margaret McGonigal were in Dublin to attend a Supreme Court ceremony marking the occasion of their eldest son Dick 'taking silk' – being admitted to the Inner Bar and becoming a Senior Counsel like his father. Life in Ireland went on.

Eoin was able to move straight from the 5th LAA Regiment RA to a junior officer (subaltern) posting with the RUR – having spent just one year studying law at Trinity College Dublin, he was now in training for war.

The RUR were the local regular infantry unit in Belfast, and many of those who enlisted in it would have been known to the brothers. A good lot of the so-called 'rugby crowd' headed to the RUR, for example Sammy Walker, Harry McKibbin and Bob Alexander, who were all on the 1938 Lions tour. Historically, the regiment (when called the Royal Irish Rifles) had recruited mainly but not exclusively from Ulster. This continued even after Partition, when the name was changed to the RUR in 1923; it continued to draw recruits from both sides of the border and was made up of both Catholics and Protestants.

The RUR's motto, '*Quis separabit*' ('Who shall separate us') was forward-looking in that the men of the regiment made a point of proudly sticking together in good times and bad – there was no internal partition. Indeed, Colonel Robin Charley noted that such was the camaraderie in the RUR that Catholic and Protestant soldiers would sing each other's sectarian songs.

The Royal Irish Rifles was formed in 1881 from two 'Regiments of Foot': the 83rd (County of Dublin) Regiment and the 86th (County Down) Regiment, which again attracted men from all corners of the island. Like the regiment in *Sharpe's Rifles*, it was seen as a more 'robust' unit of fighting men than, for example, either the Royal Irish Fusiliers in Armagh or the Royal Inniskilling Fusiliers in Omagh – and therefore not an obvious choice for two Clongowes-educated sons of a judge.

RUR badge.

Ambrose and Eoin were both posted to the RUR's ITC at St Patrick's barracks in Ballymena and forged a strong friendship with fellow officer Robert Blair ('Paddy') Mayne. Being from Ireland, he was always referred to as 'Paddy' in the Army, but the brothers usually called him 'Blair' (or 'Mayne'). Despite being from opposite sides of the religious divide in Northern Ireland, the brothers and Blair had much in common that was important to men of their age, such as rugby and downing pints of Guinness in the local Adair Arms Hotel. They became firm friends, visiting each other's families during the odd weekend or holiday. Ambrose had, in fact, first come across Blair when he was at Queen's – both played rugby and both were in the Queen's

RUR's St Patrick's Barracks, overgrown, prior to redevelopment.

OTC. When Ambrose arrived, Blair was already an established member of the all-conquering QUB 1st XV team of 1937. It included two other Lions players, Harry McKribbin and George Cromey, and went unbeaten for the entire season (the 'Invincibles' of its time). Fresh out of school and just under three years younger than Blair, Ambrose had played for the Queen's 2nd XV before leaving to study law in Dublin. Coincidentally, Queen's and the RUR weren't Blair's first encounter with the McGonigals. In September 1938, the brothers' cousin David McGonigal, a solicitor who had left Belfast to begin a new career as a sports editor for the *Cape Times* in South Africa, hosted Blair and the other seven Irish members of the Lions rugby team that toured South Africa that year to an evening of Irish food and drink (Appendix J). Then, on 28 June 1939, John McGonigal was the presiding judge when Blair was introduced at the Belfast Quarter Sessions to commence his practice as a solicitor with the firm of GL MacLaine & Co (having trained with TCG Macintosh, Newtownards).

In time, Blair would become one of the most decorated officers of the Second World War, winning four DSOs as well as the *Légion d'honneur* and the Croix de Guerre from the post-war French Government. Controversially, having already been recommended for a Victoria Cross by his superior officers (including Field Marshal Montgomery), the award was downgraded by a person or persons unknown to a third DSO on grounds thought to be related to one or a combination of his Irish background, the unconventional nature of the SAS's methods (e.g. a lack of senior witnesses) and his lack of respect for authority. Or quite simply that in October 1945, with the war

The Adair Arms Hotel, Ballymena.

drawing to a close, Britain no longer had need of any further heroes. As it was, by the time the three men joined the RUR, Blair had already lived a life made for the cinema. A former amateur boxing champion, eight-handicap golfer and Irish rugby international, as well as member of the British and Irish Lions team that toured South Africa in 1938, Blair did nothing by halves and recognized in Ambrose and Eoin two kindred spirits.

Also based in the north at the same time as Ambrose and Eoin was Colonel Corran Purdon, who later took part in the legendary Commando raid on St Nazaire, where he was captured and then held as a PoW at Colditz Castle. Colonel Purdon, who was born in Cork, was also commissioned into the RUR in 1939 but found his way there via the Royal Military Academy at Sandhurst. Purdon wrote of his time with the Depot of his Regiment at, initially, Armagh, and later with the RUR's ITC in Ballymena:

I was quartered in a former granary in the Mall at Armagh where a number of us subalterns shared stone-floored, freezing-cold, bare rooms, sleeping in our bedding-rolls on wooden-framed, canvas camp beds. The legendary Blair (Paddy) Mayne was also there … I played scrum half for the unit rugby team behind a pack which included him (he was a well-known Irish International Rugby forward), and a number of top class players, among whom were the brothers Eoin and Ambrose McGonigal.

Paddy was a giant of a man. Eoin was a very good looking chap, as was his brother Ambrose – Ambrose died recently as Northern Ireland's senior Roman Catholic judge. The McGonigal sisters were Irish beauties and one of them, Letty, was married to [Colonel] Jack Carson (later to command 1 RUR in action in France, Germany and Korea), a charming, quiet man and a distant relation of mine.

Letty's two brothers – like most of us subalterns – were wild young men, and it amused them, when full of good cheer, in the small hours of the morning, to ring up Jack Carson. This brought a raging sister to the telephone and Letty would give her brothers a piece of her mind. Little did she know that the receiver was held out for the rest of us, convulsed in mirth, to hear what Letty thought of her brothers!

I remember one night in Ballymena Castle where our ITC Officers' Mess was established. The anteroom after dinner was filled with uproarious characters and Mess rugger 'broke out'. Our CO, the burly, gallant Victor Crowley, was bullocking around in the midst of his younger officers. Among them were the huge and powerful Blair Mayne, the McGonigal brothers, the Nixon brothers, the May brothers, Runce

Rooney, Desmond Woods, all of whom were to distinguish themselves in the war (Desmond had already won his first MC in Palestine).

In the midst of the melee the tall, lean, dark figure of Ambrose McGonigal appeared behind the CO, a large heavy oblong silver tray held in both hands. This he brought down with force on the Colonel's head and the burly figure of our leader sank to his knees, but tough guy that he was, he got up again almost immediately. By then Ambrose had disappeared and the slight, wiry figure of my batman Rifleman Henry, former boxing champion of the China Station, was at my elbow. 'Come outside, Sir, and help me with Mr. Ambrose, please.' I went out to where an unconscious shape lay, and with Henry taking his arms and me holding his legs, we carried him down the drive and across the Square to the Depot Officers' Mess where, having undressed him and put him into his pyjamas, we placed him in his bed. 'Did he pass out?' I asked my batman, who had been chauffeur to Mr. Justice McGonigal, Ambrose's father. 'No, Sir. I doped him, Sir, to keep him from any further trouble!' said the champion boxer. Fortunately, Colonel Crowley never knew who or what hit him!'

This was an enjoyable and formative time for the subalterns, especially the brothers – later, when training with the SAS in Egypt, Eoin wrote to Ambrose reminiscing about his time in Ballymena and wishing he could be back there to enjoy a few pints of Guinness over Christmas. Blair also later wrote to his own brother in similar terms about how he missed Ballymena.

Ballymena Castle in 1887, since demolished.

Eoin used his time there to develop his interest in writing – he was an enthusiastic short story writer, sometimes under his own name and sometimes under the pseudonym 'Ian O'Donnell'. About fifteen drafts have survived. It would seem he may have harboured dreams of becoming a writer and perhaps unusually, given his love of rugby and subsequent selection for the Special Forces, most of what he wrote (at least initially) was romantic in nature, often concluding with some kind of twist or surprise ending.

In one story (with faint strains of *Cyrano de Bergerac*), the main character is fed questions by a more knowledgeable friend so he can carry himself off as an authority on Homer's *Iliad* in order to win his lover's hand in marriage. In another, the local village beauty declines the chance of a country cottage life with one of the well-intentioned and respectable but fawning local boys, in favour of spending time with a one-legged, garrulous and crude seaman who whisks her away in the middle of the night with the promise of impassioned argument and adventure. And in a third, a poet seeking inspiration in trying to win over his beloved, takes the advice of a dream-like spirit of 'nymphal charms'; fed up with endless, hackneyed poetic allusions, he decides that 'to write about love and to talk about love is a feeble alternative to loving and being loved.' As a result, the struggling poet throws away his rhyming dictionary and sends a wire to his girlfriend announcing that he is leaving immediately to see her later that night. He is transformed into a decisive man of action, but we do not learn whether this new strategy was successful. Such scenes were unusual themes for someone who was in fact a man of action and leader of men – or as his future Commanding Officer, David Stirling, later said of him, 'a huge character of a guy'. However, the stories are all the more charming for the contrast, and Eoin reveals himself as an imaginative young man, perhaps a little innocent but with a strong romantic and idealistic streak.

It is not clear how long Eoin continued to write – he had certainly started while at Trinity College, since a number of his stories were written by hand in university notebooks – but it is clear he was still producing them after enlisting; one of his drafts (typewritten) is based around the discovery by the main protagonist that his wife is having an affair with a man called 'Mayne'. Quite what Blair (who was said to have harboured dreams of becoming a writer himself) might have thought of this role we can only imagine. It appears in a story entitled 'The Escape' by 'Ian O'Donnell' and uses, in fact, a great example of the on-the-spot resourcefulness and ingenuity that would later be demanded of the original SAS recruits. Upon discovering by chance the dead body of an unknown man floating in a river, a group of whiskey-drinking old friends quickly decide to take advantage of the situation. They pretend it is in fact one of them, the main protagonist of the story, so that he can say goodbye to his old life and escape what turns out to be a bad marriage to a former cabaret dancer (she who had succumbed to the irresistible charms of 'Mayne') and a mountain of bad debts. It is all decided upon and accomplished within a matter of minutes, with identifying evidence planted on the corpse for the benefit of the police. After this inventive albeit drastic solution to his everyday problems, the protagonist is last seen strolling away towards the train, contemplating his new life while lighting a cigarette. As a big admirer of the songs of Percy French (*The Mountains of Mourne* and *Are Ye Right There, Michael?*), Blair is bound to have been impressed by this display of verve!

The Cameronians (Scottish Rifles)

In between the socializing and his writing, Eoin managed to complete several courses of instruction – these included field engineering and mortar courses at Grey Point Battery, Antrim, a 'Young Officers Course' in Aldershot and a month spent at the Small Arms School in Hythe. However, in late spring 1940, the 2nd Battalion, Cameronians (Scottish Rifles) asked for officers on attachment from the RUR. Both Eoin and Blair immediately volunteered and on 14 June 1940 found themselves in Huntly, Aberdeenshire.

'June 1940 before going to Cameronians' – the last photo of Eoin with his father, John. Eoin died the following year, and John not long afterwards.

Eoin armed with a shepherd's crook and pipe – not a look that was repeated much in North Africa!

Joining the Cameronians was not a difficult decision. They had been training with the RUR in Ballymena for some time and after a season of rugby and Guinness were keen to take any opportunity to alleviate the boredom of routine training. They were concerned that if they didn't get involved in the war soon, it might all be over. It was not a transfer but a secondment and it led, just two months later, at Galashiels (on 8 August 1940) to Eoin's volunteering, with Blair, for the newly formed No. 11 (Scottish) Commando – at the time, they were the only two officers from an Irish regiment to have done so. Ambrose, who was further ahead in his studies than Eoin (and had broken his leg while motorcycling in training, not to mention having just met his wife to be), opted to remain in Ireland with the RUR.

Chapter 8

11 (Scottish) Commando in Arran

For Eoin, joining the Commando held out the prospect of being able to get involved in a more independent and to his eyes more intelligent form of fighting, where stealth and strategy were key. It represented something more modern, far removed from the trench warfare of 1914–18. A paraphrased extract from the Commando Veterans website provides some background to the beginnings of the Commando:

> The first call for volunteers for 'service of a hazardous nature' was in the early months of 1940 and for the new Independent Companies … Winston Churchill wanted his own Corps of 'shock troops' to start afresh. Lt Col Dudley Clarke, who was then Military Assistant to the Chiefs of the Imperial General Staff, is generally credited with the initial outline plan of their formation. His plan was approved and the name agreed on. Thus the 'Commandos' were formed.
>
> It should be noted that at this time these early Commandos were all Army Commandos rather than Royal Marines. A total of twelve Army Commando units were initially raised. This unique record of the Army Commandos owed more than anything to the fact that every man was a volunteer. He was, moreover, a picked volunteer, selected by officers who trained him and led him in battle. Those who failed for one reason or another to measure up to the most exacting standards of training, discipline and conduct under fire, would be 'Returned to Unit' without hesitation. Many were. Nobody who survived it would question the practical severity of this ordeal … The men who organized the Commandos were content with nothing short of perfection. From the first day they set about learning the tactics and techniques of war, and devising new ones; no detail was too insignificant. And yet, though no plan was too bold, mere foolhardiness was generally condemned. This attitude, evoking a certain spirit of emulation in the field army, helped in some measure to disperse the clouds of convention that had afflicted military thinking in 1939; a new approach to winning the war was demanded.

In any event, as resistance by the French and Belgian Armies collapsed in May 1940, the British Expeditionary Force withdrew to Dunkirk, where it was evacuated between 26 May and 4 June. Britain was on the defensive, but Churchill saw that it was important to introduce an offensive component into the equation. On 3 June he wrote to his Chiefs of Staff: 'The completely defensive habit of mind, which has ruined the French, must not be allowed to ruin all our initiative. It is of the highest consequence to keep the largest numbers of German forces all along the coasts of the countries that have been conquered, and we should immediately set to work to organise raiding forces on these coasts …' [And on 5 June, continuing] 'Enterprises must be prepared with specially trained troops of the hunter class, who can develop a reign of terror first of all on the "butcher and bolt" policy … [to] kill and capture the Hun garrison … and then away. I look to the Chiefs of Staff to propose me measures for a vigorous, enterprising and ceaseless offensive against the whole German occupied coastline. Tanks and AFVs must be made in flat-bottomed boats, out of which they can crawl ashore, do a deep a raid inland, cutting vital communications, and then back, leaving a trail of German corpses behind them.'

Therefore, barely six weeks after Churchill had challenged his Chiefs of Staff to propose measures for a 'ceaseless offensive' against the German-occupied coastline, men from a variety of regiments started volunteering for action and adventure in 'service of a hazardous nature'. Eoin and Blair were among the first.

Those who put their names forward were literally taking a step into the unknown. There was no existing blueprint for the Commando; the development of the concept and the standards for recruitment, selection and training would be determined by the Commanding Officer. To streamline the selection process, some basic criteria were set: all potential Commandos had to be trained soldiers, physically fit, able to swim and immune from sea- and air-sickness. Their personal attributes had to include courage, physical endurance, initiative, resourcefulness, marksmanship, self-reliance and an aggressive spirit towards the war. As at 9 June 1940, the requirements stated:

Volunteers will be employed on fighting duties only, and Commanding Officers should be assured that these duties will require only the best type of officers and men … They should be young and must be absolutely fit. They should be able to swim and be immune from sea sickness … (b) Officers: Personality, tactical ability and imagination … The officers selected as Commando leaders should be capable of planning and personally leading operations carried out by parties chosen from their own Commandos. These officers should be selected entirely for their operational abilities.

This was elaborated upon in the Special Service Training Instructions:

Mental as well as physical alertness. As a general definition: what is required is the man who is quick in thought and quick on his feet. Rather than a man who, though he may be exceptionally strong, is slow in his mental reactions and in his movements … Physical fitness and endurance will be an essential element of every operation, not only because of the difficulties of the terrain over which the troops may be called upon to move, but because great speed in reaching the objective will almost invariably be required.

Special Service selection placed a heavy emphasis on an individual's ability to play sports or games to a high level, because 'a good physique was important'. A high level of physical fitness was demanded from the start. Therefore, it is not surprising that the Special Service Application forms document men with strong sporting backgrounds – applicants were asked about their physical abilities and in particular whether they could ride, swim, mountaineer, ski, shoot, run, bicycle long distances or box.

The unit that Eoin had volunteered for was called No. 11 Commando, 'The Scottish'. They wore Balmoral bonnets with a bobble on the top and a black hackle supported by the badge of the trooper's home regiment. According to Bill Fraser, a future SAS 'original', the unit's so-called 'Scottishness' was further enhanced by the age-old theory that the wearing of a black hackle indicated you 'had a quarrel with someone'. Eventually, and despite some opposition from the Army Council, a green beret became standard issue for all Commando forces. However, the 11th Commando retained their Balmoral bonnets until disbandment.

No. 11 was first formed at Galashiels in the Borders, and all of the volunteers came from Scottish, English and Irish regiments. The Commanding Officer chosen to lead them was Lieutenant Colonel Richard 'Dick' R. Pedder (of the Highland Light Infantry) and he quickly set about the task of putting his unit together. Pedder was a no-nonsense officer with a mind of his own who knew exactly what he wanted for the unit – he was the ideal choice for developing the Commando blueprint. With Churchill's call to arms the bar had been set high, but Pedder intended on exceeding it; Churchill had demanded specially trained troops for service of an undefined hazardous nature, and so from those who applied Pedder ruthlessly culled both officers and men he thought unsuitable. As time went on, No. 11 Commando gained a reputation as the most disciplined and highly trained of all the newly formed Commando units.

Pedder set up his headquarters in the Douglas Hotel in the border town of Galashiels and first went about selecting his officers, before then interviewing the men. Both Eoin and Blair were selected as junior officers.

Training in Galashiels soon got under way in earnest. Reveille was set for 0630 hrs, followed 30 minutes later by one hour of Physical Training (PT), before the men had breakfast at 0800. Breakfast was followed by morning parade, with a kit inspection at 0900. PT then continued throughout the

Lt Col Pedder with the HLI in 1924. (*Commando Veterans Association*)

morning, usually in the form of fast-paced 8–10-mile route marches (with arms and in full battle dress), as well as cross-country, map and compass work, moving through cover, etc. The men who got through those early weeks and

Eoin and Blair wearing 'The Hackle' of 11 (Scottish) Commando. (*NMS*)

months very soon came to grasp Pedder's passion for route-marching – they were continually on the move. After lunch, PT would continue in the form of swimming, running and more exercise until tea at 1630. This would be followed by lectures until 1800, after which, unless on company duties, the men's time was their own. However, conditions were primitive, and few were impressed; as one volunteer would later record: 'Galashiels in 1940, what a dump, disused woollen mills … We finished up in Netherdale Mill … the washing facilities were awful – the latrines were pre-Domesday Book – the food was atrocious – to wash our eating irons we had to use a horse trough.'

The approach bore little or no resemblance to how things were done in the regular army. The Commando represented a complete revolution in the concept of soldiering. There was no bullying and no sergeant major shouting at the men every minute of the day – you were told where to be and expected to get there under your own steam. No normal barracks or regimental HQ was established – there was no point wasting soldiers' training time with fatigues – instead, men were expected to find digs in a nearby town. It was a meritocracy, and the officers had to lead by example, on the basis that 'if they can do it, then so must we.' Men were encouraged to see themselves as being just as important as anyone else in the army, whether that was their immediate captain or a brigadier – each man counted as much as the next. Their approach to training was also new; they didn't do the usual PT exercises in gym kit, but conducted most of their training in full kit, under live fire, replicating the conditions and challenges they would have to face in the field. Their methods were radical for the time, but many of them are still

The view from Goat Fell, the highest peak on Arran Island.

being used today. As their standards were so high, they ended up creaming off some of the best men from the regular regiments, and as a result, the military establishment did not like them; some COs tried to stop their men from volunteering. And although not all the recruits were lantern-jawed, natural-born killing machines, they had all been prepared to volunteer for an unknown 'service of a hazardous nature', which of itself spoke volumes. They were a mixed bag of individuals, but through training, discipline, being afforded a degree of self-responsibility and the natural weeding-out process of selection, those who succeeded did so because of their individuality, intelligence and initiative. They were also resilient.

The initial intensity of the training was a shock to the system for many of the volunteers, but for Pedder, Galashiels was only a gentle introduction. He was soon making plans to move the unit to a more demanding training ground; the Isle of Arran off the west coast of Scotland, during the winter.

Eoin arrived on Arran on 11 September 1940 (just over a year after enlisting) and save for one short period spent on manoeuvres in Falkirk preparing to oppose an anticipated German invasion via Norway, and a round trip to the Straits of Gibraltar in December 1940 (with the Commando being lured there on the promise of action in Pantelleria), he ended up training on the island for almost five months.

Arran's mountainous form dominates the open waters of the Firth of Clyde. Its jagged peaks, huge corries and miles of rugged coastline would prove the ideal training ground for the Commando recruits. With more volunteers than he required for operational strength, and given the island's challenging terrain, Pedder contrived a plan to separate the sheep from the goats. No stranger to pushing men to their limits, and well-known for his 50-hour toughening exercises at the end of infantry training courses, he ordered 11 Commando to march 100 miles (as the crow flies) from Galashiels to Ayr in preparation for the move to Arran. This was to be the first of many tests of physical and mental endurance. Many of the recruits found the march too demanding, and as one recalled:

> We marched twenty to thirty miles a day and slept in the hedgerows. I changed my socks at every stop and washed through the pair I had taken off in a burn. Many of the men developed blisters and when they could not walk any more they got to ride in the transport that carried our kit. I remember them crowing to us as they passed. When we got to Ayr, they were all RTU'd [Returned to Unit].

With bagpipes playing they began their march, and it would be six days before they finally 'bedded down' at Ayr racecourse. Each troop took the

Arran in winter
(Bellevue Farm)

lead in rotation, with the pipers borrowed from the Cameron Highlanders playing them along. The only food was bully beef (corned beef in a can) and biscuits – unlikely to be mistaken for a staple diet. Water for washing and drinking was taken from burns and was therefore undoubtedly refreshing. Sleeping arrangements entailed bedding down wherever they could, and on most nights this meant sleeping in the open air under whatever cover they could find, often in hedgerows. It was a hard routine but one that would come to typify the Commando attitude. As the troops leapfrogged each other on a westerly bearing, Pedder marched alongside, scrutinizing his officers, measuring up his men and looking for those worthy of being a part of his elite unit. He permitted anybody who did not have the physical and/ or mental endurance to complete the march to travel to Ayr on the back of one of the supply trucks. However, he then instantly issued all those who had taken a lift with a 'Return to Unit' chit, sending them back to their original units – it was a humiliation felt by some to be far more painful than any blister.

This entire period was a shock to the system for most, but there was method in Pedder's madness. One trooper recalled that more nights were spent out on the hills than in bed, but 'At the end,' he said, 'we felt there was nothing we could not undertake.'

The Commando initiation and training was tough because they were intended to be the army's elite troops, the aggressive part of the service in the early years, when the war was still primarily a defensive one. Churchill wanted to use them to change the momentum, putting into practice the adage that the best form of defence is attack. The aim was therefore to filter the group down into athlete-soldiers – those who had the intelligence, the resilience and the physical attributes to live up to Churchill's demand for 'specially trained troops of the hunter class, who can develop a reign of terror … leaving a trail of German corpses behind them'.

As one of Eoin's fellow junior officers, Tommy McPherson, recalled:

> From the very beginning, entry into the Commandos carried with it huge kudos, so I was incredibly pleased when, in due course, my name was accepted … I'm not aware that many regretted the decision to join the Commandos, but for any who might have had second thoughts there was a powerful incentive to succeed, because being returned to your unit, or RTU'd, was a humiliating mark of failure for soldiers who didn't make the grade.

This was a long way from life at Clongowes (except perhaps for the invariably cold boarding-school showers), but Eoin revelled in the physical challenges – in letters to Ambrose, he was clearly proud of his developing fitness (and slightly baiting his big brother who was stuck at home with a broken leg). He had always felt stronger than most and as an officer he was determined to lead by example. Having been used to (and proud of) standing out at school as 'our deputy from Belfast', and now being one of only two officer representatives from an Irish regiment in Arran (the other being the almost superhuman Blair Mayne), Eoin was determined to succeed.

Glen Rosa Valley, Arran.

In Blair he had an older-brother figure to try and outdo, just as he had competed with Ambrose at school. And as a junior officer of just nineteen (albeit that the average age of Pedder's officers was only twenty-one), he was resolute in wanting to justify his place in this elite force on merit. He recognized the responsibility that would soon come in leading his men in battle and did not take it lightly. He loved the feeling of independence, of doing something important, and was stirred by the love of his country to stand and defend it, as had the legendary Irish youth Cuchulainn, his boyhood hero. This was a chance to make a real difference.

Still, mythology aside, many aspects of the Commando training on Arran continued much as before. The unit would rally at the blast of a whistle or horn and come running from their billets early in the morning for their daily PT regime. This consisted mainly of cross-country runs and marches, and they were expected to maintain the same speed going uphill as on the flat or going downhill.

From Lamlash in the east, where 11 Commando were all billeted, the men would head south to Whiting Bay, before cutting across and up Ross Road, then striking off left and up the great hillside. There they would run through moor and bog until they reached the loch on the top, before turning to come back down again. However, on more occasions than they could remember, Pedder would send them northwards, to the top of Goat Fell, the island's highest peak. Often wet and exhausted, they would then return to their billets and their welcoming landladies, only to be turned around and sent to the summit again, returning in the middle of the night. They would then be up for reveille to start it all over again at the crack of dawn the following morning. It was relentless. And Eoin loved it.

Eoin relished the mental and physical challenges set by Pedder – as youngsters growing up in Ireland, he and Ambrose had often spent their holidays hiking around the hills in the north and around the coastline of North Donegal, Inishowen, where his grandfather was born. North Donegal is a wild place exposed to the best and worst of nature – it has a reputation for being one of the windiest, most exposed parts of Ireland, where very little grows apart from heather and gorse. Arran is similarly rugged but better protected and blessed with a unique microclimate as a result of lying in the path of the North Atlantic drift. It is famous for the diversity of its plant life, but for Eoin and the rest of 11 Commando it was just bloody wet. All of the time. The days were short at that time of year, with the nights almost blending into one, and there seemed to be a constant gale which picked up as each day went on, but Eoin didn't mind the elements. He loved the isolation of the hills and valleys they marched through, with just the roaming wild

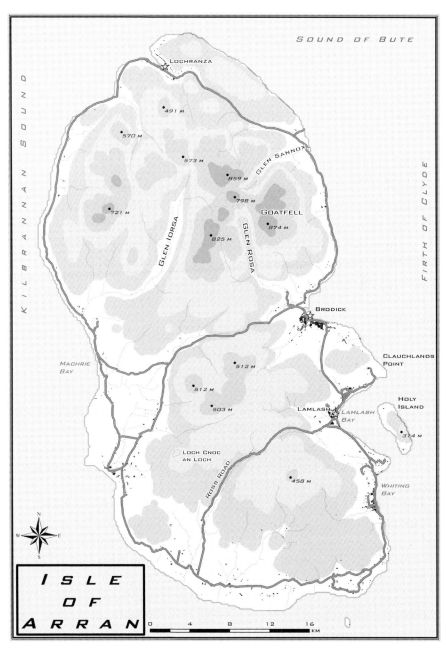

Map 1.

stags for company. The only tricky bit was marching through pathless valleys where the men constantly found their feet sinking down into unseen gaps between rocks overgrown with grass; there were more than a few sprained ankles as a result, but the pace still had to be maintained.

A deceptive-looking Goat Fell, Arran.

Still, with flat country in the south, rolling hills in the middle and steep mountainous country in the north, the island was an ideal place for the Commando to train. The seashore and shingle beaches were perfect for all forms of amphibious training, whether diving in full kit off Lamlash pier or swimming to Holy Isle and back from Lamlash Bay (a 2-mile round trip avoiding the large local community of seals along the way). The options were numerous and the training was unyielding. Swimming was one of the few activities at which Blair did not excel. Pulling his heavy frame through the waters of the Clyde in full kit was not high on his list of favourite pastimes.

In addition to the normal routine of PT, map-reading, initiative tests, picking locks, blowing safes, mock operations, demolitions and exercise by night and day (incorporating both speed and route-marches), Pedder incorporated a further range of specialist skills: rock climbing, unarmed combat, the use of explosives and a knowledge of transport beyond that required of the ordinary regimental soldier. Comprehensive weapons training was also covered, for which Eoin (and Blair) was responsible – this was Eoin's area of expertise from his time with the Ulster Rifles and the Cameronians (Scottish Rifles) in Aberdeen. He had always been considered an excellent shot.

Toggle rope.

Commandos using a toggle rope bridge under live fire in training. (*Commando Veterans Association*)

While training, each man carried a flask of whisky and morphia tablets as part of his kit. He also carried a 'toggle rope' – a short length of rope with a bight at one end and a toggle at the other. These short lengths could be joined together for climbing cliffs (Ambrose would put them to good use later in the war), for making rope bridges or as safety lines when crossing rivers in spate.

Other items that Pedder insisted were carried at all times included toilet paper, first-aid bandages, lengths of string and cheese wire – it was not unusual for him to stop a man during training and ask him to produce any one of them. A failure to do so meant trouble.

Eoin was well known for carrying one further item which made him a much sought-after comrade – his silver cigarette case. A little unconventional perhaps, but its contents were always appreciated. A present from his grandparents, he felt it brought him luck and it reminded him of home.

The skills training undertaken by the Commando stretched endurance levels to the limit, and despite the winter weather, the training continued regardless. The northern highlands of Arran at that time of the year can be a wild and unforgiving place, and the winter of 1939/40 managed to excel in this regard. Nevertheless, day after day, night after night, Eoin's unit marched and manoeuvred over mountains and through glens (usually in the rain); they waded through rivers that had burst their banks, and had to repeat simulated beach landings almost every single night. It meant that on most days when they returned to their billets they were soaked through – much to the displeasure of their landladies. The training was unremitting and men were being RTU'd on a regular basis – it was like a considerably more brutal 'X Factor' selection process, with music in the form of the marching bagpipers but not so much singing in the rain.

To add to the challenges faced, the men were dressed not in the breathable, waterproofed Gore-Tex gear of today's mountaineers but woollen battledress that unhelpfully acted as an excellent sponge in the wet and took their landladies forever to dry out. The kit became heavier as they marched, and the wet socks did not do much for blistered feet. In fact, even in decent weather, the uniforms, when new, were not popular – they were coated with a chemical substance designed to protect from some of the effects of a gas attack, but it meant that until the battledress was broken in, its wearers used to itch like flea-stricken dogs. Actually, a good soak in some Arran rain apparently helped soften them up … a (wet) silver lining!

On top of everything was the frustration of waiting for action and not knowing when (if at all) their training might be put to use. At one point it appeared that the Commando would finally be engaged on an operation;

early in the autumn of 1940, with the threat of a possible Axis invasion from Norway, several Commando units were moved to Falkirk as a defensive measure. However, nothing came of it, and they soon returned to Arran to continue training. It was beginning to become frustrating.

One observer of the unit's training at this time was Admiral Sir Walter Cowan KCB, CB, DSO, who had joined the Commando to improve the men's boat work. He recounted:

> Coming back after a night landing and a mountain to climb at speed, they would, at dawn, making for the beaches and breakfast, come in perhaps seven miles with full equipment, machine guns and all, averaging five and a half miles an hour without effort, not a man falling out … the training of the two Scottish Commandos 9 and 11 in Arran during the autumn and winter of 1940 was the most vigorous and ruthless I have ever seen … the pick of the Scottish regiments, and they laughed at hardship – wet through at least five days out of seven and often up to or over the waist … they practised landing in merchant ship life boats, heavy and unhandy to a degree.
>
> Most of the men had next to no knowledge of boat work, and started learning to pull in these unwieldy craft with heavy oars – it was a wonder it didn't break their hearts … Sometimes the weather became very bad before they were ready to re-embark, and one evening it so happened that we might easily have drowned two boatloads in the primitive life boats. I have never forgotten it.

Holy Isle as seen from Lamlash, showing naval ships in the deep channel. (*Isle of Arran Heritage Museum*)

They 'attacked' Clauchlands Point at the northern end of Lamlash Bay dozens of times that winter. As the landing craft came in to the beach, Admiral Cowan would tell them, 'Far too much noise – you must do it again', and this they did until they learned to keep 'as quiet as mice'.

It was an ideal location for such work, as the channel between Holy Isle and Arran's east coast is especially deep; the island was used as a naval base throughout this period. In fact, because of the naval presence, there are very few records of the Commando's time on Arran – photographs were not permitted either of the Commando or the effect of the war on the island in 1939/40.

Admiral Cowan. (*NMS*)

It is thought that Admiral Cowan may have been the inspiration in part for two of Waugh's characters, Colonel 'Jumbo' Trotter and Brigadier Ritchie-Hook in *Officers and Gentlemen*. Based on Waugh's wartime experiences, the book describes the main character's time spent training on a Scottish island before moving to Egypt with a new Commando unit. Admiral Cowan (then aged seventy) made a great impression on the men, and one of those who shared the Landour billet with Eoin and Blair described him as

> incredible. Small, slight and amazingly fit, he had the heart and courage of a lion; he accompanied the Commandos on training exercises, mostly at night, involving long distances over mountainous terrain in atrocious weather and, later on, operations in the Middle East.

Despite serving in Benin, Nigeria, West Africa and in the Mahdist and Second Boer Wars, the First World War and the Baltic amongst others from 1886 through to retirement in 1931, Cowan immediately took a lower rank in order to volunteer for the Commando in Arran and help train them in small-boat handling in 1941. He went on to see action in North Africa, was captured at Tobruk and, after release, rejoined the Commando and saw further action in Italy. He was both the canny old hand and a Great War veteran who was determined to go out in a blaze of glory. As remembered by Lieutenant Colonel Carol Mather MC, 'The little admiral … having spent his retirement in the hunting-field, [Cowan] now [in his seventies] wanted to end his days on active service. In fact his greatest ambition was to be killed in action. This was not granted him.'

Similarly impressed, Waugh described his fictional characters in terms which must have been informed by Cowan's extraordinary service: Colonel 'Jumbo' Trotter 'retired with the rank of full colonel in 1936. Within an hour of the declaration of war he was back in the barracks.' And Ritchie-Hook: 'That ferocious Halberdier, he was sure, was even then biffing his way through the jungle on a line dead straight for the enemy.' Admiral Cowan was the archetypal old campaigner and much admired by the men of 11 Commando – an admiration which was clearly mutual based on his subsequent assessment of their involvement in the Litani River Battle in Syria.

Chapter 9

Landour Spirit: 'I'll shoot you, Blair'

The unremitting weather and relentless training apart, life on Arran was not all bad. For many, this was their first time away from home (or boarding school) – it was an adventure, and the training had created strong bonds. The young men felt a growing sense of independence and of doing something important for their country. Ironically, it may have felt for some as though life was just beginning.

No. 11 Commando's billets were all located around Lamlash village or on nearby farms on the east coast. Beds were allocated in volunteer homes, with four or five men per house. The senior officers rented the 'White House' from the Duchess of Montrose as an officers' mess and were allowed one day off per week for sport when they (as well as junior officers such as Eoin) were given access to some of the Duchess's shooting (which according to Waugh involved on occasion some remarkably fine stalking and shooting of deer with tommy guns). Eoin shared a billet called Landour Cottage in Lamlash with Blair and three other members of No. 11 (Gerald Bryan, Walter Marshall and one other), where they were very well looked after by their landlady, Ann McGowan. By way of pay, in addition to daily allowances for food and lodging, officers were given 13/4d (66.5p), while the other ranks (ORs) were allowed a more modest 6/8d (33.5p) – by the standards of the day, this was generous.

Of course, some managed to make rather more of their time on Arran than those with No. 11. Two of those with No. 8 (Guards) Commando, known as 'the Blue [blood] Commando' or more commonly 'the Guards', were the author, Evelyn Waugh and the PM's son, Randolph Churchill. Some of the officers of No. 8 were better known for their social activities than their preparation for war, spending as much time drinking and gambling as training. There was an informal division amongst the Guards officers between the professional soldiers and the so-called 'dandy officer brigade' recruited by Lieutenant Colonel Robert Laycock from the gentlemen's clubs of London, specifically White's in St James's. There was a distinct element of elitism in No. 8 Commando – Laycock seems to have ignored formal recruitment channels: 'I had a list of volunteers given me, but I did not

Landour Cottage, where Eoin was billeted at Lamlash, Arran.

rely on it. I called on my friends whom I could trust.' This led to varying standards; Guards No. 8 Troop's were considered to have fallen too low, and it was therefore disbanded in its entirety, with the men returned to their original units. David Stirling, the officer behind the birth of the SAS whom Eoin and Blair would soon encounter in Egypt, was with the Guards and known to enjoy an evening spent drinking and gambling – a nickname he came to earn, the 'Great Sloth', reflected his lack of enthusiasm for training.

The same issues could not be said to have afflicted No. 11 Commando in any way. As Waugh later noted in his diary, '11 Commando were very young and quiet, over-disciplined, unlike ourselves [No. 8 Commando] in every way, but quite companionable. They trained indefatigably.' Nonetheless, despite the standards they maintained and the arduous training, the men of No. 11 were extremely well looked after by their landladies – they were provided with up to four meals a day and could have a bath at least once a week. With space being tight in the billets, however, they had to adhere to strict routines. Cold water was used mainly for washing and in some cases for bathing. They used various farm buildings, boiling water in old boilers and taking baths in turn, with the last man left to swill the place out. The landladies would dry the troop's saturated kit after each day in the field – the men seemed to be perpetually soaked, and without the modern conveniences of today this was a daily slog. The landladies were paid, but their almost five months' work was a real war effort and one that has often been overlooked.

In a letter written to his mother in late 1940 and headed 'Sunday Night, Machrie Bay', Blair described Arran's weather during the first night of an endurance march – and the generosity of the local volunteers:

We left Lamlash about two o'clock and walked over here, about seventeen miles. For the first four miles there were odd showers. They didn't hinder us much since we quickly dried, but after it wasn't so good as the final shower lasted for the last thirteen miles, and there was a regular gale blowing off the sea into our faces. I waded through a river the other night and I don't think it was any wetter! This book [the letter was written on blotched sheets torn from a squared notebook] was in my pocket and is still wet. We got in here about seven o'clock and then started to find somewhere to sleep. We were carrying nothing except some food, we would not demean ourselves by carrying blankets. It is a smallish hamlet, eight or nine houses and I started going to them to find somewhere for my twenty-five men to dry their clothes. They were all decent, one old lady reminded me of you. I knocked at the door and the girl who opened it seemed scared. I think at first she thought I was a Jerry parachutist, though Father Christmas would have been more like the thing, what with all the equipment I had on. At any rate, I told her who we were, that we intended sleeping out and wondered if she could get some clothes dried. She rose to her feet. 'You'll not stop outside as long as I've a bed in my house,' she declared, and then went into a huddle with her two daughters and her clatter of children and then announced that she could take six. To cut a long story short, I am sitting in borrowed pyjamas and an overcoat made for a much smaller man than myself, so much so that when one of my lads saw me he said, 'Let Burton dress you!' [the slogan of a then well-known department store.]

On another occasion, Blair marched his 7 Troop off the end of the pier at Lamlash into deep icy water in full kit. He then marched right in after them. This would be the first of many marches off the end of the pier. It was proof of discipline, but not one appreciated by the soldiers' landladies. Blair was soundly berated by the indignant women, who looked after the soldiers in their care like mothers and were already getting fed up washing and drying the few spare uniforms on an almost daily basis.

Another feature of Pedder's unorthodox approach to training Eoin's unit was that they were among the first to conduct exercises and drills with live ammunition fired over their heads. They were also often seen and heard carrying out live mortar practice on the moor between Sannox and Corrie in the shadow of Goat Fell, disturbing the local stags. Unlike in the stricter regimental systems, the Commando enjoyed easy access to ammunition and explosives. Much of it, as a result of their being responsible for weapons training, was stored away under the beds in Eoin's and Blair's billet at Landour – much to the concern of their landlady, who had begun to wonder just how far her patriotic duty was expected to run. As Blair noted in a letter to his mother, the ammo came in very handy for splitting the bigger lumps of coal for Landour's fire. It was also not unknown for the men, in particular Blair, to improve the ventilation in the cottage by shooting out window panes. The local glazier was kept busy.

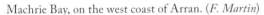

Machrie Bay, on the west coast of Arran. (*F. Martin*)

The pier at Lamlash, with Holy Isle 'in the distance' to the left.

As for distractions, the village had only one pub for the 500 troops from the three Commando units based on Arran in 1940, and the landlord would continuously run his two taps into a zinc bath from which he kept up his supply of pints of beer. There were three or four dances a week in the Village Hall, and the hall-keeper, John Martin, used to send to Glasgow for records of the St Bernard's waltz, the slow foxtrot and the quickstep. A particular favourite was *The Woodpecker's Song* by Glenn Miller and his Orchestra, a big hit throughout Britain in 1940, and girls came from around the island to dance to it with the soldiers.

So, despite the challenges presented by weather and training, the men soon began to feel at home on Arran. Blair wrote to his mother:

> I like this place – we are very comfortable here and the mess is fine. I don't live in the mess as I think I told you. Five of us are in a small parlour house, only for sleeping of course. I prefer it. We keep a fire going, have a gramophone, and there is a pot of tea made in the evening. I think this is the sort of place I'll live in. No women about it, and clothes lying about all over the place, dirty teacups on the floor, wet boots in the oven, a rugby jersey over one armchair and your feet on the fender, a perfect existence. We have lots of labour-saving devices also, e.g. the coal is in very large lumps. To split it we just fire a revolver shot into it, it cracks it wonderfully.

One of those who came later to share the billet at Landour was Gerald Bryan, an expert mountaineer before the war who was later to lose a leg in the Litani River operation in Syria (No. 11 Commando's first operation in

June 1941). Coming from the Royal Engineers in Chester and later the newly formed No. 9 Commando, Bryan was seconded to No. 11 Commando at the request of Pedder in order to help train some of the men in mountaineering and establish a cadre of properly trained rock climbers – he was formally posted to No. 11 in December 1940. With his arrival, Landour began to take on a distinctly Ulster character, as not only did Bryan originally come from Belfast, but for a period his family home was on Malone Road, not far from the McGonigals.

Bryan recalled that on New Year's Eve 1940, not long after Eoin had turned twenty, he, Eoin and the other two men from the billet went out to celebrate at the local hotel with some girlfriends from the Women's Voluntary Service (WVS). Blair wasn't interested in a Hogmanay party and remained in the billet alone. At about 1.00am, as the nominated duty officer, Bryan had to leave the party to inspect the guard at Brigade Headquarters. Having completed his inspection, he thought he would call into Landour on the way back to the others to wish Blair a happy new year. Blair was still alone. However, from his appearance, it was immediately clear he had seen the New Year well and truly in. Belligerently, he held out a jug to Bryan and ordered him to 'Get me some water.'

Bravely (or perhaps foolishly – Bryan was only 5′ 7″ and Blair 6′ 2″), Bryan demurred: 'Look, Paddy, I've been out and about for the last bloody hour. Get your own water.'

Whereupon, as Bryan recalled, 'Paddy picked me up and hit me in the face, sending me flying across the room against a wall where I collapsed on to the floor. When Paddy went out of the room to fetch some water, I slipped out of the house and ran off into the darkness pursued by Paddy firing at me with his Colt .45 automatic pistol [more probably a revolver].'

It was a somewhat exhilarating start to the New Year!

I joined the others in the WVS billet. One look at my face and everyone agreed it would be prudent to remain where we were for the rest of the night. We got back next morning and found three things. Paddy was sitting there, surrounded by thirty-six small bottles of cherry brandy, one side of beef, one leg of lamb and two loaves of bread. All the windows were shot out. He was sober. We said, 'Blair, where the hell did you get all this stuff? Get up that track and hide the lot.' We discovered later that he had nipped over to Brigade HQ and purloined the lot. But that morning he just stared at my bruised and swollen face with genuine concern. 'Who hit you?' he asked. 'Just you tell me and I'll sort the bugger out.'

Bryan was convinced that Blair had no recollection of the night before. In fact, the whole affair was successfully hushed up and they just managed to get the windows replaced before the police arrived to interview Bryan (as Duty Officer) about the theft from the Brigade Headquarters and the shooting. Nevertheless, Bryan recalled how, a few months later in Cyprus, their CO Dick Pedder turned to Blair one night in the officers' mess and said, 'By the way, I know who broke into Brigade HQ on New Year's Eve and stole the drink.'

Gerard Bryan. (*NMS*)

'Do you?' replied Paddy, with what Bryan described as a mischievous smile. 'Do tell us, because it was a great mystery at the time!'

Apparently, Pedder gave him an exasperated look and in typical fashion marched out of the room. Blair liked Pedder but he did not always get on with his superiors – he had his own way of doing things that didn't always meet with universal approval.

Bryan also told how a favourite game at Lamlash was for Blair to stand in the middle of the room while the other four advanced from the corners and tried to bring him down. They never succeeded, and it could become rough – shooting at Landour was not just confined to splitting lumps of coal.

'The only person who was able to control Paddy when he cut loose was Eoin McGonigal. Eoin had been known to point a revolver at him and say, "I'll shoot you, Blair." Paddy would stop because he knew that Eoin meant it.'

An early life spent dealing with a wild older brother had prepared Eoin well.

As attested by its owners, the walls of Landour were still marked with bullet holes many years after the war. Eoin was described as a 'super shot', and because both he and Blair ran the Commando shooting range packages (pistol and tommy gun training) during their time on Arran, they had access to virtually unlimited ammunition, and according to Bryan, 'They were not slow to use their pistols around [Landour] house.' It seems they took their work seriously and were not averse to putting in some extra shooting practice at home. It was possibly one of the most dangerous periods of the war for any of them and a miracle there were no mishaps!

Chapter 10

Longing for a show: 'the best trained, disciplined and soldier-like unit of the whole lot'

By the last few weeks of 1940 the men were more than ready; all they needed was a suitable operation. During the previous autumn, as the German invasion scare reached a climax, the Commando took part in various exercises connected with the defence of Britain. However, it was a frustrating time, with operations being planned and then cancelled on several occasions – the false alarm in early autumn over the attack via Norway was followed by the promise in late December of another operation, code-named Workshop, involving the capture of the Mediterranean island of Pantelleria, situated between Sicily and Tunis. The island was strategically positioned to give control of the Gibraltar, Malta and Alexandria convoy routes – its occupation by the Axis had become a serious obstacle for the Allies. Pantelleria is a small island, approximately 32 miles square, but at the time boasted its own airfield with underground hangars and held about eighty aircraft. Bays had also been created for a flotilla of German E-Boats. It was protected by about eighty guns of various calibres and garrisoned by around 11,000 Italian troops. Capturing it would be no easy task. Nevertheless, in the latter half of 1940 Admiral Keyes proposed to Churchill

that its capture by amphibious landing by the Commando was feasible. Taking it would restore Allied control of the East/Central Mediterranean, and ease the transport of essential supplies to the vital island fortress of Malta.

It would also mean that the use of the alternative 'safe' route around the Cape of Good Hope to Port Said and Alexandria in Egypt would no longer be necessary. This would reduce the return trip to just over 6,000 miles – a saving of 18,000 miles. The Commandos would soon see for themselves that this would have been a very desirable saving.

(*Commando Veterans Association*)

The plan was to run the gauntlet of Axis forces in the Mediterranean en route to Malta, before peeling off to seize the island. Once ashore, it was thought that the two sides would be so enmeshed that the Italian air force would be unable to intervene, at which point the odds would favour the Commando.

The Commando were taken from Lochranza on Arran by the *Royal Scotsman* under the guise of yet another exercise – however, preparation for the 'exercise' was such that nobody believed it. The convoy was ready to sail on 18 December 1940, and due to pass through the Straits of Gibraltar on the 28th. However, at literally the eleventh hour, German dive-bombers were re-deployed in Sicily, leading to an initial postponement of the operation before it was abandoned altogether.

So, almost as quickly as the excitement had built, the Commando returned to Arran and disembarked. Another damp squib. The operation did eventually go ahead, but not until 1943 and not with 11 Commando.

As was noted by their Captain at the time, 'The men were longing for a show.' Evelyn Waugh was a little more explicit in referring to this period of near-misses in *Officers and Gentlemen* (also sometimes referred to as 'Professional Soldiers and Scum Dandies' – Waugh never had the means to match the social exploits of some of his fellow Guards officers):

> There should be a drug for soldiers … to put them to sleep until they were needed. They should repose among the briar like the knights of the Sleeping Beauty … This unvarying cycle of excitement and disappointment rubbed them bare of paint and exposed the lead beneath.

At last, however, a plan was formed to capture Rhodes. This would require a lengthy voyage (which the attack on Pantelleria would have avoided). The men were therefore given one week's leave, from 14 to 21 January 1941. Eoin spent his with his family in Belfast – he had just been promoted to lieutenant and wanted to say goodbye before heading off for what looked like being an extended tour overseas. As it turned out, this would be the last time he would see his parents.

In the week after Eoin returned from leave, 11 Commando planned and carried out a successful mock raid on an aerodrome on the mainland. The guards were distracted by two of the Commando dressed as women, while the others cut the perimeter fence and gained entry to the site, where they carried out a simulated attack on the officers' mess with un-primed Mills bombs (hand grenades used in both world wars).

A few days later, on 31 January, using converted infantry landing vessels, they departed Arran for the last time. The ships were owned by the Glen Line and capable of sailing at up to 23 knots – they had previously been used as fast traders out to the Far East. They were painted battleship grey and

Eoin with John and Margaret McGonigal (prior to joining the Cameronians in 1940). Margaret is holding her grown-up son's hand.

had their holds converted to provide accommodation for the troops, with the decks used to store the landing craft that the men had been training with in Arran. Half of 11 Commando sailed on HMS *Glenroy* along with 8 Commando, while the other half sailed on HMS *Glenearn* with 7 Commando.

No. 7 Commando was drawn from Eastern Command, and by the time its ranks were deemed full there were fifty-eight different Corps or Regiments represented in its ranks. As a result, it developed a reputation as an undisciplined unit, the antithesis of No. 11, the Scottish, who if anything were criticized in some quarters for being over-disciplined and over-trained. In contrast, No. 8, the Guards (comprising the Grenadiers, the Welsh and Coldstream Guards, etc – although in fact most were not Guardsmen) were thought by some to be comprised of quite a few 'good time Charlies', primarily drawn from various London clubs. As Gerald Bryan recalled, 'The sight of the Coldstream Guards officers sitting down to breakfast and lunch with their hats on caused us plebeians some merriment.'

In this context, Admiral Cowan later wrote of No. 11 Commando:

[The forthcoming Litani River action in Syria] … was by far the best achievement of any of the lot [i.e. of all the Commando units] we journeyed out with and ensured the success of the advance, and it was so fitting that it fell to that battalion [11 Commando] to carry it through as no one can contest the fact that they were by far the best trained,

disciplined and soldier-like unit of the whole lot and the earnestness
and selflessness and grit of all of [them] was a perpetual marvel.

High praise indeed from the 'little admiral'. The two ships sailed from Arran
in company with the cruisers HMS *Kenya* and *Dorsetshire* as part of a larger
convoy of frigates and destroyers that was going around the Cape. They set
off from the mouth of the Clyde and sailed past the northern tip of Ireland
out into the Atlantic. Eoin would have looked wistfully over at the Irish
mainland as they passed Malin Head at the tip of Inishowen in Donegal –
just along the coast from his grandfather's childhood home and a place he
had hiked around with Ambrose on family holidays. They were heading out
into a dangerous and uncertain world and leaving their families behind, both
literally and in terms of any regular communication. Many, including Eoin,
would not return. Of the 500 Commando in the convoy, by the end of the
war only about fifty had escaped imprisonment, wounding or death – they
were to be quite literally decimated by the events to follow.

It was a lengthy voyage made worse by the weather – they encountered
Force 9 storms and were forced into making a wide loop out into the Atlantic
before turning south. Carrying an assortment of landing craft, derricks and
heavy weapons as deck cargo, the Glen ships were unstable and swayed
mercilessly in the stormy seas. As the ships rolled, so did the Commando,
suffering accordingly; instead of 'heaving-ho', they simply heaved. It was
not pleasant.

The weather and need to avoid German U-Boats extended the journey
significantly, and so the men occupied themselves as best they could with
regular sessions of P.T. on the cramped ships' decks. A boxing tournament
was also organized but, inevitably, card games served as the main source of
entertainment. In this regard, Jock Lewes of 8 (Guards) Commando, the
future training officer of the soon to be born SAS, noted the enthusiasm
that David Stirling (the principal founder of the SAS) demonstrated for
gambling during the voyage:

> In the trip out I saw [Stirling] first as the promoter of (to me)
> astronomical gambling at roulette and baccarat, willing to make or take
> a bet on anything in amounts which I would reckon in months or even
> years of work: clearly he does not think of money thus.

On the whole, however, as recalled by one of Eoin's fellow junior officers,
Lieutenant Tommy McPherson, the voyage was testing:

> For days we heaved our way through the stormy ocean under grey,
> rain-swept skies. The weather was so vile that all we could do with

the men was to make sure that they kept their quarters clean and remained alive, even if many of them were so ill that they felt they would rather die. Then suddenly, gloriously, the sun came out … and before we knew it we were off the African coast. We eventually put into Sierra Leone for supplies, fresh vegetables and water, and although we [No. 11 Commando specifically – not the other two Commando] were forbidden to go ashore or have any truck with the locals, because of the extremely dubious security situation in the country, it wasn't long before Sierra Leone came visiting. As we lay off the deep-water harbour in Freetown, we were immediately surrounded by Africans in canoes of all sorts trying to sell us things. Even though we [again, only No. 11 Commando] were confined to ship, it was still wonderful to see the green waving palm trees above the sandy beaches, to feel the warmth of the sun and to see fresh fruit and vegetables coming aboard in the sort of quantity that nobody had seen in Britain since the very earliest days of the war.

The fresh fruit and vegetables were a welcome relief from an outbreak of diarrhea that had swept through the troops' ranks. Finally, after a brief stop in Freetown, Sierra Leone, they reached calmer waters, where they saw dolphins and flying fish following in their wake, and even a single albatross flying overhead. It is not known how many of the men may have recalled Coleridge's *The Rime of the Ancient Mariner* and, for seafarers, the shifting symbolism of the albatross. ('… what evil looks Had I from old and young! Instead of the cross, the Albatross about my neck was hung.') And although any temptation to shoot the bird was resisted, hot and humid conditions persisted, with the result that they could smell quite easily the stench of rotting vegetation and human waste from the land which saturated the warm air. Given that most of those on board had never before been out of Britain, this came as a shock to their senses with some wondering if it was an omen of worse to come. The memory of Lamlash was already quickly fading.

They then headed for Cape Town, where they spent a couple of weeks. On arrival Pedder, ever the disciplinarian, immediately put No. 11 Commando through a four-

Lt Tommy McPherson. (*NMS*)

Soldiers exercising
while onboard a later
voyage to Cape Town.
(*C. Beaton*)

hour route march in full kit – although after spending so many weeks on board ship, where exercise was limited to the ship's deck, this was a welcome return to solid ground. Moreover, they could 'show their own swagger' to the crowds who turned out to watch them march to the distinctive pulse of the pipes.

In contrast, the other two Commandos, Nos. 7 and 8 (the Guards) were allowed a period of liberty to enjoy what the city had to offer. Pedder's stricter approach would never let him bend this far, and Eoin's No. 11 Commando were required to maintain discipline and mostly remained on board. Evelyn Waugh observed in his diary the differences in approach to training (or as he put it, enjoying the 'cruise' down south), noting that No. 11 Commando were over-disciplined and 'trained indefatigably all the voyage. [In contrast, w]e did very little except PT and one or two written exercises for the officers.' Of course, this was only when interruptions to their card games were tolerated (or they ran low on funds).

In fact, the Guards in particular enjoyed observing No. 11's adherence to discipline – thought to have been the inspiration for Waugh's 'B Commando' in *Officers and Gentlemen*. The troops were all met in Cape Town with great reception committees and something was laid on for almost everybody. However, as Waugh wrote:

> It didn't do B Commando much good. They've been taken on a route march, poor devils … there was a sterner sound. The soldiers on the pavement, reluctant to lose their holiday mood, edged into doorways and slipped down side turnings. A column in threes in full marching order, arms swinging high, eyes grimly fixed to the front, tramped down the main street towards the docks. Guy and Claire saluted the leading officer, a glaring, fleshless figure.
>
> 'B Commando,' said Guy. 'Colonel Prentice.'
>
> 'Awfully mad … Enclosing every thin man, there's a fat man demanding elbow room. No doubt he's enjoying himself in his own fashion. One way and another, Guy, Cape Town seems to have provided each of us with whatever we wanted.'

Could Colonel Prentice have been based on Colonel Dick Pedder?

Lt Col Dick Pedder. (*NMS*)

On the odd occasion when Eoin's unit were allowed out, they came across examples of the racial segregation that was to blight South Africa for decades to come. While institutional segregation in the form of apartheid was still a few years away (1948), the men still encountered several examples of minority white rule. Blair had seen this before when on tour with the Lions in 1938, when he famously freed some convicts being used to build a stand at Ellis Park (rugby) Stadium. The *Irish Times* noted:

> The famous Ellis Park stands were in the process of being erected by convicts from a local prison who slept in a compound beneath the scaffolding. Mayne and Travers [a Lions teammate] engaged one convict in conversation asking what he had done to be imprisoned. The answer was stealing chickens, for which he got seven years. The Lions' players christened their new friend 'Rooster' and decided to help him and a friend fly the coop. That night Mayne and Travers returned with bolt cutters and clothing and set free the convicts.

However, most of the others in No. 11 had not encountered segregation before and were amazed to see the not-infrequent notice boards bearing the words 'Whites Only'.

To Eoin and Blair the concept of segregation was, sadly, a little more familiar – albeit as the self-imposed religious segregation which had seen the divide between Protestants and the minority Catholics across schools, public housing and employment in Northern Ireland grow wider since Partition. It was not until the late 1970s that the British Government sought to reduce job discrimination in Northern Ireland with the Fair Employment Act.

Blair's supposedly natural antipathy towards Catholics has been the focus of 'theories' by various writers – despite his great friendship with the McGonigal brothers, Stirling and the many Irishmen he had under his command over the years. In reality, perhaps the more interesting question is how the brothers viewed their place in Belfast and the British Army as part of the Catholic minority in an increasingly hostile Six Counties, where their father's career had gone sideways. However, there is no evidence that they ever paid these matters any real heed. They were clearly alive to the issues – in one of his letters home Eoin asked how the Falls Road was bearing up and whether the forces were sparing 'the papists', but it was never a question of choosing between being Irish, Northern Irish or British. Indeed, they used these terms interchangeably on their various forms for university and the army – it seemed to be more a question of convenience rather than religious or political ideology. They took people as they found them, decided what they believed to be the right thing to do, and then did not look back. This non-partisan approach to life will have been informed by the mixed (and at the time highly unusual) religious background of the brothers' grandparents (as well as several uncles and aunts), combined with their education in the south but roots and home life in Ulster.

The same could also be said of Blair; despite the description of his father by a Mayne biographer as 'a diehard Unionist who amassed an arsenal to fight Home Rule', there is no evidence that Blair was guilty of any religious bigotry. On the contrary, it is acknowledged that Blair was passionate about Ireland and, like many Irish people living overseas, loved everything that reminded him of home. He was keenly aware of the country's history and culture and a huge fan of Ireland's traditions in music and poetry. He had played rugby for Ireland, celebrated St Patrick's Day and had a batman whom, it has been said, he primarily kept on for his ability to sing a great range of Irish songs. No doubt, as a proud Ulsterman who like the brothers had been born before Partition, he may have been suspicious about southern 'taigs' and 'papists', but that is a long way from saying that he was sectarian-minded. Regional rivalries are common in most countries. Malcolm Pleydell, a medical officer with the SAS put it well:

> Yes, Paddy was Irish all right; Irish from top to toe; from the lazy eyes that could light into anger so quickly, to the quiet voice and its intonation. Northern Irish, mind you, and he regarded all Southerners with true native caution. But he had Southern Irishmen in his Irish patrol – they all had shamrocks painted on their Jeeps – and I know he was proud of them; he never grew tired of quoting the reply given by one of the Southerners in answer to the question, why was he fighting in the war: 'Why?' he had replied. 'Of course it's for the independence of the small countries.' (Malcolm James, *Born of the Desert*)

Even in letters home to his sister Babs, Blair would refer to plans for St Patrick's Day – in January 1942 he wrote, 'I hope this Shamrock you are sending arrives in time' – and in a letter of late February 1942 he acknowledged receipt of some blue packets of Gallaher's cigarettes (made in Belfast in the biggest cigarette factory in the world)

Piper Lawson on the Fort at Famagusta

from the RUC, and said he was 'keeping a packet for the 17th [St Patrick's Day]'. He was planning to have a ceremony, he wrote, each time he lit one.

Like one of his favourite singers, Percy French, Blair avoided sectarian preference, appearing instead more than capable of placing himself 'betwixt and between' his duty to the King as an officer in the British Army and his love of Ulster and all things Irish – best illustrated by French's parody of the Queen's advice to one of her Lords before a visit to Ireland:

> 'Remember and steer', sez she,
> 'Uncommonly clear', sez she.
> 'I know what you mean', sez he,
> 'Betwixt and between', sez he.
> 'Up wid the green', sez he,
> And 'God save the Queen', sez he.

As Pleydell's comments make clear, Blair was adept at sidestepping any overt political comment and, again to quote French, would use humour instead:

> There was an old man of Kilcoole
> Who married a wife, quite a fool.
> 'Twas a Union', he'd say,
> 'That I wanted that day,
> But begorrah I'm getting Home Rule!'

In any case, after a couple of weeks the troops were back on the ships again and en route to Egypt. During the voyage, Piper Jimmy Lawson composed the first two parts of the tune *The 11th (Scottish) Commando March*, to which the following words were added:

> From a' the crack regiments cam oor men
> The pick of the Heilands and Lowlands and a'
> And stout-hearted Irish frae mountain and bog
> And stout-hearted Irish frae mountain and bog
> And gunners and infantry gallant and braw
> And noo we're awa', lads, to meet the foe
> And noo we're awa', lads, to meet the foe
> We'll fight in the desert, the hill and the plain,
> And though as yet we've no honours to show,
> They'll ken the 'Black Hackle' afore we cam hame.

Until that time *Scotland the Brave* had been the regimental march, but this new march was written to be played before it to give 11 Commando a more distinct identity. Apparently, Lawson had originally wanted to name the march after Colonel Pedder, but typically, Pedder was having none of it – 11 Commando wasn't one man.

Chapter 11

Egypt–Cyprus: 'C Battalion of Layforce'

E oin and the rest of No. 11 (Scottish) Commando finally disembarked in Suez on 7 March 1941. Three days later, the Commando units were moved on again, taking a train to Geneifa, where they began to prepare for the invasion of Rhodes.

To Eoin it felt slightly surreal. Only six years earlier, his parents had stopped off at Port Said, having approached Egypt from the other end of the Suez Canal through the Mediterranean, en route to a longer trip to Asia. The circumstances could not have been more different. He recalled them talking about being greeted by a crowd of touts looking to sell trinkets to the well-heeled visitors. His parents had returned with several Japanese netsuke and other Chinese and Japanese figurines, including a small monkey for Eoin, reflecting the year of his birth (and perhaps the more mischievous elements of his personality).

In contrast, the Commando units were welcomed by General Archibald Wavell on 12 March 1941. The then Commander-in-Chief Middle East Forces addressed them, explaining that the three units would from that point on be known as 'Layforce' and would come under the command of Lieutenant Colonel (as he then was) Bob Laycock. For security reasons, primarily a fear of alerting the enemy to the Commando's presence in North Africa, use of the name 'Commando' was now prohibited and 11 Commando was temporarily renamed 'C Battalion of Layforce'. Maintaining secrecy in order to achieve a surprise attack had become a particular concern with the news that the Afrika Korps had recently arrived to reinforce the ailing Italian army. The stakes were rising and so, based in Alexandria from 7 April 1941, preparations for the invasion continued.

However, yet again, events overtook their preparations when on 6 April the

Japanese monkey with a green jacket.

Germans invaded Greece and Yugoslavia. In the Western Desert Rommel, who had arrived in February, also launched an offensive, reoccupying Cyrenaica by early April and capturing Bardia. The Rhodes operation was therefore cancelled, adding to the men's frustration; Layforce were all desperate to fight, but circumstances kept intervening to prevent their involvement in anything meaningful.

As a result, even though some parts of Layforce were being utilized on smaller actions, this period was generally one of frustration, with hastily planned operations repeatedly being even more hastily cancelled. An example was the unrealized plan (at least initially and so far as 11 Commando were concerned) to conduct a raid on Bardia – an operation code-named Addition. The plan envisaged 11 Commando (C Battalion of Layforce) attacking the Sollum–Sidi Barrani highway on the Mediterranean coast east of Tobruk and west of Bardia in Cyrenaica. The hope was that they could also attack and destroy any motor transport they came across and take prisoners. They would then be in a position to destroy a stores depot which lay in the west of this area. The planned duration of the raid was approximately three hours. So much for the plan.

Several nights were spent on board the *Glenearn*, in and around Port Said and Alexandria, and on 16 April, along with four troops from 8 Commando, they embarked on the raid. But yet again, before even reaching their target – on this occasion due to adverse weather conditions – the raid was cancelled, forcing a return to Alexandria. Any sense of a so-called elite, special-forces purpose was being badly eroded; with the false starts while in Arran, the cancellation of the Rhodes operation (the primary reason for their move to the region), and now the cancellation of Operation Addition, it felt that the powers that be were struggling to find an appropriate role for the Commando. Some men started openly discussing requests to be returned to their original units. They had volunteered well over eight months earlier for 'service of a hazardous nature' – they had not expected it would consist solely of training and repeated false promises of action.

A few days later, the raid did take place but was dramatically scaled down, with No. 11 playing no part in it. The operation, undertaken by 7 Commando, was not deemed a great success: the intelligence did not pan out, and although the landings were unopposed, targets were hard to identify and/or did not exist and just under seventy men were captured as a result of miscommunication (confused directions). Moreover, one officer was mortally wounded as a result of 'friendly fire' by an over-anxious sentry.

Famously, an inscription was found scratched on to the troop deck of the *Glengyle*: 'Never in the whole history of human endeavour have so few been buggered about by so many' – a sentiment with which even Laycock expressed sympathy in a lecture given in the UK at the end of 1941.

Equally famously, Evelyn Waugh, who took part in the raid, painted a wholly unflattering picture in his personal diaries (published in 1976), calling it 'incompetent execution by the commandos against virtually no opposition'.

In any case, on 23 April Eoin and the newly-named C Battalion then moved from Alexandria, crossing the Suez Canal at Kantara, before entraining again and proceeding to the lush fruit groves of Palestine. At the end of the month they were transported by ship from the port of Haifa to Cyprus (on board the SS *Warszawa*, a Polish merchant vessel), arriving at Famagusta on 29/30 April 1941 to bolster the garrison there against the threat of a (half-) expected Axis invasion. They got to work establishing 'fields of fire', digging 'slit trenches' and preparing buildings for demolition. Along with a battalion from the Norfolk Regiment and the usual ancillary units, C Battalion would provide the only defence available if an attack did come. Fortunately, all that the invasion threat amounted to was a considerable number of nuisance raids by the Axis air forces. And so they remained, awaiting orders …

Having first established a camp on the site of the ancient city of Salamis, the Commando were soon dispersed around the island, and life settled into a regular routine with little to remind the men of war. Bored, over-trained and over-disciplined, frustration began to set in; they were a long way from fulfilling Churchill's demand for men of 'the hunter class' who would 'butcher and then bolt' – instead, they were just bored. Having put in so much hard training, they were straining at the bit. And although they were well looked after, the fact was that due to the lack of any action, morale was low. The bars and brothels of Nicosia and Famagusta experienced more trouble from them than the Axis forces did, as the soldiers took out their frustration on one-shilling bottles of Cypriot wine. An oft-repeated anecdote from the time which highlights the mood concerned, perhaps inevitably, Blair Mayne – he landed himself in some trouble during a dispute with the owner of a nightclub over his bar bill. Like a scene from a classic Western, after an evening's drinking with Eoin and others, Blair is said to have threatened the owner with his revolver by shooting around the man's feet and making him dance. True or not, it paints a picture of the general atmosphere of disenchantment and boredom at the time. This was soon to change.

Chapter 12

Litani River, Syria: Commando Assault 9 June 1941

E ventually, following the invasion of Crete by 15,000 German paratroopers in late May 1941, the Allies decided to advance into Syria (into an area that is part of modern-day Lebanon) and mount a seaborne assault on the Vichy French positions. It was hoped that there would be little resistance. The spearhead would be the 7th Australian Division, which had been held in reserve for the defence of Egypt. The plan called for the main thrust by the 7th Division along the coast road towards Beirut starting on the morning of 8 June 1941. Naval support would come in the form of the cruisers *Ajax*, *Phoebe*, *Coventry* and *Perth*, and the destroyers *Kandahar*, *Kimberley*, *Janus* and *Jackal*. The French had built up a strong

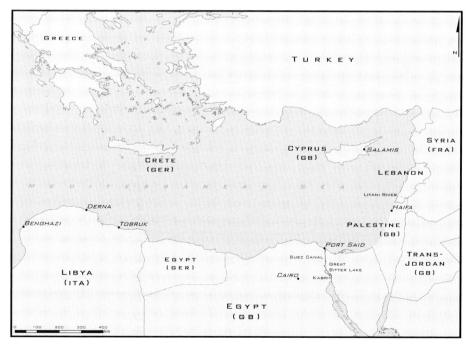

Map 2: The region where Eoin spent the final nine months of his life (Cyprus, Syria, Lebanon, Egypt & Libya).

River Litani.

defensive position on the line of the Litani River, where the vital Quâsmiyeh Bridge was known to be mined.

So finally the men of 11 Commando/C Battalion of Layforce were being called upon – their task would be to land north and south of the Litani River and capture the Quâsmiyeh Bridge, intact, to facilitate the progress of the Australian 21st Infantry Brigade (part of the 7th Division), who were leading the advance. The attack by C Battalion was planned to coincide with the main thrust by the Australians along the coastal road. It was code-named Operation Exporter.

Eoin and the men of C Battalion left Cyprus on 4 June 1941 and transferred to Port Said. They then sailed, again on board HMS *Glengyle*, on 7 June (escorted by the destroyers *Hotspur* and *Isis*) and arrived off Aiteniyé at the mouth of the Litani River in brilliant moonlight. This was obviously far from ideal. There was a heavy swell running that made lowering and unhooking the landing craft very difficult. At this stage, an advance party reached the rendezvous point in a patrol boat and indicated that the element of surprise may have been lost. There were enemy patrol boats in the vicinity and much activity on shore. HMS *Glengyle* had been visible in the moonlight while still eight miles off. In addition, heavy surf would make landing difficult.

Colonel Pedder and his fellow C Battalion officers were keen to press on regardless and attempt a landing. Their orders indicated that in view of the vital nature of Operation Exporter, synchronization of the timing of their raid with the advance of the Australians was paramount, and casualties in such conditions would therefore be expected and acceptable. Moreover, they were not at all convinced that even if HMS *Glengyle* had been spotted, the enemy were in fact aware that a raid was imminent or that at that early stage they would be prepared to defend against one.

However, the captain of HMS *Glengyle* was not persuaded, and despite it causing the men great difficulty, recovered the landing craft and ordered the return of the ship to Port Said. With some very disgruntled passengers on board, she arrived there at 1500 on 8 June.

In the meantime, the Australians had begun their advance into Syria. The Vichy French retired to their defensive points on the Litani River line and blew up the Quâsmiyeh Bridge. This changed the situation immediately, and so no sooner had HMS *Glengyle* re-moored at Port Said than she was ordered to sail again and carry out the landing operation that night instead. One can only imagine the nature of the discussions on board during this journey. The upshot was that they performed a nautical and tactical U-turn, this time escorted by HMS *Ilex* and *Hero*. Dick Pedder modified the original attack plan so that the whole Commando force would now be landed north of the Litani River at dawn, and this time the plan would obviously not include the taking of the Quâsmiyeh Bridge.

HMS *Glengyle*. (*Blair Mayne Association*)

The remains of the
Quâsmiyeh Bridge.
(*Australian War
Memorial*)

The Litani River landing in Syria was C Battalion's baptism of fire. It was the first opposed landing ever attempted by the Commando and viewed with foreboding by Eoin and the other officers. This had not been part of their training on Arran and did not accord with the Commando concept of highly trained, small, elite units engaged in guerilla warfare, covert raiding operations, blowing up installations, capturing prisoners and reconnaissance. Instead, they were now faced with a plan that was ill-conceived and no real alternative. Having already lost time, and with the Australians on the move, C Battalion had to get in fast to provide support.

The plan was for one group of C Battalion to capture the French positions on the Litani River and hold them long enough for the advancing Australian Brigade's sappers to build a pontoon. At the same time, another Commando party would capture the still intact Kafr Badda Bridge on a stream or tributary, about three miles to the north of the Litani River and on the enemy's main coastal supply route from the north.

The 27 officers and 456 men of C Battalion were divided into three groups, one commanded by Dick Pedder, the second by Geoffrey Keyes and the third by Pedder's adjutant, Captain George More of the Royal Engineers.

Keyes would lead the main attack with Nos. 2, 3 and 9 Troops. They would land just north of Aiteniyé Farm and take the enemy defensive positions overlooking the Litani River from the rear. A smaller party under Captain More, with No. 4 Troop (commanded by Eoin) and No. 10 Troop (commanded by Lieutenant Tommy Macpherson), were to land about a mile and a half farther up the coast and seize the still intact Kafr Badda Bridge. This formed part of the enemy's main supply route, so More's party was tasked with disrupting communications, preventing enemy reinforcement

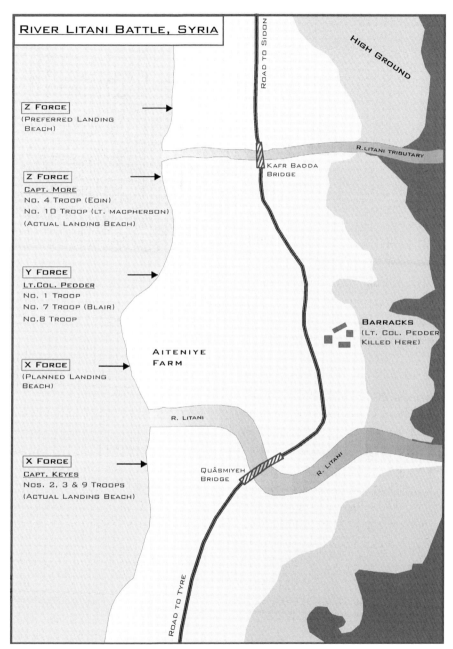

Map 3: Eoin was in command of No. 4 Troop in Z Force to the north.

and re-supply, and then reinforcing the centre party. Pedder's party, with No. 1 Troop (in which Gerald Bryan commanded a section), No. 7 Troop (under Blair's command) and No. 8 Troop, would land in the centre to attack the enemy barracks and act as reserves. No. 5 Troop and part of HQ Troop remained in Cyprus, and some but not all of No. 6 Troop were left on board HMS *Glengyle* and manned the AA guns, as space on the landing craft was limited.

While this attack was progressing from the sea, the Australians who had reached the Litani defences would, under cover of an artillery barrage, build a pontoon bridge. They would then cross the river to advance, with their light armour, through the Commando positions. The password chosen for the operation was 'Arran'.

Each party was equipped with a portable wireless set for communications, and a medical orderly. Each man wore a khaki shirt and shorts, steel helmets camouflaged with sacking (painted green and brown) and rope-soled boots, and camouflaged his face and hands with streaks of burnt cork. They were armed with Lee Enfield rifles and bayonets, revolvers (Webleys but possibly also Enfields or Smith & Wessons), grenades and a knife. Some also had 110 rounds of ammunition and spare magazines for the Bren light machine guns and tommy guns. Some sections also had a Boys anti-tank rifle.

Eoin, of course, was also fortified with his cigarette case.

HMS *Glengyle* reached the Syrian coast, for the second time in three days, at 0300 on 9 June 1941 just as the moon was setting. Conditions by then were calmer, and the eleven available landing craft were launched without difficulty. The northern and centre parties landed at about 0420, but the main party to the south went in slowly and did not land until 0450.

The problem was that having embarked in their ALCs with a full moon setting behind them, the Commandos found themselves landing at first light with the rising sun in their eyes and in full view of the enemy. There was nothing smart, let alone stealthy, about this strategy but it was unavoidable in the circumstances. Moreover, despite the calmer sea conditions, the actual landings on the most northerly beach by George More's group (with Eoin's No. 4 Troop) were far from smooth. As the ALCs carrying them came nearer to the land, two of them hit sandbars and foundered, forcing the Commando to clamber out into neck-deep water. As a result, More's wireless sets were wrecked, leaving him out of contact with the other two groups.

Captain George More. (*NMS*)

Assault Landing Craft ('ALCs') During Training Operations. (*www.combinedops.com*)

To make matters even more interesting, they had been landed on the wrong side of the enemy and faced the prospect of a frontal assault to take the bridge. They would have to move across open ground against an enemy positioned on higher ground and supported by AFVs (armoured fighting vehicles).

For a first opposed landing, this was quickly becoming a study in how not to approach it. Nevertheless, they pressed on.

Corporal H. Butler, a Bren gunner with Eoin's No. 4 Troop, recalled:

> We waded ashore in a heavy sea over rocks and each wave breaking over our heads and shoulders. We covered the last 40 yards to shore under machine-gun fire and advanced 150 yards inland without casualties, took cover and discarded lifebelts and haversacks as previously planned. Then we advanced in open formation due east … I spotted a machine-gun nest at our rear and took aim. The Bren refused to fire, so I made for cover and stripped it down, found it full of water and sand …

Captain More and Eoin conferred and agreed that they should attempt to cross the river near to where it entered the sea. But by 1600 the enemy was in position and in force, with no fewer than fourteen AFVs and four machine-gun posts flanking the approaches to the bridge and commanding the surrounding area. An intense action followed, and when the enemy engaged Eoin's Troop with both two-pounder guns and medium machine guns, Eoin had to lead a fighting withdrawal of his men.

Jimmy Lappin recalled:

> We had just cleared the beach and were lying in scrub grass. It was just after dawn on a beautiful clear morning. The air was still and when I looked over to the next two blokes, MacKay and Hurst, a couple of yards away, they had just lit up cigarettes. I could see two thin columns of blue smoke rising and I thought that I would have a smoke too but, just as I got my cigarettes out, the whistle blew for us to advance. These two blokes never moved, they were both hit, the smoke gave away their position. Cpl. MacKay was killed outright and Hurst died later in the day.

Nevertheless, with support arriving in the form of No. 10 Troop, Eoin led his men back in, and the Kafr Badda Bridge was eventually in the hands of the Commando by 0600. It had not been mined and so was captured intact. The position was reinforced against a possible counter-attack and a large number of prisoners was collected and taken under Eoin's charge to the hills to the east. At this point, at around 0800, Captain More could hear shelling in the direction of Aiteniyé and, with no radio communications, left on a motorcycle to try to make contact with the centre party.

A counter-attack commenced at around noon with the arrival of eight more AFVs. No. 10 Troop held them at bay until about 1600, when a further six enemy AFVs appeared from the east. These engaged Eoin's No. 4 Troop and, as a result, some of the prisoners escaped and were able to rejoin the action. At around 1730 both Nos. 4 and 10 Troops were forced to begin a withdrawal. Captain More then returned and, in the darkness, they attempted to make for the Australian lines. Most of Eoin's men made their way into the hills to the east, crossing the swiftly flowing water above the bridge with little further incident. However, a party led by Captain More made for the mouth of the river, where they were engaged by the enemy and suffered a number of casualties before having to surrender.

Lieutenant Eoin McGonigal, Officer Commanding No. 4 Troop, reported:

We landed in two ALCs – one sub-section under 2Lt Richards and three sub-sections under myself. 2Lt Parnacott was with me. We crossed the beaches with a few stray shots above our heads and no casualties, and made due east to the road. 2Lt Richards' party had not joined us. We crossed the road about 300 yards south of the enemy MT [Motor Transport] whose personnel took no notice of us. Gaining the rising ground, we saw the remaining troops of our fighting party engaging the MT on the road. As long as possible we gave them supporting fire from the rear. Then, when they had captured the trucks, we pushed northwards along the hills towards Kaffa Badr Bridge. On the road running east from this bridge we engaged one armoured truck, and an armoured car. The truck we destroyed and the car escaped to the east. Some twenty enemy retiring to the north were engaged by our small arms at 300 yards with good effect, and then … [we] … combined with Captain More's party in the capture of the French guns and trucks in the long valley which runs due east from the Kaffa Badr Bridge.

Capt. More consolidated the position and placed 10 Troop on the high ground above the Kaffa Badr Bridge and … [my] … Troop on the hills overlooking the valley some 500 yards east of 10 Troop. We occupied this position till about 4 o'clock in the afternoon, and set up a very temporary RAP [Regimental Aid Post] and had, under our care, a large body of prisoners. During this period we saw small bodies of the enemy to the eastward, all of these retiring northwards, and a French reconnaissance plane made repeated flights over us in the early afternoon. We could hear the sounds of 10 Troop on our left engaging enemy AFVs on the main north road and at about four o'clock, six armoured cars appeared on the road running to our east about 1400 yards away. These AFVs engaged our area with two pounders or some similar gun, and medium Mgs. They inflicted heavy casualties on our French prisoners. It had been impossible, owing to the flat nature of the ground around the road, to put any anti-AFV obstacle on the road and so, on the approach of the AFVs I withdrew my main body, consisting of one section of 4 Troop and some dozen men from Nos. 1, 7 and 10 Troops whom I had formed into another sub-section.

One sub-section and two anti-tank rifles stayed in our area and were driven out by the AFVs some fifteen minutes later. We reformed in the hills and with 3 sub-sections and two anti-tank rifles we moved to the support of 10 Troop. During the action with the AFVs, many French prisoners were killed attempting to disarm our men or escape. One sub-section was now sent to hold a main ridge covering our rear and the main road about 500 yards south of No 10 Troop and with the remainder of the troop I reported to Capt MacDonald and placed myself under his orders, this force being meantime augmented by a section of 8 Troop. Capt More arrived and took command of this fighting party.

Capt More ordered a withdrawal on the Litani River direction, using the ridges as bounds, and … [my] … Troop and 10 Troop alternated as forward troops. The enemy were bringing heavy but inaccurate fire to bear on us and, as far as can be checked, we suffered no casualties during the withdrawal. Eventually Capt More held a conference and it was decided to try and cross the river where it entered the sea. For this purpose we held a position till an hour after darkness and then it was found that 10 Troop and … [my] … Troop had retired in the direction of the high ground eastwards. It was by this route that most of … [my] … Troop got out of the fighting area and crossed the river above the main bridge. The remainder of Capt More's fighting party descended to the beach, where eventually we were caught by enemy MGs and suffered seven casualties, including 2Lt Parnacott killed. We eventually succeeded in surrendering, movement forwards or backwards being impossible. Next morning the French commander handed his post over to Capt More and we rejoined the main body of the Commando under Major Keyes.

The centre party of Nos. 1, 7 and 8 Troops (Blair was in charge of No. 7), with eight officers and 145 men in four landing craft, came under heavy machine-gun fire as they approached the beach. As a consequence, the landing craft went astern almost immediately after grounding, and most of the men were landed in water above their waists. Nevertheless, they struggled ashore and cleared the beaches quickly, losing only one man killed in No. 7 Troop.

The headquarters troop with Colonel Pedder crawled off the beach through a dry stream-bed and crossed the coast road without being detected by the enemy as they made for the barracks. They reached a valley north of the barracks and captured a number of prisoners who were guarding ammunition stores but then came under heavy machine-gun and mortar fire. They were pinned down until support arrived from another section led by Lieutenant Farmiloe which helped to put the machine gun and mortar out of action. They then moved on to a rise to the north-east of the barracks, where they again came under very heavy machine-gun fire and accurate sniping, which resulted in a number of casualties. Colonel Pedder ordered a withdrawal to try to contact the main force under Keyes which should have been to the south. They attempted to return to lower ground with better cover, but at around 0900 Colonel Pedder was killed, and shortly thereafter, Lieutenant Farmiloe was also fatally wounded.

It became apparent that all the officers of the headquarters party had either been killed or seriously wounded, and therefore Regimental Sergeant Major Tevendale assumed command. He planned a withdrawal in the direction of the Litani River but realized that enemy activity would make this difficult. The remaining men positioned themselves above the main road to the barracks and consolidated their situation, waiting for an opportunity to withdraw and in the meantime disrupting enemy communications.

They remained this way until about 1000, when the two large French destroyers *Guerpard* and *Valmy* joined in bombarding the beaches. However, these were soon chased off by the British destroyers *Janus*, *Jackal*, *Hotspur* and *Isis*.

At about this time the Australian artillery began a barrage on the French defences which allowed the forward units of Nos. 2 and 3 Troops to launch a boat. Captain Eric Garland and six men from No. 3 Troop crossed to the north bank of the river, and the boat was returned by two Australians. The enemy barrage and small arms fire continued until about 1130, pinning them on the south shore, unable to reinforce the crossing party.

In the meantime, over on the far bank, Captain Garland and his men were cutting wire and exchanging fire with the French positions less than 100 yards away on higher ground. At about 1145 Captain Highland got across with another boatload, and shortly thereafter, a French officer walked out of the post with a white flag.

With the enemy guns silenced, the Australians crossed the Litani River on the sand-bar at its mouth and grouped to attack Aiteniyé. The advance

Australian forces, Litani River, Syria. (*Australian War Memorial*)

began about 2100 but was repulsed in just over an hour. However, daylight on 10 June brought an end to the engagement as the French in Aiteniyé surrendered to Captain More. More and a French officer walked through the French defences to reassure the troops that the action was indeed over, and they gave up their positions.

By midday on the 10th it was pretty much all over – the Australians had finally made their crossing and were now advancing through the positions that were held by Geoffrey Keyes' X Party. C Battalion's part in Operation Exporter came to an end and they made their way to a transit camp at Haifa in Palestine. War correspondent Alan Moorhead would recall seeing the 'Jocks', exhausted but nearly all smoking and enquiring about their comrades, picking up stragglers on the way and mourning their dead.

The rest of the day was spent tending to the wounded and burying the dead, and on 14 June 1941, after a period of leave in Haifa, they set sail on the SS *Rodi* for Cyprus, reaching Famagusta the following morning.

Chapter 13

Aftermath: 'my silver cigarette case'

Operator Exporter was a success despite the hard lessons learnt. The toll on 11 Commando was heavy – casualties were unacceptably high, and the dead included their CO Dick Pedder. Five officers and forty other ranks lay dead, with nine missing, presumed dead, and a further three officers and forty-seven other ranks were wounded (i.e. 104 casualties out of the 395 who took part in the landing). Gerald Bryan, with Pedder's No. 1 troop at Litani, was one of the unlucky ones; shot in both legs, he ended up having one of them amputated. He was alive, but it would be the end of his mountaineering career. However, even when lying on a stretcher in a Beirut hospital, one of his first thoughts was for his treasured cigarette case: 'When I arrived at the hospital in Beirut my shirt was covered in blood and … was cut off. I was then completely naked. Remarkably, my silver cigarette case was returned to me.'

Blair's troop lost one man on landing and another crossing the coast road under heavy machine-gun fire. The official account of the action, attributed to Blair (but written and signed on his behalf by Captain George More), is brief:

> 0700 Passed Lt. [Bill] Fraser's section [a future 'L' Detachment SAS Brigade 'original']. Took 25 prisoners at French explosive store. (Colonel Pedder's troop had already passed that way and frightened them into staying put.) 0730 Attack on strong mortar post covering river. There was also some form of observations post beside this. Another thirty prisoners taken. 0800 Pinned down by Bren gun fire from Australians on other side of river. No notice taken of white flag. 0900 Had to retreat to obtain cover. 1000 Collected and concentrated all prisoners. 1100 Started to move east from explosive store. 1200 More prisoners, mostly mule drivers taken. [1200 to 1700 not accounted for except by march.] 1700 Reached river after long detour. 1730 Again fired on by Australians, one O.R. killed. 1800 Reached small house beside river – spent the night there. French still sniping. 0430 Crossed pontoon bridge and marched down to Australian camp. Prisoners escorted to Tyre.
>
> Signed Lt. R. B. Mayne, R.U.R.

However, in a letter to his brother dated 15 July, Blair elaborated on the operation:

I have left the Scottish Commando now – it was not the same when the CO [Dick Pedder] got written off. Nearly a year I was with it and I liked it well, but I think the Commandos are finished out here. We did a good piece of work when we landed behind the French lines at the Litani River. We were fired on as we landed, but got off the beach with a couple of casualties. Then we saw a lot of men and transport about 600 yards up the road. I couldn't understand it as they seemed to be firing the wrong way, but might have been Aussies. There was quite a lot of cover – kind of hayfield – I crawled up to thirty yards or so and heard them talking French. So I started whaling grenades at them and my men opened fire. After about five minutes, up went a white flag. There were about forty of them – two machine guns and a mortar – a nice bag to start with.

We had only a couple of men hurt. They had been firing at McGonigal's crowd who had landed further north. We left those prisoners and pushed on. McGunn, a Cameronian, was in charge of my forward section and he got stuck, so we went around him. I had about fifteen men. It got hilly and hard going and Frenchies all over the place. Eventually, we came to a path which we followed and came on a dozen mules and one knew that there must be something somewhere and we came on it just around the corner. About thirty of those fellows sitting thirty yards away. I was round first with my revolver, and the sergeant had a tommy gun – were they surprised! I called on them to '*jettez-vous à la plancher*' but they seemed to be a bit slow on the uptake. One of them lifted a rifle and I'm afraid he hadn't time to be sorry.

This was a sort of HQ place, typewriters, ammunition, revolvers, bombs and, more to the point, beer and food. We had been going about six hours and we were ready for it. While we were dining the phone rang. We didn't answer but followed the wire and got another bull – four machine guns, two light machine guns, two mortars and fifty more prisoners. We lost only two men (sounds like a German communiqué). It was a long time since I had a day like it. Eventually, about eight hours later, we came back through the Aussie lines. We were rather tired so the prisoner laddies kindly carried the booty and equipment. The rest of the story can keep until I see you. I am getting rather tired of this country [Egypt]. The job is not bad, but I can't stand the natives!

While ultimately the operation was effective in achieving its objectives, it had come with the loss of many men. Much of the blame for what had gone wrong was laid at the door of the navy. However, naval incompetence was, according to Lieutenant Macpherson, 'compounded by progressive snags that developed as a result of the long round-trip caused by the postponement. The landing was late and the landing craft hit the beaches in clear visibility after dawn instead of an hour or 90 minutes before.' Almost a third of Layforce were casualties, but by far the majority of these had resulted from Keyes' order to advance to contact against a defended position in broad daylight. Jim Gornall, one of the few who crossed the Litani, commented:

> Keyes was the officer commanding our unit. He had no artillery support. He hadn't recce'd any of the area. He knew nothing of the south bank of the river. And yet he made a frontal attack. There were three Troops of us landed on the beach – about 150 men – but only 14 of us crossed that bloody river. Not all of the rest were casualties, but a lot of them were. And that was down to Keyes and his frontal attack.

Having been landed on the wrong side of the Litani and in action for the first time, Keyes was in a dilemma. The plan had been for the Commando to assault the enemy from the rear, under cover of darkness, taking them by surprise – as per their training. Instead, Keyes was faced with either doing nothing or advancing to contact in a classic frontal attack against troops who were dug in behind barbed wire with artillery and machine guns. This was not at all what the Commandos should have been brought in to do: a frontal attack in daylight smacked more of the outdated tactics of the First World War. 'It certainly was most dangerous,' he wrote later. 'I had to make a decision whether to try and cross or go home!' And so he ordered his Troops to advance to contact.

Very soon therefore, his men had the curious experience of passing through the lines of the 2/16th Australian infantry battalion, the men for whom they had been meant to clear the way but who had actually arrived before them. The Australian CO was astonished to see them. Keyes took the opportunity to enquire if they had a boat the Commandos could borrow; the CO was glad to oblige but showed no inclination to join the attack. Only minutes after passing the Australians, the carnage started. 'We were going through the Aussie lines,' Jim Gornall recalled, 'and the Aussies were saying "Go on Jock, give 'em hell!" And then we got a couple of hundred yards in front of them and all hell was let loose – on us! We had no artillery support. The Aussies had artillery, but there was no one to coordinate it, because we weren't expected – we'd been landed by mistake on the wrong side of the river.'

Eoin – photo taken by Blair in what is believed to be Cyprus.

It was a disaster. And the tragic consequences of that frontal attack played no small part in the subsequent decision to disband Layforce. With their Commanding Officer killed, Keyes and More, the two remaining senior officers, reported to Jerusalem and were congratulated on their efforts. Lieutenant Colonel Laycock visited the men and commended their performance. Arrangements were then put in place for them to return to Cyprus where they would guard the dock areas and await new orders – essentially, they were posted there on garrison duty.

As it was, only a portion of C Battalion sailed back to Cyprus. The others were sent to the Commando base at Geneifa, where they were involved in other work. However, within a few days towards the end of June, it became apparent that Layforce/11 Commando would be disbanded. Both 7 and 8 Commando had already suffered that fate. Replacement troops, suitably trained, were difficult to obtain, and the resources available at the eastern end of the Mediterranean precluded the type of operations for which the Commandos were best suited. With no mission for which to train, the unit disintegrated.

There was friction among some of the officers and dissatisfaction with their new commanding officer. Keyes, with little experience, was over-zealous, and this, combined with grumblings of nepotism relating to his rapid rise as CO, meant that morale suffered. Some of the officers and men returned to their original units. Others graduated to the Long Range Desert Group (LRDG) or considered travelling to Asia to train the Chinese in guerrilla warfare tactics in their fight against Japan – something that both Eoin and Blair discussed. After all the expectation built up through the establishment, recruitment and training of 11 Commando, and the sacrifice of so many at Litani, it was an undeservedly sad end for this adventurous and pioneering group of special forces soldiers.

11 (Scottish) Commando comprised: 1 Lieutenant Colonel; 10 Captains; 24 Subalterns [junior commissioned officers, primarily different grades of lieutenant such as Eoin]; 2 Warrant Officers; 42 Sergeants; 81 Corporals; 122 Lance Corporals; and 250 Privates.

Collection of photos compiled by Walter Marshall of 11 Commando Officers. (*National Museums Scotland*)

Collection of photos compiled by Walter Marshall of 11 Commando Officers. (*National Museums Scotland*)

Chapter 14

Blair v Keyes: 'a truculent Irishman'

Unfortunately, friction in the unit led to various incidents, some of which involved Blair and Keyes. The reports are not all reliable, but it is said that when Eoin and Blair were playing chess one evening, Keyes tried to interrupt their game and Blair either knocked him unconscious or hit him and chased him out of the officers' mess at the point of a bayonet. When he came round, or things calmed down, Keyes threatened to have Blair placed under close arrest. However, knowing all too well Blair's standing amongst the men, Keyes never followed through. Instead, it would seem that he bided his time until another opportunity to dismiss Blair from No. 11 Commando came about.

Whatever the truth of the matter, their mutual antipathy was well known. Blair considered that the aristocratic Keyes would never have been accepted into the Commando if his father, a Great War hero, had not been the director of Combined Operations. Keyes, on the other hand, considered Blair a loose cannon who drank too much and couldn't control his temper.

In any event, it wasn't long before another incident involving Blair happened, this time in the form of a dispute between Blair and a fellow officer, Charles Napier, the son of another high-ranking military officer and Keyes' second-in-command. It ended with Blair allegedly attacking Napier and thereby presenting Keyes with a further opportunity to engineer his dismissal – an opportunity which some felt he appeared all too ready to seize.

On 21 June 1941 (less than a week after getting back from the Litani River operation), Blair was accused of beating up Napier following an evening of drinks at the officers' mess at Salamis on the east coast of Cyprus. Keyes had stayed the night elsewhere and only arrived at Salamis the following day, when the trouble was already over. Keyes states in his diary that he conducted an investigation and concluded that Blair 'must' have been responsible; that after drinking heavily in the mess, Blair had allegedly waited by Napier's tent and assaulted him when he returned that evening. The events have been reported (in Michael Asher, *The Regiment*) as follows:

> On 21 June … Lt. Col. Geoffrey Keyes returned to his HQ at Salamis on Cyprus, to find an 'appalling scandal' in progress. The previous evening

had been Guest Night at the 11 (Scottish) Commando's officers' mess, and one of his subalterns, twenty-six-year-old Lt. Robert Blair 'Paddy' Mayne, Royal Ulster Rifles, had drunk himself into a frenzy. Called to order by the commando's acting 2IC, Major Charles Napier, Gordon Highlanders, the scion of a well-known military family, Mayne had growled threats and became 'very bolshie'. Later, as Napier returned to his tent, he was set upon by a 'huge unknown assailant' and severely thrashed. Napier was certain it was Mayne but was unable to identify him in the darkness. Geoffrey Keyes, Royal Scots Greys, son of the Director of Combined Operations, First World War hero Admiral Sir Roger Keyes, was a bespectacled Old Etonian, who at twenty-six was reportedly the youngest battalion commander in the British army. He investigated the assault on Napier, and by next morning was satisfied that Mayne was responsible. On 23 June he hauled Mayne in front of the divisional Commander, Brigadier Rodwell, who promptly RTU'd him. The orders session is recorded in Keyes's diary:

> June 23: Produce Paddy before Div Commander, and he is rocketed and removed. Very sorry to lose him as he did awfully well in the battle and is a great fighter. He is however, an extremely truculent Irishman when he is 'drink taken' and is as strong as a bull.

As a result, Blair was sent to the Commando Base Depot in Geneifa, Egypt. There he went down with a bout of malaria and was confined to No. 19 General Hospital, Canal Zone to recover.

However, it seems that this account may not be entirely accurate or complete. It has since been noted that Blair and others in No. 11 had a grudge against Napier. According to a then serving member of 11 Commando, Napier, who had not taken part in the Litani River operation, had shot (or ordered the shooting of) Blair's dog while Blair, Eoin and the rest of 11 Commando were mounting their attack in Syria. Blair was attached to the dog (it was in fact a stray which had been adopted by his troop) and was furious about this. It led to an argument in the mess between Blair and Napier and the subsequent allegations of assault.

Nonetheless, some questions remain about the surrounding circumstances. For example, it is not clear what would have prompted Napier, Keyes' second-in-command, to have shot Blair's dog (or ordered it shot); and why would Blair not simply have challenged Napier in the open rather than lie in wait for him in the dark at his tent – a most unlikely course of action for somebody as direct and bold as Blair, a man who had little respect for any authority unless earned? Blair had already demonstrated his willingness to challenge his superiors on more than one occasion – a fact to which Keyes himself could only too happily attest. It is therefore difficult to understand why, with drink taken, Blair would suddenly have become more circumspect and calculating.

Moreover, it is odd that Napier was unable to identify Blair, despite it being alleged at the time that Blair was in a state of so-called 'drunken frenzy' and therefore unlikely to have been capable of acting with much stealth (let alone restraint in waiting in the dark to assault Napier). It is also notable that Blair neither denied nor accepted responsibility for the attack and was only dismissed on the basis of circumstantial evidence – essentially, Keyes' investigation into the fact of the argument between Blair and Napier in the mess. ('Later,' Keyes wrote in his diary, 'Charles got beaten up, by a large unknown assailant. Paddy suspected, and Charles sure of it; but <u>no proof</u>.' [Emphasis added.]) Bearing in mind that Blair was later given responsibility for dispensing troop discipline within the SAS and did so by taking on insubordinates in the boxing ring, it is difficult to accept that he would have attacked Napier surreptitiously, particularly while under the influence.

An alternative view (albeit a purely speculative one) is this: given the anger with their commanding officer for shooting the troop's mascot while the troop were engaged in such an attritional operation as the Litani River action (an operation Napier had avoided), others were involved in issuing some informal troop discipline, but Blair was insistent on taking responsibility for what happened.

Capt Keyes and Lt Napier. (*NMS*)

Regardless of what actually happened or the motivations involved, the fact is that there was genuine tension between several of the officers – both because of this incident and the allegations of nepotism and favouritism generally. Few had forgotten that despite not completing the 100-mile march to Ayr from Galashiels, Keyes had not been RTU'd like others who had failed to finish it. Instead, he had complained of sore feet, taken a lift in a supply truck and later been promoted as Pedder's second-in-command. There were many who felt that he should not have been admitted into the Commando, let alone put in charge at Litani River. In this regard, it is interesting to note Asher's description of the man in *Get Rommel*:

> All his life, Geoffrey Keyes had striven to emulate his father and to live up to his reputation, a particularly difficult task for him because he was not cast in the robust mould from which heroes are supposed to be made. Suffering from poor hearing and eyesight, he had been obliged to give up boxing at Eton because of potential damage to his ears, and to ditch rowing because of curvature of the spine. His mother, a woman who believed that to show affection to a child was to spoil it, obliged him to wear various contraptions – all of them unsuccessful – to cure this ailment, which only added to his sense of inadequacy. During his first term at Sandhurst he was rated below average physically, and he was never more than a mediocre shot.

Regarding Keyes' posting to the Commandos Asher wrote:

> The influence of the British ruling class worked in ways more subtle than official wires. The interviewing officer, Major Bruce Ramsay, was of First World War vintage, and even if he had not received a wire [one was sent by Roger Keyes directing the posting of his son Geoffrey] … he was certainly aware that he was interviewing a national hero's eldest son. [A similar predicament to that faced in the future by David Stirling when dealing with a request to join the SAS by Randolph Churchill.]

In any event, Blair had run foul of the wrong people at Salamis. It was clear there was no love lost between Keyes and Blair – eleven days after his appearance before the Brigadier when he was RTU'd, Blair wrote to his mother on 4 July 1941 [incorrectly dated 4 June] explaining how he had 'applied to get out' and since 'left' the Commando, and complaining about Keyes: 'I have left the Commando now, I was sorry in a way, but they are all breaking up. I couldn't stand the person who is acting C/O [Keyes] a young pup of a lad. So I applied to get out, I am not sure what I'll do now, but I am getting rather tired of this country.' However, after taking on the sons of

A later photograph of Blair and another stray.

such high-ranking members of the military establishment, Blair would not have been easily forgiven, regardless of his standing amongst the rank and file. Therefore, following the disbandment of Layforce after Litani, Blair was close to joining British Military Mission 204 in the then British colony of Burma (the mission tasked with helping train Chinese militia in their expected fight against the Japanese across the border in Yunnan). Blair had applied and was waiting to find out if he had been accepted – if it hadn't been for the opportunity presented by David Stirling and his fledgling SAS, Blair might well have gone east. It would be a choice between the jungle's humidity and leeches and the desert's hot sand and flies – neither particularly comfortable for any Irishman.

Chapter 15

'Blooded'

Eoin was equally unhappy and frustrated at the way things had gone at Litani. They had lost a lot of good men using methods that ran counter to everything they had trained so hard for on Arran. It was desperately disappointing. Gerald Bryan, the mountaineering expert from Belfast who had shared the billet with Eoin and Blair on Arran, had lost a leg and would never climb again. The death of their leader, Dick Pedder, had also hit hard. Eoin was disappointed and despite restrictions on what he could say made this clear to Ambrose when he wrote to him from 'C' Bn. Layforce, Middle East Forces on 26 June 1941 (eleven days after returning from Litani/Haifa):

Dear Ambrose,

I am now beginning to get some letters through, but unfortunately they are all very old. For example, I got one to-day dated the 27th February from Mother, and that is the latest that I have received so far. However, I am hoping that you will soon get air mail letters like these which are meant to get home inside a fortnight.

As you probably saw from the papers, the Scottish Commando have been blooded, and blooded was the only word for it. The McGonigal carcass is still undamaged, I'm glad to say; but I do not suppose we are allowed to say anything more about it.

How are you getting on? Are you back with the Regiment yet? You seemed to be having rather a sticky time in February; let me know as soon as possible how you are getting on and whether you are back in circulation.

If you do stay with the Rifles … for goodness sake don't volunteer for this Commando business again. I'll probably be arrested as a Fifth Columnist if I give reasons but certainly this job has not planned out as we were led to hope it will.

I am going to pull every string to get home, but chances are minute. However, the thought of Winter in Ballymena is worth a lot of hard work.

Best wishes,
Eoin

The harsh reality of war was hitting home. Eoin, the other officers and all their men had worked hard in training and were looking forward to being properly deployed. Instead, having experienced the frustration of repeated false starts, wasted time, a poorly executed mission when it finally came and the loss of so many comrades, the men were extremely disillusioned.

Thoughts of their time at the RUR's barracks at Ballymena was a common theme. Blair also wrote home to his mother, 'I wouldn't mind a spell in Ballymena at the moment, but I want to see a little more fun yet before I come back.' They were torn between wanting to stay and finish what they had come to do, and wishing they could spend some time back home. It would seem that in the aftermath of Litani and the uncertainty surrounding their future direction and existence as a special Battalion, Eoin and Blair had probably been discussing how nice it would have been to be back with the Rifles in Ulster.

This was reflected in Eoin's writing – not just his letters home but his short stories. While the precise timing is not clear, it is very noticeable that as time went on the tone of the stories became distinctly darker. Gone were the light-hearted romantic tales, to be replaced by markedly colder stories of murder and extortion. These included an account of a robbery carried out by some nefarious Chinese characters in Japanese-occupied Shanghai involving a series of particularly callous and unnecessary murders – a hanging and the cutting of the throats of the victim's wife and two children. After killing the wife, the culprit explains his actions, commenting that he 'never did believe in orphans … They have a dog's life' and so he immediately slits the throat of the son, just to the side of his Adam's apple, and metes out the same treatment to the daughter. Then in a scene reminiscent of a Quentin Tarantino film, members of the gang 'playfully' carve the hero's name into his forehead with their knives. The contrast with Eoin's earlier stories is stark, and a calmly considered and executed desire for revenge emerges ('a cold anger outlived the scars on his forehead and he lost no time in weeping for the past but settled down to what was, at least, a duty'). All that was needed was an outlet, a focus for this desire.

While it may be a little simplistic to draw a direct connection between the brutality of events in Syria and this change of tone in Eoin's writing, it is difficult not to think it was an important factor. There was a palpable sense of disenchantment. It seemed that any thoughts of foreign adventure had disappeared the moment the ALCs hit the sandbars at Litani and his men had come under fire. This was not helped by the lack of news from home – for many, including Eoin, thoughts of home were hard to keep at bay. The fact that up until 26 June 1941 he had heard nothing from home for well over four months could not have helped.

All the men were desperate for mail – they had had very little news since leaving Arran. The weight and bulk of letters meant that correspondence was taking between three and six months to get through. For today's connected generation this would be quite literally unimaginable. For young men like Eoin the expectations were entirely different, but it nevertheless made life incredibly difficult. Having originally feared that the war would be over if they did not immediately get involved, they now found themselves spending more time waiting for action and waiting for news from home than they had previously thought the war would last. In one sense, the fact that there were less frequent reminders of home perhaps made it easier to focus on what they were there to do and created a sense of camaraderie, but the challenge of homesickness and loneliness was very real; the feeling of life suspended and the desperation to experience the normality of everyday things – commonplace interactions with loved ones, a trip to the local newsagent for some cigarettes and a paper or a few pints in the Adair Arms Hotel in Ballymena. Without regular action, the men were finding it difficult to dispel thoughts of home, and the dearth of news from family and friends only intensified these feelings.

However, the introduction of airgraphs that summer improved things considerably. These forms, upon which the soldiers' messages were written, were photographed and then sent as negatives on rolls of microfilm. At their destination, the negatives were printed on photographic paper and delivered as airgraph letters by the normal Royal Engineers (Postal Section), also known as the Army Postal Services (APS). It was estimated that 1,600 airgraph letters on film weighed just 5oz, whereas 1,600 ordinary letters weighed 50lbs – this allowed the average delivery time to be reduced to a mere two or three weeks.

The maximum length of a message that each form could hold was only a few hundred words, but at just 3d (less than 1½p), they were inexpensive and therefore extremely popular (at least initially). The first shipment comprised some 70,000 letters, 350,000 messages being sent during the first month of the service and over 500,000 in the second. Still, there was a drawback; the form was not to be folded, and had to be handed in at a post office, where it would first be handled by censors, and then by sorters and other processing personnel. As a result, some soldiers grew to dislike them, as anything personal could be read by those screening the messages. So, when sufficient aircraft capacity became available, use of the airgraph declined in favour of the more expensive but more private air letter.

Alongside the technical advances made in speeding up deliveries, Eoin and Blair did their bit in 'encouraging' those involved in processing the men's correspondence to do so as quickly as possible. Again, the tale is difficult to confirm, but it is said that in response to complaints from the men that the mail from home was being delivered late, Eoin and Blair took it upon themselves to give their unfortunate postmaster and his colleagues 'a good thrashing'. Whether it improved efficiency is not known but it probably did the men's morale no end of good …

Chapter 16

'L' Detachment SAS Brigade:
a new breed of dervishes

The extended garrison duty in Cyprus did little to repair the damage caused by the Litani experience or to stop the men of 11 Commando thinking of home. It was therefore most timely that just as many Commando members of Layforce were being returned to their original units, getting ready to join the Long Range Desert Group (LRDG) in North Africa or, as with Blair, applying to join the British Military Mission 204 in Burma, an opportunity arose to join a nascent parachute unit being formed by a member of 8 Commando – Captain David Stirling.

The details were thin, very little was known about the new unit – it was all supposed to be a bit 'hush-hush'. However, recruits were promised an opportunity for action of the type for which they had trained so hard with Dick Pedder. For Eoin and the other members of the now disbanded Layforce considered good enough to be accepted, the decision to join 'L' Detachment, Special Air Service Brigade, as it was then known, was an easy one – return to their original units and traditional warfare, or do justice to their training and the Commando ethos of 'operating by night, fighting alone or in small groups, killing quickly and silently, using independent initiative and thinking only in terms of attack' (Lieutenant Colonel Clarke). If Stirling was to be believed, 'L' Detachment represented the kind of independent, irregular warfare they were looking for when they volunteered for the Commando – they would be taking part in clandestine operations behind enemy lines in North Africa. As highly skilled Commando, this might very well be their last chance to make a real impact. Moreover, for Eoin it provided a clear focus with which he might dispel some of his recent misgivings.

Of course, it might also prove to be another specialized unit which spent most of its time waiting and training, punctuated by repeated instances of cancelled or poorly conceived operations. It was a choice between taking this leap in the dark but with ambitious objectives and renewed purpose, or returning to the RUR; looking forward, not back. Stirling's pitch to potential recruits was that they would be taking the fight to Rommel, the 'Desert Fox'

– parachuting in behind enemy lines in the Western Desert and going after enemy installations and aircraft. Some of the original members of the unit have since recalled it being described around Base Depot as a group of 'do or die boys'. The Allies had nothing in the region, no air force or ground troops. Stirling wanted to deploy small units covertly behind enemy lines, attacking airfields located along the coast by approaching from the desert and destroying aircraft on the ground. The Germans and Italians would not expect ground assaults from inland, so the strategy offered both the advantage of surprise and a safe retreat back into the desert after a mission was completed. It was intended to be a parachute regiment and presented those accepted with a chance to put their dormant skills to real effect. For Eoin, it was a chance to look forward.

Stirling had already identified some of the men he wanted to speak to, and there were two officers in particular that he was hoping to persuade to join: Lieutenant Jock Lewes and Blair Mayne. Stirling would have already known of Blair because of his sporting reputation, the time spent training on Arran and his work at Litani. However, John Steel 'Jock' Lewes, a 27-year-old officer born in India and raised in Australia before moving to England for university, was central to Stirling's plans. Lewes was a fellow member of 8 Commando and had already been operating behind enemy lines in small groups in Tobruk to great effect. More importantly, Lewes was developing plans to use a small paratroop force and had managed to get hold of some parachutes destined for India that had been unloaded in error at Alexandria. As described by Jim Almonds, Lewes

> had not been blessed with the physique, strength and stamina of the average Commando but he looked keen and intelligent. He was about six feet tall with a slim build and a high forehead from which thick sandy brown hair was swept cleanly back. He had a sharp, sensitive face with the regulation neat moustache and an unconscious slight air of superiority. He was very fit. But there were some things which fitness could not prevent. His hands and arms were disfigured by weeping desert sores [lesions caused by over-exposure to the desert sun].
> (L. Almonds-Windmill, *Gentleman Jim*)

Lewes was another to have volunteered early on for the Commando with great expectations, only to end up frustrated by cancelled and failed operations. Impressed by the success of German paratroops (*Fallschirmjäger*) used en masse during the invasion of Crete in May 1941, Lewes was inspired to use their methods as a blueprint for deploying small groups of these highly trained soldiers in North Africa. Having obtained authorization from

Laycock, and armed with the misallocated parachutes, he went about setting up his own small parachute raiding unit. He pulled together three fellow members from the soon to be disbanded 8 Commando and began the first ever practice jumps in the Middle East. He also conducted experiments in desert marching, the rationing of water on marches (as a form of discipline but also to minimize the risk of illness from contaminated local supplies), navigation techniques, etc. It was all trial and error – no training, just self-instruction. The results were promising, but despite this, Lewes encountered further frustration when plans to use his new unit were continually cancelled. Stirling later wrote, 'Although Jock's operation was never executed owing to lack of decision at the top, there was never any doubt that it would have been successful.'

An account of the first of the early practice jumps and, in effect, the inception of what would later become Stirling's SAS was given by Guardsman D'Arcy. The jump took place at a small landing ground about 50 miles inland of Bagush, and the party comprised Lieutenant Lewes, Guardsmen Davies and Evans of the Welsh Guards; Guardsman D'Arcy of the Irish Guards; and, having gatecrashed the party, Lieutenant Stirling and Guardsman Storie of the Scots Guards:

> Having been frustrated in his plans for a sea-borne operation, Lt. J.S. LEWES, Welch Guards, decided to try it by parachute. He and his party first went to an R.A.F. H.Q. located somewhere near FUKA, there he discussed the details with an R.A.F. Officer who, although none of the party had jumped before, was most helpful. He showed us the parachutes we were to use. From the log books we saw that the last periodical examination had been omitted, but Lt Lewes decided they were O.K. Next day, along with Lt. Stirling and Sgt. Storie who were hoping to do a job in Syria, we made a trial flight [on 14 June 1941 – five days after 11 Commando's battle at the River Litani]. The plane used was a Vickers 'Valentia'. We threw out a dummy made from sandbags and tent poles. The parachute opened O.K. but the tent poles were smashed on landing. Afterwards we tried a 10ft jump from the top of the plane and then a little parachute control.
>
> The following afternoon we flew inland in the 'Valentia' which was used to deliver mail. We reached the landing field towards dusk, landed, fitted on our parachutes, and decided to jump in the failing light. We were to jump in pairs, Lt. Lewes and his servant [i.e. batman], Gdsn Davies first, the R.A.F. Officer was to despatch. The instructions were to dive out as though going into water. We hooked ourselves up, circled the field, and on a signal from the R.A.F. Officer, Lt. Lewes and Davies

dived out. Next time round, I dived out, and was surprised to see Lt. Stirling pass me in the air. Lt. Lewes made a perfect landing, next came Davies a little shaken. Lt. Stirling injured his spine and also lost his sight for about an hour, next, myself, a little shaken and a few scratches, and lastly Sgt. Storie who seemed O.K. Gdsn. Evans was unable to jump as the pilot decided to land owing to the approaching darkness. We slept on the landing field. Next morning we jumped again, this time a stick [a formation of soldiers jumping from a plane] of four, preceded by a bundle to represent a container. The previous night we had worn K.D. [khaki dress] shirts and shorts, but from experience we decided to put on pullovers. We wore no hats. We pushed the bundle out first and Gdsn. Evans, myself, Davies and Lt. Lewes followed as quickly as possible. The first three landed quite close to each other and doubled forward to the container, but Lt. Lewes in trying to avoid some oil barrels, rather badly injured his spine, Gdsn Evans also hurt his ankle. Sgt. Storie who jumped after us, landed O.K.

The intended operation was eventually cancelled.

[It is understood that the 'Sgt Storie' referred to here is in fact Sgt Storey – not L/Cpl Jimmy Storie of 11 Commando and 'L' Detachment. All the jumpers were from 8 Commando.]

With his plans frustrated, Lewes found himself instead posted to the besieged port of Tobruk in late June – he left Alexandria on 6 July and spent a six-week posting there, experiencing some intense combat. However, he was also able to use his down-time to refine his military skills, especially in small-party raiding and desert endurance.

In the meantime Stirling, who it seems managed to catch and tear his chute on the plane's tail wing, suffered a spinal shock-related injury and endured a lengthy stay in hospital. It was about 3–4 weeks before he could walk properly again, but he used the time to develop a proposal for a new parachute raiding force; based on Lewes' plans, it would be an independent unit operating behind enemy lines in five-man groups, attacking installations and aircraft on the ground. They would parachute in and approach these installations from the desert before retreating the same way with the help of the LRDG, which was already running reconnaissance and mapping operations by jeep.

Interestingly, although the use of five-man units to conduct irregular warfare behind enemy lines was a novel concept, the strategy of attacking enemy bases by employing surprise attacks from the desert was not. Twenty odd years previously, a famous precedent had been set when T.E. Lawrence (of Arabia) – another British Army officer of Irish descent – led Arab irregulars (Bedouin nomads) in a surprise attack from the desert against Turkish Ottoman forces in the Red Sea port of Aqaba. Crossing hundreds of miles of desert on camels (as opposed to Stirling's planes, parachutes and jeeps) and capturing Turkish posts along the way, Lawrence and a carefully chosen party of Arabs (which had swelled significantly by the time they reached their destination) succeeded in taking Aqaba, which had organized all its defences against expected assault from the sea.

In an interesting parallel to how Stirling's 'originals' were later described, Lawrence wrote about the Bedouin as a fighting force, noting that 'their real sphere is guerilla warfare. They are intelligent, and very lively, almost reckless, but too individualistic to endure commands … The Hejaz war is one of dervishes against regular forces – and we are on the side of the dervishes. Our text-books do not apply to its conditions at all.'

They were re-writing the rules, and it might be said that with the recruitment of Stirling's 'originals', a new breed of 'dervishes' had arrived.

Historical parallels apart, as soon as Stirling had finished developing Jock Lewes' ideas and after taking soundings from his brothers Peter (Third Secretary at the British Embassy) and Bill (an assistant to Brigadier Arthur Smith, Chief of Staff, MEC), Evelyn Waugh and others, he then set about using his connections to obtain permission from ME Command to put it into action and recruit the men he needed.

Stirling knew the idea would get shut down if he followed the proper chain of command – British army bureaucracy of the time was deservedly regarded as rigid. If he was going to succeed, Stirling would need to explore a combination of avenues. And so, having most likely prevailed upon his brother Bill to use his position to gain the support of Brigadier Smith, Stirling also managed to get approval for his proposal from the Deputy Chief of General Staff, General Sir Neil Ritchie (a family friend), and he in turn helped Stirling obtain the approval of General Sir Claude Auchinleck – then Commander-in-Chief of ME Command. Stirling's proposal, bearing his name and the stamp of the Chief of General Staff was dated 16 July 1941; in conjunction with permission to recruit men and create his new parachute unit, he was promoted from Lieutenant to Captain. It was a decent result.

Stirling also spoke to Laycock, the day after his meeting with Ritchie, and discussed which officers he should or at least could try to recruit from Layforce. Stirling wanted Lewes (albeit that he was not Layforce), and Laycock recommended he try to persuade Blair, Eoin and Bill Fraser (a Scot) to join as well. Blair and Eoin had acquitted themselves well at Litani, leading Nos. 7 and 4 Troops of Y and Z Forces respectively, while Fraser, although concussed at Litani and unable to make a significant impression, had significant experience serving with the BEF in France in 1939/1940. Laycock basically recommended that Stirling try to recruit as many soldiers from Layforce as remained. Stirling then set about tracking down his men. He wanted Lewes and Blair as his senior officers, in command of A and B Troops, with Eoin, Fraser and an old Ampleforth school friend of the Stirlings, Charles Bonington (father of the mountaineer, Chris Bonington) as officers in charge of the underlying sections.

Stirling first managed to persuade Lewes to come on board. This was not straightforward and took several attempts, probably because the men were so different and there was significant doubt on Lewes' part about Stirling's commitment. He may have been a fellow member of the Guards Commando, but that is where the similarities ended – Lewes was deadly serious about the war and needed Stirling to be also. Stirling had the well-earned reputation of being a gentleman commando – a 'hooray Henry' who had spent more time on Arran socializing and gambling with the Churchill and Waugh set than training. Stirling's nickname, 'The Great Sloth', gives some indication of how he was perceived, and his voyage from Arran was apparently spent either in bed or at the card tables. Nevertheless, while the original concept of small paratroop raiding units may have been based in large part on Lewes' own ideas, he knew from experience that without the right connections it would never see the light of day. Stirling's now renowned powers of persuasion and access to family friends such as General Ritchie and through his brother, Brigadier Smith, filled this gap, and so, although the two men were unlikely bedfellows, Lewes was eventually persuaded – Stirling would handle the politics and Lewes would shape the unit. Recruitment of the other four officers then started immediately.

The precise timing of events is not clear, but at this stage 11 Commando had finished garrison duty in Cyprus and on 6 August left for Egypt, from where it was expected they would then be heading off in different directions, to their original units or on assignments in Asia, North Africa and so on. It was in Geneifa that Stirling set about interviewing the officers he wanted.

The assumption therefore is that after Lewes, the first prospective officer Stirling must have interviewed was Eoin. This would probably have been some time during the week between Eoin's arrival in Egypt (Amiriyya) on 6 August and his formal posting to the new unit on 15 August – just before his departure for the 'L' Detachment training camp at Kabrit. As an officer in 11 Commando whose actions at Litani had been recognized (Ben McIntyre, *Rogue Heroes* notes that 'The one man in the unit who was neither awed nor intimidated by Mayne was Eoin McGonigal … McGonigal had also fought at Litani River, where he had won a reputation for coolness under fire'), Eoin would have also felt free to explain the circumstances surrounding Blair's dismissal from 11 Commando in candid terms to Stirling, and where to find him. This would have reinforced what Stirling already thought, and given the misconceived gossip that appears to have been swirling around at the time, perhaps also laid to rest any lingering concerns that Blair was the right person to lead one of his Troops. Stirling is quoted as confirming that he was told of Blair's whereabouts by 'a great friend of his', making clear that 'Eoin McGonigal was the one person who liked Paddy before he became a hero.'

Indeed, it has been said that it was Eoin's recommendation that helped persuade Stirling to recruit Blair:

> It was almost certainly Eoin McGonigal who suggested to Stirling that he should take on another officer of 11 Commando, Blair 'Paddy' Mayne – his best friend – who had distinguished himself at the Litani River action in June and been Mentioned in Dispatches. Stirling, who had not yet heard a shot fired in anger himself, was keen to recruit officers who had already experienced battle, and agreed to have a word with Mayne. (Michael Asher, *Get Rommel*)

As it happened, having been RTU'd on 23 June 1941 (the War Diary for 'C' Battalion Layforce simply notes, 'Lt R.B. Mayne RUR left the unit') and then discharged from hospital following almost a month's stay recovering from malaria, Blair was kicking his heels in Geneifa. He wrote to his sister Barbara ('Babs') on 3 August from 'Commando Base Depot, MEF':

> I am doing nothing this morning. I could go to church I suppose but I am too lazy. I'll write this letter instead. I haven't seen McGonigal for over a month now but I expect him to join me here sometime this week.
>
> I haven't got any news at all, haven't seen anyone from home … since about 4 months ago … As well as McGonigal there was another Belfast boy in our unit. Gerald Bryan was his name, lived somewhere on the Malone Road. He unfortunately got wounded in the foot and is, I think, a prisoner of war.

Gerald Bryan had his leg amputated while a prisoner of war. After being released he returned to England and a role with the Special Operations Executive. Blair was clearly missing being able to chat with his Ulster comrades.

Stirling then spoke to Fraser (who was formally posted three days after Eoin on 18 August but only joined 'L' Detachment in Kabrit on 1 September).

It is not clear when Bonington was brought in but it must have been at around the same time as Fraser or shortly afterwards.

On 28 August, twelve ORs from the few remaining members of 11 Commando were then posted to 'L' Detachment (J. Orton, B. Morris, B. Tait, J. Cheyne, J. DuVivier, J. Storie, J. Byrne, K. Warburton, J. Duffy, C. McCormack, D. Keith and G. White). Other members of 11 Commando were deployed on Operation Flipper, the failed attempt to capture or kill Rommel at his HQ in Libya, and so the balance of the recruits was made up of men from the other Layforce Commando units, No. 7 Commando but mostly from Stirling's old unit, No. 8 (Guards) Commando.

A Captain F.C. Thomson also joined 'L' Detachment in an observer capacity upon the orders of MEHQ (described variously as a GHQ/MEHQ Army Observer Officer, and by Stirling as his 'adjutant'). It seems that Stirling was not yet entirely trusted with his new Brigade! Training then started in Kabrit on 5 September 1941.

As for Blair, it appears that although he may have been one of the first potential officers to be identified by Stirling, he was probably the last to be interviewed and recruited, given the cloud hanging over him following the run-in with Napier and Keyes and the fact that he had been convalescing in Geneifa. A letter from Blair to his mother written on 4 July 1941 (mistakenly dated 4 June 1941) suggests he was in hospital from 4 to about 13/14 July, following which he went to a convalescent hospital for two weeks and was discharged on about 27/28 July 1941. It is not known how precisely he spent the month of August, but his letters were sent from the Commando Base Depot at Geneifa while he waited on news of his application to join the British Military Mission 204. Nevertheless, Stirling would have tracked him down after speaking to Eoin, and reference to the diary of Jim Almonds (an original member of 'L' Detachment and one of Jock Lewes' men from Tobruk) suggests that he joined 'L' Detachment just a few days after training had formally started on 5 September.

And with that, the first two officers from an Irish regiment to have joined Pedder's Commando unit on Arran then became the only two Irish officers selected for 'L' Detachment SAS Brigade. For Eoin in particular, this was a huge achievement – at just twenty he was one of the first and youngest of Stirling's original officers (all of whom were in their mid to late twenties, apart from Bonington at thirty-two). It must have been quite a challenge for somebody so young to lead men selected as much for their independence as for their determination and bravery in volunteering to take on such uncertain and 'hazardous' challenges. Bear in mind also that many of the ORs would have been pre-war regulars with more military experience than their officers. Eoin would train with them and have to work to gain their respect. The leadership skills that had marked him out for selection at such a young age had always been there: captaining sports and debating teams at all levels at school, as well as working with and training 11 Commando on Arran – all put into sharp focus when leading his Troop into battle at Litani River. However, his recruitment by David Stirling was now about to test those skills as never before.

In just over six months Eoin had left Scotland, moved to Cyprus, led a Troop in battle in Syria and been selected as the youngest 'original' officer of 'L' Detachment SAS Brigade. Just over three months later, he would be lost in the desert in Libya, never to be seen again.

Chapter 17

The Final Four Months with
a 'band of vagabonds'

By the end of August 1941 David Stirling had interviewed and signed up the five original officers he had handpicked for his new unit. This was an accomplishment in itself, because he had encountered repeated obstacles in getting the men that he wanted. As he put it himself, the 'fossilised shits' in Middle East Headquarters (MEHQ) command were still trying to run the war as though it was 1914/18 and making it hard for him to recruit. Stirling was clear that 'It was essential for me to get the right officers and I had a great struggle to get them', labelling the middle and lower levels of MEHQ as 'freemasons of mediocrity', 'unfailingly obstructive and uncooperative … astonishingly tiresome'.

In theory, it should not have proved difficult; save for Bonington, the officers Stirling wanted were all members of the recently disbanded Commando units, disillusioned and trying to find ways to make themselves useful. Nevertheless, despite his proposal having been given a seal of approval by their Commander-in-Chief, the people at MEHQ were opposed to seeing any officer, let alone those who had been trained to such a high level and 'blooded' in combat conditions, join what they viewed as an irregular, renegade, private unit. Still, one by one, Stirling got his men: Lewes, Eoin, Fraser, Bonington and finally, Blair. Despite MEHQ's reluctance to let them go, few of those selected for 'L' Detachment fitted into any of the conventional military units. Stirling's officers exemplified the sense in picking people because of their individual strengths, initiative and ability to get the job done working together, rather than as the type of soldier who would only act on orders. Stirling's concept of the SAS as a meritocracy, where the emphasis was on excellence and class distinctions were ignored, drew many rugged individualists. Stirling had his leaders:

> They were men who possessed the qualities of responsibility, initiative, individualism, and a strong sense of discipline. It is important to remember from the start that toughness was in no way a passport into the S.A.S., invariably volunteers with the above characteristics coupled with a strong will power and stamina were selected.

As Lieutenant Bill Fraser recalled, once an officer candidate was identified, the initial selection process comprised a brief interview with Stirling in a tent at the sprawling Infantry Base Depot at Geneifa. Stirling asked each potential recruit for his thoughts on parachute jumping, examples of initiative and whether he thought he could meet the basic requirements of an elite Special Forces group – the ability to stretch himself further than he had been as a Commando. It was not the most exacting of interviews but it did hint at things to come; there was no blueprint, they would not be spoon-fed – each man must be prepared to work harder than ever before,

Lt Bill Fraser. (*NMS*)

think for himself, be resourceful and adapt. He would be expected to use cunning and push himself beyond his previous limits.

With his officers recruited, Stirling then set about selecting the sixty-plus men he wanted for his force, as well as a number of camp staff. The nominal rolls at Appendices B and C, although dated 27 August and 1 September 1941 respectively, were clearly produced or amended some years later and provide some evidence that Stirling's original recruits actually numbered close to seventy all ranks, and potentially a good number more. Accurate records from the period remain elusive, but it is known that others were in camp at the time, although this has not yet been formally clarified. In fact, even the date of the first nominal roll (27 August 1941) is one day before the first twelve ORs from 11 Commando were even posted to 'L' Detachment. Also notable is the fact that neither roll refers to either Pct Ken Warburton or Pct Joe Duffy – two 11 Commando soldiers who died on an early training parachute jump with 'L' Detachment in mid-October.) In any event, the 'Layforce Diary to Disbandment' records as of 16 September 1941, '1 S.A.S. Commando (Parachutists) of 70 all ranks'.

As for the personal attributes that were sought, an extract from, 'L' Detachment, S.A.S. Brigade/Aims and Men' makes the requirements clear:

The Men 'L' Detachment wants. An undisciplined TOUGH is no good, however tough he may be. Most of 'L' Detachment's work is night work and all of it demands courage, fitness and determination in the highest degree, but also, and just as important, discipline, skill, intelligence, and training. Many of these characteristics can be acquired.

The training of 'L' Detachment is designed to foster them. But this is only possible with really keen men. It is therefore no good volunteering for this type of work just for the novelty of it or for a change. The type 'L' Detachment needs is the type of man who genuinely feels he has an aptitude for work of this nature.

As Stirling explained in a BBC interview in 1985:

> In a sense, they weren't really controllable. They were harnessable but they all had this individuality… The object was to give them the same purpose and once they were harnessed to that proposition, then they … policed themselves, so to speak, and that band of vagabonds had to grasp what they had to do which included discipline, although most of them were escaping from the conventional regimental discipline and they didn't fully appreciate they were running into a much more exacting type of discipline – but they were so united towards achieving the purpose and that really caused them to be, through this common purpose, easily handled.

The 'vagabonds' of 'L' Detachment were divided into A and B Troops, commanded by Jock Lewes and Blair respectively. Basic infantry skills were to be fine-tuned until they were perfect – Lewes would double as the Training Officer and instructor in fieldcraft. Bill Fraser would teach map reading and navigation, while Eoin ('a first-class weapons instructor', as the Jock Lewes biography notes), as in 11 Commando, was given responsibility for weapons training. In a later letter Blair wrote, 'Eoin worked very hard here and was entirely responsible for all the Weapon Training and much of the night training.'

Tellingly, despite his run-ins with Keyes and alleged assault on Napier, and in addition to overseeing gruelling PT sessions, Blair was put in charge of troop discipline. Any defaulters were treated to Blair's own unique form of punishment. After being paraded, if an offending soldier accepted Blair's decision he was promptly taken to a makeshift boxing ring to face Blair, who would administer some 'punishment' over several rounds, or fewer if necessary. All would then be quickly forgotten and the subject never mentioned again. However, if the offender could offer a good excuse, which so far as Blair was concerned meant it had to be utterly implausible, absurd or humorous, then no action would be taken. One such occasion involved a soldier who was late back to camp. In his defence he explained that he had in fact been on his way back with plenty of time in hand, but when he stopped to light a cigarette, the wind proved to be so strong that he had to turn his back to complete his task. Once his cigarette was lit, he continued on his way, only to realize too late that he had forgotten to turn round again and so had ended up back where he had started. An amused Blair, knowing it was pure nonsense but demonstrated a bit of wit, immediately dismissed the relieved soldier unharmed.

In general, however, there was to be no 'pissing about' of the kind that was to be found in the regular army – those who didn't come up to the mark in terms of performance were unceremoniously returned to their units.

Still, the experience of Litani and the listless period that followed had left their mark. Even after his transfer to the SAS, Eoin was finding it difficult to move on. On 23 September 1941 he wrote to Ambrose:

Dear Ambrose,

I am very sorry for being so slack about writing. We have been working like nothing on earth just recently.

I have just received the first airgraphs from home. They are a great improvement – arriving in three or four weeks.

Congratulations on being graded A1. It seemed as though that was never coming. Don't come out here if you can help it. This is a bloody repeat bloody part of the world. The Adair Arms [near the RUR's ITC in Ballymena] and a thick glass of Guinness and heavy rain outside haunt every moment of the day.

Eoin

It was clear that having been away for almost a year, Eoin was desperate for news from home. The reference to being graded 'A1' concerned a motorcycle accident Ambrose was involved in during training – he broke a leg, and his physical fitness had to be reassessed. In 1940 a system of health categories was instituted by the Army: 'A1' and 'A2', then 'B1' to 'B5'. These seven categories were based on vision in relation to shooting and driving, physical endurance, the ability to march and the manifestation of any other disease which would affect military duty. Categories also existed which determined both task and location worldwide: 'C' – Home service only; 'D' – Temporarily unfit; and 'E' – Permanently unfit. The Army allocated each soldier to one of these categories on the basis of the Civilian Medical Board grades.

On the same day Eoin wrote to his eldest sister, Ina – the only one of his four sisters to have been at home while he and Ambrose were growing up:

Dear Ina,

I am afraid that this is the first letter which I have written to you since I came out here.

You seem to have been having a very hectic time with air raids, in fact I expect you will be awarded the George Medal for all the bandaging you have had to do. How is the Falls Road bearing up? Are the forces sparing the Papists?

For goodness sake write! – I have not received a single letter from any of my adoring sisters!

Eoin

Christmas greetings from the desert followed soon after.

Chapter 18

Kabrit: 'Stirling's Rest Camp'

Stirling's new unit of sixty-five-plus officers and ORs had been designated 'L' Detachment Special Air Service Brigade' for a reason. Not for its size – a 'Brigade' is typically composed of three Battalions, with three Brigades to a Division (plus supporting elements in each comprising artillery, engineers, logistic units, etc.). Sixty-five or so men (plus unacknowledged ORs and camp staff) fell some way short of this. It was also not, despite the jokes, because they were all still 'Learners' when it came to parachute work. In fact, the name was part of an intelligence bluff intended to exaggerate the Detachment's small numbers and suggest a substantial airborne threat to the Germans. The hope was that the enemy's planning might be disrupted if they thought that they would have to divert resources to face a potentially significant additional force in the area.

Having recruited the members of his new 'Brigade', Stirling introduced them to their new home. Kabrit lies 90 miles east of Cairo on the edge of the Great Bitter Lake, and for those men like Eoin and Blair who had come from 11 Commando and trained in the sodden green uplands and valleys of Arran, it could not have been more different. It presented an arresting sight but not for what was on display, because there was very little to see at all: Kabrit was flat, sandy, featureless and hot – the only common denominator being that while Scotland has its midges, Kabrit has its flies, and lots of them. However, it was an ideal place in which to locate the training camp for a new unit, because there was little else to do. There were no distractions – no bars and brothels, just sand, more sand, the ever-present flies and a wind that blew in from the lake and invaded every nook and cranny with yet more sand. In fact, there wasn't even a camp; the men arrived at various stages throughout late August and early September 1941, to be greeted by a desolate and totally barren site. They were literally starting from the ground up. As one of the recruits recalled, 'It was a desolate bloody place, there was a pile of hessian tents and we were told … to shut up and put them up.'

There were several RAF airbases dotted about the surrounding area. The nearest to the Brigade's camp was RAF Kabrit; to the north was RAF Kasfareet, and to the south, RAF El Shallufa. On the banks of the Great

Eoin outside his tent at Kabrit.

Bitter Lake was HMS *Saunders*, the first Combined Operations Training Centre to be established outside of the United Kingdom and, despite the name, a naval shore base. All of these bases were in the vicinity of the large and sprawling Fayid Army Base. In contrast, 'L' Detachment had no camp as such, apart from one large marquee tent which served as the Quartermaster's store. The Company Quartermaster Sergeant, Gerry Ward, was one of the camp's administration staff attached to 'L' Detachment and slept in the QM store tent alone. Also to be found were a few 'EPI' tents. These were hessian affairs made in India for European army personnel. If the men wanted a camp, they would have to build it themselves.

The meagre supplies reflected the sometimes barely concealed hostility Stirling was battling at MEHQ – the quartermaster sergeant responsible for supplies had plainly already been briefed. Stirling was informed that, apart from a couple of tents, there would be a wait of six months for supplies from England; everyone was expected to take their turn, and while Stirling may have been given permission to recruit his men, he would be required 'to queue at "Q"' for supplies.

The men were tasked with digging in and erecting the few tents available. This led to some unhappiness amongst the ranks as the 'gentlemen' NCOs, mainly from the Guards (No. 8 Commando, Stirling's old unit), oversaw this work. Many of the men refused and requested that they be returned to their parent units via the Commando Base Depot at Geneifa – this was exactly the kind of work they had been promised would not be a part of 'L' Detachment. Some men broke camp, found a local bar and had a few drinks. In their opinion, they weren't there to be treated as labourers. When they returned with bottles of beer, Jock Lewes climbed on to a table and addressed the men telling them that whatever they believed, there was a method to this madness and they would just have to deal with it. Raising the stakes, he also then famously declared that if they didn't, they were cowards with a long streak of yellow down their backs who just couldn't take it. It was a gamble and one that almost ended in open rebellion – some of these men had just come back from seeing action in Syria, Tobruk and Crete, and they were stunned. He challenged them to prove that they would do everything he did – and in return, he would do everything they did. No officer had ever spoken to them like this before, but it worked and, eventually placated, the men were persuaded to return to the work of putting the camp together. (It is not reported if Jock Lewes helped to dig!)

Six men were allocated to each of the tents and, for the time being, most stuck with the men that they had already soldiered with. To say that at least initially (if not for some continuing period) there was tension between the men and, in particular, the NCOs would be far from overstating the matter – it would take time for the men to bond and for some of the initial ill-discipline to disappear. The reluctance to mix remained; for example, the Seaforths stuck with the Seaforths and the various Guards with the Guards. However, given the nature of the environment and their circumstances, there was little room for such divisions to take hold.

Gradually, things settled down and the men began to grow accustomed to their new routines and environment. Blair wrote home to his sister Babs on 9 September confirming that both he and Eoin had settled in: 'I wrote to Mother a couple of days ago probably arrive about the same time as this, I mentioned that McGonigal is here with me, he is fine also.'

It is an apocryphal story now, but the Brigade's first 'operation' came after the QM suggested to some of the men that if they wanted anything more luxurious in the way of living quarters, they might want to visit the neighbouring encampment. This camp had been put up for New Zealanders, but they were first ordered to Crete and were wiped out defending the island against the invading Germans. So all that 'L' Detachment had to do was drive in and take whatever they wanted. They were already adapting to their new environment, making the most of what they found around them – an early recycling policy by the British Army!

They also appropriated a large pile of bricks from one of the RAF bases and used it to build a canteen. This was furnished with scavenged chairs and tables as well as a selection of beer and snacks sourced by Lance Corporal Kauffman. He was an artful Londoner who seems to have been a far better

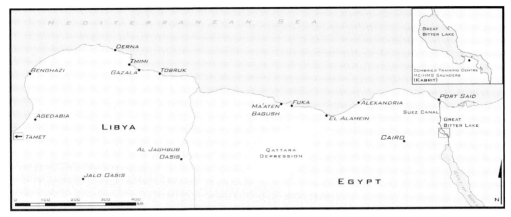

Map 4: 'L' Detachment's training camp at Kabrit (see inset box), temporary desert bases at, initially, Al Jaghbub Oasis and then Jalo Oasis, as well as various enemy airfields (in particular, Gazala and Tmimi).

Stirling in front of the officers' mess with the parachute training frame in the background. (*C. Beaton/IWM*)

scrounger than he was a soldier, since he was soon RTU'd for not making the grade; but his canteen lasted longer than he did and was the envy of the five officers and Stirling who had to make do with a tent as their mess.

Despite Kauffman's efforts, supplies were in fact generally pretty meagre – bully beef, biscuits, herrings and porridge were not sufficient fuel for what these men were expected to do. And despite occasionally stealing from the nearby Army stores and selling things on to the locals, or bartering to acquire what they needed to supplement their rations,

The indefatigable 'Bully beef'.

on the whole the standard of nutrition remained poor throughout. An oft-repeated memory is of the constant promises by the officers of a full plate at the next feeding time. The refrain, 'Better food tomorrow', was too familiar, and while of course, 'tomorrow' usually did come, it was rarely accompanied by 'better food'. The solution? 'Tomorrow!' Humour which rapidly lost any appeal it may initially have had.

In any event, there was little time for the men of 'L' Detachment to sit around and gorge themselves in their canteen. Despite the sign that had been erected in jest at the camp's entrance reading, 'Stirling's Rest Camp', they would have just two and a half months to prepare for their first operation – one that would involve parachuting and long marches across desert terrain, skills that most of the men had yet to master. In fact, few of them had ever even been in a plane before – let alone jumped out of one. Stirling recalled:

> In our training programme the principle on which we worked was entirely different from that of the Commandos. A Commando unit, having once selected from a batch of volunteers, were generally committed to those men and had to nurse them up to the required standard. 'L' Detachment, on the other hand, had set a minimum standard to which all ranks had to attain and we had to be most firm in returning to their units those who were unable to reach that standard.

In the end, several were requested to leave. In this regard, when referring to the need for a Commando unit to nurse recruits up to the required standard, Stirling was of course speaking of his experience with 8 Commando on Arran – this was not the policy employed by Dick Pedder, who was known for regularly returning members of 11 Commando to their parent units if they did not meet the standard he required of them. In any event, this is a core SAS recruitment principle which carries through to today's volunteers, as is illustrated by the ongoing debate as to whether allowances should be made to render it easier for women to overcome the notoriously high threshold for acceptance into the SAS.

Training was to be harder than that of the Commando, but on operations discipline would be of a more relaxed nature. Stirling was a six-foot-five-inch aristocratic Scot with a gentle stoop and quiet voice who never seemed to order anyone to do anything. Instead, he was known to suggest to his men that 'Perhaps this would be a good idea' or ask, 'Could you possibly do this?' Of course, if the request was not met to the full, the individual could expect to be unceremoniously returned to his original unit. On 4 September 1941 Stirling paraded his men to tell them what he expected of them: self-discipline and discipline on the parade ground (although saluting every time another rank came into contact with an officer was waived), personal motivation, modesty, the highest standard of turnout and behaviour, and one hundred per cent devotion to having a crack at 'the Hun'. The Army's ritual cleaning of personal weapons for the parade ground and inspection was put to one side, to the relief of all.

Lewes taught them first and foremost that the desert should be respected but not feared. The men learned how to navigate using the most basic of maps, how to move noiselessly at night, how to survive on minimal amounts of water and how to use the desert as camouflage. They developed the confidence to navigate their way across hostile terrain with little in the way of food and water. Night confidence and night shooting (in time, both overseen by Eoin) were essential, as movement and offensive operations would take place only in darkness. They practised night movement blindfolded during the day, crawling and feeling objects, so that their instructors could watch them and point out mistakes. They also learnt to recognize sounds, so that moving about in the desert at night on moonless nights would become second nature.

In time, the men came to respect the earnest and ascetic Lewes. 'Jock liked things right, he was a perfectionist,' recalled Corporal Jimmy Storie. 'He thought more about things in depth, while Stirling was more carefree … Stirling was the backbone but Lewes was the brains, he got the ideas such as the Lewes Bomb.'

Training also included speed route marches – both day and night, covering distances through the desert of between ten and thirty miles, carrying packs full of sand. Some men used to empty sand out to lighten their loads and only refilled them close to the end of the march. Jock Lewes soon caught on to this and had the sand replaced with stones, but the men found a way of discarding and replacing these as well. As a result, although initiative was valued … Lewes eventually had the stones numbered in order to foil any further attempts.

Before dawn the men were roused, and while it was still dark their first task of the day was a route march or a long-distance run. Following this they would play a game of rugby in which each section would try to knock the other about a bit – tactics at which Blair excelled. While he was sometimes visibly uncomfortable when addressing the men in more formal group settings (he did not have Eoin's natural affinity for impromptu debating), he was a man transformed when it came to physical challenges of any description and completely at ease with a ball in hand. And for the men to be facing off against a member of the Lions was just thrilling. (Although, according to Jim Almonds, what really impressed them was the rumour 'about him having "smacked" his last CO during an argument, actually knocking him down'.)

Bonds between the men soon developed, and they quickly became accustomed to the new regime, surpassing the initial training thresholds. As a result, three-day exercises comprising a sixty-mile hike covering twenty miles each night and then lying up during the day became the norm. Each man would scrape a hollow in the desert sand and lie in it covered by his smock. Food was minimal, comprising dates and hard rations plus personal water bottles. Lying up in this fashion was better than when some of them had had to use the deluged ditches of Arran, but still sleep did not come easy; the presence of poisonous snakes such as adders or kraits did not help them to relax. Map reading and compass work was also essential, as was medical knowledge. Training even included instruction on how to perform an amputation, although like fishermen who traditionally do not learn how to swim, the recruits were reluctant to tempt fate by gaining such expertise.

The classic children's memory test, 'Kim's game', was also used to help train them to get map references and other information by heart. In Rudyard Kipling's 1901 novel *Kim* the eponymous hero plays the game during his training as a spy – a number of miscellaneous objects are placed on a table, inspected, then covered and he attempts to recall them.

Weapons training, for which Eoin was responsible, was essential; all ranks had to be fully conversant with all weapons, not only the British but also the German and Italian ones. In this regard, the SAS again adopted a more independent approach – there was a small weapons range down by the canal where men could pick whichever weapons they wanted to master and practise on their own. A strict regime was not imposed. They were also able to make their own choice of personal weapons. The Middle East

Commando knuckle-duster knife was produced locally in Egypt, sometimes from refashioned 6-inch bayonet blades with 5-inch brass knuckles. These were primarily issued to Nos. 50 and 52 Middle East Commando (locally raised Commando units that were drawn from British forces stationed in the Middle East at the outbreak of war), but are thought likely to have made their way into the hands of the SAS and LRDG as well. A later favourite, and one made famous by the Commandos and SAS, was the FS knife or dagger – a double-edged fighting or thrusting knife with a 7½-inch blade and 4-inch ribbed grip. It is not clear what Eoin used, but it may have been an independently sourced blade, as in a letter to Blair, Eoin's mother referred to the fact that Eoin's 'dagger' was missing. This suggests something like the FS knife, perhaps an early version, although it is thought they had not been made available to 'L' Detachment at that time – most men just brought their own knives. Lieutenant Colonel Carol Mather (of 8 Commando, Layforce and later, 'L' Detachment) recalls some officers equipping themselves with extra weaponry and in his own case remembers 'carrying a sketch of a dagger to Wilkinson's, the swordmakers in Pall Mall, which afterwards became the standard pattern for the commando knife.' They also went into battle with grenades, various revolvers (usually Webleys, but Enfields and Smith & Wessons were also used), the short-magazine Lee Enfield Mk III rifle (SMLE), Bren guns and Lewes bombs.

Operating behind the lines, it could help to have some understanding of the enemy's language and so time was spent learning the rudiments. Water discipline was of high importance – no man was allowed to share his bottle, and no one was allowed to drink until the order was given. However, it was expected that when men returned from a march, their bottles would still be

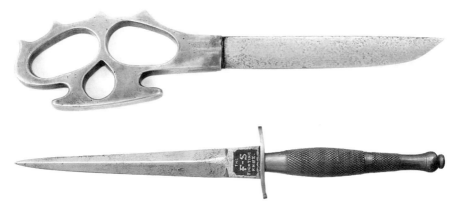

The Middle East Commando knife (aka 'death's head' given the grip's resemblance to a skull) and the Fairbairn-Sykes fighting knife (FS knife) made by Wilkinson Sword Co

Webley Mk VI 455 revolver.   Bren Mk 1 LMG.

SMLE Mk III rifle.

full; some believed it was the comfort of knowing that they had water if they needed it which helped them get through the marches. This is not a practice that is advocated today.

At the end of each day's training the men would return to their tents to write up notes on the day's activities, and these would be checked at various times by Lewes to see how well the lessons were being absorbed. It was possible to bathe in the nearby salty Great Bitter Lake, which the Suez Canal went through, but great care had to be taken – if you swallowed any water by accident, a trip to sick quarters for some jabs was essential.

Schemes were set up to start at night after a full day's training, and after a beer with their food, the men would be called out to participate in whatever scheme Lewes had planned for them. Lessons in explosives led to the demolition of local buildings, and all would become experts in destruction. Lewes made a habit of goading the men, calling them 'yellow' and pushing them to prove they were worthy of inclusion in 'L' Detachment. He felt that being confrontational would help them to learn how to think and act under pressure. To progress they needed to be constantly challenged and made to feel uncomfortable.

Much emphasis was also put on night work, but the exercises that Eoin conducted during these periods gradually became easier, as David Stirling believed that the key to successful night fighting was a soldier's self-confidence. During demolition training they were joined by an Egyptian

Railways employee who showed them the best places to plant explosives in order to destroy train and track. For example, planting explosives at a curve in the track would almost certainly cause a derailment. This would also make it more difficult for the enemy's repair teams, as it was harder to replace a curved piece of track.

It was a comprehensive programme, and as the training progressed, the spirit and humour amongst the men noticeably improved. There was a belief the new training regime was being delivered with real purpose, and it was a vast improvement on the recent months of limbo. It also became clear that after the months of training on Arran, the attritional operation at Litani, the raids at Tobruk and elsewhere, and perhaps Stirling's unorthodox system for selecting the men he wanted for his new unit, 'L' Detachment now comprised some of the best-trained soldiers in the British Army. They were working hard and enjoying it. Moreover, and possibly even more importantly from Eoin's perspective, the airgraphs had speeded up the delivery of news from home considerably, and with it, the men's morale improved. Eoin was no longer reading what had felt like distant historical accounts of life in Ireland, and he went from warning Ambrose off from coming anywhere near the Middle East to wishing he could join him in Kabrit. On 8 October 1941 he wrote to his brother:

Dear Ambrose,

These Airgraphs … are really a grand invention. It is a big improvement getting news through inside three or four weeks. You feel at last that you are in contact and are hearing about things which are actually happening, not things which are three months old.

This unit I am in now is first class. I have never had better men under me, all mad keen to get a crack at Jerry or the Italians. They've all been well 'blooded' and are fairly howling for more. I only wish you could get out here and come in too, with some Ulster Riflemen.

I am going off for three days shooting this week-end, taking my S.M.L.E. [Short Magazine Lee Enfield rifle] and seeing what the desert will yield up, living in a truck and getting well away from uniforms. It should be good fun. I am sorry that there are no lions or tigers here, and I could make some good 'safari' stories. Likely the biggest thing I hit will be a desert rat …

By the way, I am about teetotal now and am in very rude health. You wouldn't know me. Doing night marches through the desert of 30 miles and P.T. every morning at 6 o'clock. I don't know how long it will last, but just now I feel very virtuous.

Good luck and send my love to Paddy [Patricia Taylor, Ambrose's fiancée].

Eoin.

It was clear that the effort put into training was beginning to pay off – the men were beginning to see a return on all their hard work and had turned a corner following the disappointment of Litani and the disbandment of their Commando units. Eoin in particular was sounding like a new man, feeling fitter than ever and working with a group of men of which he was immensely proud – they were the best he had worked with, confident and champing at the bit to see some action. Writing home at exactly the same time as Eoin, and expressing the same sentiments, Jock Lewes proudly noted that both he and Stirling would 'back them against any unit in the Middle East, friend or foe'.

The atmosphere had improved immensely and the introduction of airgraphs had played their part in this but in doing so had also increased Eoin's workload. One thing a subaltern is told when joining a Scottish regiment is to, 'look after your Jock's' – the well-being of your men was of primary importance and it certainly seems that from his time with 11 (Scottish) Commando, Eoin adopted this tenet throughout. For Eoin's other role at Kabrit was that of the camp's chief letter writer – many of the men were not well-educated, or may have been injured or feeling down generally and so sometimes needed his help when writing home to wives, girlfriends and family. Eoin's love of writing was well-known – he would spend long hours with his notebooks working on his short stories (most of them romantic) – and given his age and as Blair used to say, his 'Irish gift of the gab', he may have been seen as the most approachable of those likely to be interested in helping the men out. Having written a short story inspired by Cyrano de Bergerac, Eoin must have loved this role. Only twenty years old and exercising his creativity in helping to give voice to the men's feelings for their loves back home – the possibilities were endless. The man who recounted this said that he never used Eoin's services himself because his wife would have spotted it a mile away – the letters were far too romantic to have come from him!

In any event, in time, they were put into groups away from their regiments and original commando units; these would be the squads within which they would operate. After much debate between Stirling and Lewes, it was eventually agreed that there should be four-man sections. These would each be known as a patrol, and each member of the patrol would be a 'specialist' – a driver/mechanic, a medic, a navigator and a demolition expert. The members would then be dependent on each other. They would be further split into two pairs of 'muckers', so no man would be left on his own – although as would be seen on the unit's first operation, this was not an absolute but best practice; the mission still came first.

Throughout the course of the training, and keeping up his end of the bargain, Lewes earned the respect of the men because he never asked them to do something that he was not prepared to do himself. He would often complete a scheme or exercise on his own first and then, if necessary, tweak it before calling on his men to perform it. He led by example.

During the initial training, Lewes tested the men's self-confidence to its limits. They trained for nine or ten hours a day and often, just as they thought they could crawl back into their beds, Lewes would order them out on one of his 'night schemes' –

Jock Lewes. (*J. Lewes*)

forced marches requiring successful navigation across the desert. Any soldier Lewes considered not up to scratch, either physically or emotionally, was RTU'd. For those such as Eoin and Blair, who had come through Dick Pedder's training on Arran, night-time training on top of daytime endurance marches was nothing new. What was new was the terrain and climate – the days could be suffocatingly hot and the nights surprisingly cold. Some recruits performed astonishing feats of endurance. On one 60-mile march, the boots of Private Doug Keith, an 11 Commando veteran, disintegrated after 20 miles, so he completed the remaining distance in stocking feet with a 75lb pack on his back.

Chapter 19

Parachute Training: 'nice and soft in the sand'

What most of the men disliked above all else was parachute training, and without an aircraft, Lewes had to improvise. To start with, he constructed a wooden platform and trolley system from which the men leapt to simulate hitting the ground at speed, then rolling. Next, he discovered a length of narrow-gauge railway unused in a nearby old quarry. Accompanied by about five men in a 3-ton truck, he collected about 80 yards of track and sleepers, as well as one of the hoppers, and took them back to the base. The sleepers and track were re-laid down the side of a sand dune, and decking was added to the hopper so that a man could balance on the top of it. The hopper was then pushed to the edge of the dune with a man on top and set in motion hurtling down the slope to the bottom of the dune. As the hopper hit the far side of the dune the man on board would jump off and try to land safely with a forward roll. This was parachute training kamikaze-style and unsurprisingly, injuries were common, with broken collarbones top of the list – so much so that it was not clear they would still have a full complement of men by the date of the operation.

Lewes then decided that even this was too tame and resorted to throwing himself off the back of a moving truck. As one recruit recalled, 'There were a great number of injuries during ground training jumping off trucks at 30–35mph.' Protected by what was described as American baseball gear, with helmets and knee and elbow pads, Reg Seekings remembered jumping off at about 35mph and trying to land on his feet rather than rolling. 'I ploughed up the bloody desert with my face,' he recalled. 'I was in a hell of a state. That was the last time I tried to be clever. Paddy Mayne jumped out and you could hear his head hit the deck half a mile away.'

Several recruits broke wrists and other limbs leaping backwards from the tailgate of a truck and ending up in hospital as a consequence of Lewes's 'ingenious' training schemes. In all, more than half the detachment suffered injuries (comprising at least half a dozen broken limbs). Nevertheless, hurling oneself backwards from a moving vehicle was considered by some to be preferable to jumping out of an aircraft at 1,000–2,000ft. In a cruel

'L' Detachment
'Parachute' training.
(*C. Beaton/IWM*)

(*Mil.Surps.Com/J Lewes*)

irony (given what was to follow), Eoin was one of the few who actually looked forward to jumping. As he commented in a letter to Ambrose on 8 October 1941: 'By the way, how do you like my new rank – Parachute-Lieutenant? The jumping is damn good fun, nice and soft on the sand.'

Nevertheless, even Eoin suffered the occasional injury; while the sand itself may have been soft, the speed of impact, the surrounding terrain and whether you could gauge the approaching impact when jumping at night could all make a significant difference to the success of a landing. In many parts of the desert the men had to contend with landing surfaces strewn with gravel and rocks as well as sharp acacia scrub. Indeed, just a month

Eoin wearing parachute training overalls.

before the Brigade was due to embark on its first mission, Eoin managed to strain his arm in training.

Lewes then acquired the use of a Bombay Troop Carrier from RAF Transport Command at the nearby airfield of Khanka. It was a collector's item, but soon the men were jumping from this near-obsolete aircraft. A hole was cut in the bottom of the fuselage to allow them to exit, but due to the small size of the hole, most of those jumping took a hefty blow to the

Eoin wearing a 'fore & aft' with his arm in a sling after parachute training.

face as a result of their packs snagging on its sides. Some also managed to get caught up on the tail wheel, so it was not an easy exercise to perform.

Actual parachute jumps were carried out on 16 October 1941. Tragically however, two of the early jumpers, Ken Warburton and Joe Duffy, lost

Parachute training under the gaze of Stirling and Randolph Churchill amongst others. (*C. Beaton/IWM*)

their lives. They were both former members of 11 Commando and were on the second training flight. First out was Warburton followed, with some hesitation, by Duffy – he had sensed something was not quite right with Warburton's chute. It was reported by Ernie Bond that Duffy had spotted his mate's chute had not opened and the static line that should have pulled it open had disappeared. Nevertheless, with shouts of encouragement from the dispatcher and other waiting jumpers ringing in his ears, Duffy went ahead and jumped – he would perhaps have felt humiliated if he had refused. It was only then that the dispatcher saw that the snap-links on the men's static lines had buckled and come off the plane's rail. Static lines attached to a rail within the aircraft were supposed to pull open the men's parachutes as they left the aircraft, but something had gone wrong and the lines were failing to catch as the men jumped. The dispatcher pulled back the next man to jump, Billy Morris, but it was obviously too late for Warburton and Duffy. Jimmy Storie was one of the party detailed to bring back the bodies – they

Members of 'L' Detachment boarding an RAF Bristol during training on 7 Nov 1941. (*Lts Smith & Clements, Army Photographic Unit/IWM*)

were found lying on their backs, side by side, as if awaiting burial. There were signs that Duffy had attempted to pull open his own canopy as he fell. 'When we got to Duffy, his parachute was half out, he had tried to pull it out but couldn't twist round and get it out,' recalled Storie. 'After that we all used to give the static line a good tug first before jumping.'

It must have been a terrifying way to go. Blair, on the drop-zone at the time, said later that he had heard the men screaming as they fell. Their bodies were brought back to Kabrit by boat – the first two names on the SAS roll of honour.

Meanwhile, Stirling had missed out on virtually all of the parachute training. Distracted by his ongoing 'negotiations' with MEHQ in Cairo, he had only managed to spend a week or two in camp, while Jock Lewes devised and oversaw all of the training. However, on hearing what had happened he signalled back immediately that after fixing the problem, everyone would jump the next day and he would be returning to jump with them. Lewes took the parade at Kabrit that evening and told the men that the accident was due to the fact that the RAF had put the fittings in the hands of the Egyptians, and through no fault of their own, the sizings were not correct. He said that this would be put right for the following day's jump. The RAF would deal with it. He then relayed Stirling's order but said that anyone who wanted to leave could do so.

Nobody left, but that night proved to be the severest test of the entire period of training for some. In those days parachuting was relatively novel and unnatural enough on its own, but a chute that failed to open at only 900ft was any parachutist's worst nightmare – there would be so little time to pull it out before hitting the ground. Few got any sleep that night.

For once, Eoin's supply of smokes from his ever-present silver cigarette case was undisturbed as the men were issued with tins of fifty Players' Navy Cut cigarettes and spent most of the night chain-smoking. It was a long 24 hours. 'We tried not to think about it,' Pct (parachutist) Bennett said, 'but we did.'

Cigarettes.

The next morning at 0530 hours, Lewes, Stirling and all the officers hooked up for what were probably the most crucial drops in SAS history. Bennett recalled that when 'action stations' was called, everyone began tugging frantically on their static lines. As the Brigade's Training Officer, and in line with his philosophy of never asking the men to do anything that he was not also prepared to do, Jock Lewes jumped first, followed by Pat Riley (an NCO who in time, following Jock's death, took over responsibility for the Brigade's training). Stirling, the other officers and the rest of the men all followed suit. The whole detachment jumped in five successive lifts, from 1,000ft, without a hitch, forming a daylight constellation of white button mushrooms as they floated back to earth. There was relief all round – it couldn't have gone better. Pct Bennett was so euphoric going down that

despite temporarily blacking out he apparently started playing his mouth organ as soon as his chute opened and he regained consciousness.

The men were due to do four day and two night jumps, as well as one into the Suez Canal, but in the end they did five day jumps and one at night. Warburton's and Duffy's deaths were not in vain. The fact that not one man then backed out of the jumps proved to be an important morale-booster – according to Bennett, the men felt that they were at last in a unit that really meant something. They were determined to see this through to the end.

On a lighter note, while they soon came to be known as 'Stirling's Parashots', this was later crudely modified by the LRDG to 'Stirling's Parashites'.

The events also improved Stirling's standing amongst the men – the fact he had made a point of returning to camp to join them for the jump made a strong impression. Until then, Stirling had been seen as a rather distant leader, preoccupied mainly with his dealings with MEHQ in Cairo while Jock Lewes ran the camp. (Bear in mind also that Stirling was remembered from 8 Commando days as a member of the so-called 'Silver Circle Club' in Cairo, gambling on the horses and drinking at the bar in Shepheard's Hotel with Evelyn Waugh and Randolph Churchill, both so-called gentleman soldiers.) As Lewes wrote at the time, 'David has been … absent more than not and I have been in command the while … we have fashioned this unit; he has established it without and, I think I may say, I have established it within.'

Stirling, who had been more than shaken by the accident, admitted later that he hated parachuting (probably as a result of the literally earth-

Parachute training at Kabrit. (*J. Lewes*)

Gathering in a parachute and post-jump discussions on 7.11.41. (*Lts. Smith & Clements, Army Photographic Unit/ IWM*)

shattering attempt made with Lewes in June which left him in hospital for several weeks) but he recognized the importance of being there to encourage his men. Moreover, while outwardly he remained his usual nonchalant self, inside he was livid with the British Army parachute training school at Ringway, Manchester, who had ignored his numerous appeals for assistance. 'I sent a final appeal to Ringway,' he reflected after Warburton's and Duffy's deaths, 'and they sent some training notes and general information, which arrived at the end of October … included in this information we discovered that Ringway had had a fatal accident caused by exactly the same defect as in our case.'

The Wizard's 'sticky' bomb

In tandem with overseeing the training programme, Jock Lewes was also working on what was to become an essential part of SAS kit – the eponymous 'Lewes bomb'. Having been advised to 'stop dreaming about the impossible' by an explosives expert from GHQ and to 'make the best with what he had', it was a problem that Lewes had been trying to solve for some time; and in October 1941, after many hours of frustrating and solitary endeavour, eventually he did. Despite the 'expert advice', he knew it was a problem to which there had to be an answer and he didn't stop experimenting until he'd found it. His aim was to create a bomb that was light enough to carry on operations but powerful enough to destroy an enemy aircraft on the ground.

Spending most of his spare time alone in an improvised shack of a 'laboratory', earning the nickname 'the Wizard', Lewes designed a 1lb device made from thermite (used in incendiary bombs) and plastic explosive ('Nobles 808') rolled together with motor oil and steel filings. It was a stodgy, 'sticky' lump about the size of a large tennis ball into which was pushed a 'No. 27' detonator, an instantaneous fuse and a time pencil. The time pencil looked a bit like a biro, comprising a glass tube with a spring-loaded striker held in place by a strip of copper wire. At the top was a glass phial containing acid that had to be squeezed gently to break. The acid would then eat through the wire and release the striker. The thicker the wire, the longer the delay before the striker was triggered – the pencils were colour-coded according to the length of fuse. It was all put into a small cotton bag, and although crude, proved to be very effective when stuck on to an aircraft's petrol tank. The combination of thermite and explosive resulted in a destructive explosion and the ignition of the petrol tank, sending the entire aircraft up in flames.

The importance of his invention cannot be underestimated – the Lewes bomb became indispensable to the success of the SAS in North Africa and was soon adopted by others such as the SBS in raids in Europe.

Chapter 20

A Monstrous Scheme:
'desert marching is not meant for Irishmen!'

B y the second half of October 1941 training had progressed far enough for Stirling to be able to offer a £10 bet that his men could simulate an attack on the RAF airfield at Heliopolis even though the airfield's security was warned. An RAF group captain informed Stirling that his chances of creeping on to a British airfield undetected were 'practically non-existent'. Stirling disputed this. It would involve a march from Kabrit to Cairo and then across the desert to the airfield – a total distance of roughly 100 miles. The journey recalled the trip Dick Pedder's Commando hopefuls took from Galashiels to Ayr en route to Arran, but the terrain and conditions were decidedly different. Moreover, there would be no passing trucks on which the injured or exhausted could hitch a ride. Airborne patrols would be out looking for them, so they would only march at night while

Desert terrain and makeshift camp. (*Blair Mayne Research Society*)

lying up camouflaged during the day. It would serve as good practice for the Brigade's forthcoming first 'real' operation – Operation Squatter. The bet was duly accepted.

The men were divided into five groups, each comprising ten-man sections that were further split into two-man teams. Each group was commanded by one of the five officers expected to be in command for Operation Squatter: Lewes, Blair, Eoin, Bonington and Fraser. (As it turned out, Bill Fraser was unable to take his place on Squatter due to an injury sustained in an intervening training exercise. Instead, he went on to take command of the rendezvous party for Squatter, with Stirling taking charge of Fraser's group for the operation.)

For supplies, each man carried four water bottles, 3lbs of dates, ½ lb of boiled sweets and some Army biscuits nicknamed 'sand channels' because they were hard enough to drive a jeep over and resembled the implements used for digging. They wore khaki drill (like the Germans), used Italian haversacks which were far better than the standard issue British ones and carried a piece of hessian with which they could camouflage themselves from the prying eyes of the aircraft. To simulate the bomb load that they would be expected to carry on Operation Squatter, stones were put into the men's haversacks; most carried the equivalent weight of eight Lewes bombs weighing around 1lb each.

On the morning of 23 October Eoin wrote to his brother for what would be the last time while preparing for the practice mission:

Dear Ambrose,

Another of your airgraphs has just arrived. They are coming very regularly now. This one was written just after you joined the 8th [the 8th Battalion RUR was raised in 1940]. It seems to be quite a good battalion, certainly there are a lot of regulars in it. Has Crook recovered yet? Give him a severe ticking off from me for being drunk in charge of a car.

So you are going to get married in December. Well done! When you wrote about it first, about a month ago, I did not think that you would ever be able to go through with it.

We are starting this evening a monstrous scheme across the desert. Marching up to 100 miles, lying up during the day, sweating, thirsty, overloaded, not quite seeing any point in it. I am becoming very expert in what to take and what not to take. I have just been making out a list of what I will carry. It is: 2 water bottles, 2 pairs of socks, 1 pair of shorts, 1 shirt, 1 blanket, 2 books, cigarettes, flask (very full), chocolate. I can't think of anything else just now, but by the end of the morning the list will read like a stock in a department store. Then round about four o'clock this afternoon, when I start packing the ruck-sack, the total weight will be 100lbs and McGonigal will discard blankets, books, shorts right, left and centre.

Moral: Don't come to the Middle East: desert marching is not meant for Irishmen!

Eoin

Despite describing the exercise as a 'monstrous scheme' and suggesting he couldn't quite see the point in it, there is no mistaking the tone of anticipation in Eoin's final letter – the kit list is not dissimilar to what he would have taken on a great adventure or holiday hiking around in Ballygally or Inishowen. Of course, this was no holiday, but even as Eoin jokes about Irishmen marching through a desert, there is a sense that he felt he was more than up to the challenge and was looking forward to it. Here at last was the precursor to finally putting all the months of training and route marching into effect. Obviously, this was not something he could put in a letter to his brother, but it had been almost fifteen months since he and Blair had joined the Commando, and once this practice operation had been completed, the SAS would be undertaking its first real mission.

On the evening of 23 October the groups started out on foot from Kabrit on their 'monstrous scheme'. They marched in their separate groups, arriving at the airfield at about midnight on the fourth day. According to Jimmy Storie, who was in the group led by Jock Lewes, they did well to 'overcome the risks of hallucination and deprivation in the cloudless skies that burned the parachutists during the day and froze them during the nights'. They achieved this by camouflaging themselves under hessian sacking in the shadow of rocky escarpments during the daylight hours and marching when the sun went down. However, it was a hard march, and the fairly extreme water discipline employed at the time meant that the men struggled with thirst – they were so parched that talking was kept to a minimum. One of the men in Blair's group recalled that as he lay on the hard desert that last day, covered with sacks, he could see nothing in his mind's eye but a tap of running water.

Once they were finally all in position, they broke through the airfield's perimeter wire and successfully planted stickers marked 'bomb' on all of the aircraft. Not one man was detected. Indeed, none of the groups had even seen each other, but all of the aircraft had been tagged, some with more than one sticker! By dawn they were out of Heliopolis and on their way to Abbabasyia

Barracks with the bet duly won. On arrival at the barracks, with their five-day beards, unwashed, dishevelled and carrying Italian haversacks, they were at first taken to be Italian deserters or prisoners of war. However, the Officer Commanding arranged to have them transported back to base at Kabrit, exhausted though happy in the knowledge that their exercise had been a complete success. They had been apprehensive, but having accomplished it so smoothly, Stirling, the other officers and all of 'L' Detachment knew they could make this concept work. Only one man from the whole party fell out during the exercise and he was duly returned to his parent unit. They were now ready for the real thing.

At the same time that Eoin was writing home singing the praises of the men, about how fit they all were, confident and champing at the bit for a chance to take on the 'jerries', Jock Lewes was also writing:

> We are a team and we are friends and we are soldiers. David and I are willing to back them against any unit in the Middle East, friend or foe. We have shown what we can do in training: soon, please God, we shall show what training can do in battle. And our men are brave: we have many who have often gone up to the sky in aircraft and have never come down in one yet. That surely is a record to be proud of.

A later photograph of Stirling (standing) and members of 'L' Detachment in modified Willys MB desert jeeps with twin-mounted Vickers guns.

Cap badge and wings.

Following their return from the Heliopolis airfield exercise, Stirling organized a competition to come up with a badge and motto for the Brigade. The basis of the badge was designed by Corporal Bob Tait and further modified by Jock Lewes before being accepted – nobody seems to know for sure, but it represents either the 'flaming sword' of Damocles, pointing down, or King Arthur's Excalibur (and not a winged dagger as many mistakenly believe). The motto, 'Who Dares Wins' was finally coined by Stirling himself.

The new albeit 'arrogant badge' (as described by Jock Lewes in a letter to his parents) would overcome one of the problems that had affected the Commandos – that they had no symbol to identify them and to identify with. Stirling wanted something to foster regimental pride, and the new SAS badge made all the difference in the world. This and their Parachute Wings, which were inspired by a fresco seen at Shepheard's Hotel in Cairo and modelled either on the Ibis 'Wings of Egypt' (the goddess Isis) or a stylized Egyptian scarab beetle, would be manufactured by John Jones and Co, the English hatters in Cairo. The men were given the option of wearing the Wings they had been awarded for their parachute jumps either straight away on the shoulder or after they returned from the operation on their breast. They all opted for the latter, although for many this option never materialized and it increased the Wings' value for those who got to wear them later. The final item was the famous SAS sand-coloured beret – a distinct improvement on the white 'ladies' beret that Stirling first had the men wear. The white version was quickly withdrawn after twenty-one men went on leave in Cairo and came back with 128 police charges, having got involved in multiple fights with men from other units (mainly Australians) who enjoyed telling the SAS how fetching they looked in their intimidating headgear.

Chapter 21

The First (and Last) Parachute Mission: Operation Squatter

10 November 1941

Stirling received preparatory orders marked 'Most Secret' on 9 November 1941 and on the following day, his final orders marked 'Secret and Personal': the Eighth Army Operational Instruction No. 16. Directed to the attention of 'Comdg. "L" Sec 1 S.A.S. Bde' and named 'Operation Squatter', 'L' Detachment's first and Eoin's last mission would be to parachute at night into the Northern Desert, Libya behind enemy lines, attack three coastal Axis airbases on foot at Tmimi and Gazala (Gazala 1 and 2), before heading south back into the desert to a meeting point, from where the LRDG would bring the survivors back to camp by a route that ran along the Egyptian coast.

LRDG and the desert terrain. (*Lt Graham, Army Photo Unit / IWM*)

This was it – the SAS' first operation behind enemy lines. Their attitude and the way in which they approached this would set a marker for all to follow.

Stirling was given authorization to send a force of fifty-four, including his five officers. He had originally wanted to take sixty, but because of injuries and a lack of space on board the aircraft following modifications to accommodate additional fuel tanks, he was limited to a total of fifty-five – which included his 'adjutant', Captain Thomson, the observer from MEHQ, who would not be jumping. The men were divided into five 'sticks' of between nine and twelve men each, under Stirling (in place of the injured Fraser), Eoin, Jock Lewes, Bonington and Blair (in order of departure). They were tasked with the destruction of enemy aircraft at the target airfields on a coastal strip about 100km long, west of Tobruk. Eoin's stick was to attack one of the two airfields at Gazala, a small, sparsely populated village about 60km west of Tobruk and 40km east of Tmimi.

Wadis Ghessina and Auda, Tobruk, September/October 1941. (*Australian War Memorial*)

The area was inhabited by Bedouin of the Awlad Ali, semi-nomads who kept camels and sheep and hitched their camels to ploughs in the rainy season. It was not desert 'proper', but a flat, rocky plain with well-frequented tracks running east-west, grooved by shallow *wadis* and covered in some parts with sharp gravel, sedge, esparto grass and thorny acacia bushes.

Wadis are dry riverbeds that only fill during the rainy season. The desert environment is characterized by sudden but infrequent heavy rainfall, often resulting in flash floods. Crossing *wadis* at certain times of the year can be dangerous or even impossible.

Being close to the coast, annual precipitation in the area is not generally high (if compared to Arran perhaps an unfair comparison), but it is variable and it tends to fall over a small number of days between October and January. Charts from 1941 are not readily available, but looking at average rainfall

Derna, 'Wadi El Khaleej'. (*Ahmed Bousneina*)

Wadi Bu Al Gharas near Tmimi. (*A. Reiter*)

figures in a ten-year period for Derna (just north along the coast from Tmimi and Gazala) produced by World Weather & Climate Information, the below chart highlights how timing can be crucial – particularly in an area known for flash flooding.

Average monthly snow and rainfall in Derna in millimeter

This is the mean monthly precipitation over the year, including rain, snow, hail etc.

Show average precipitation in Derna in Inches »

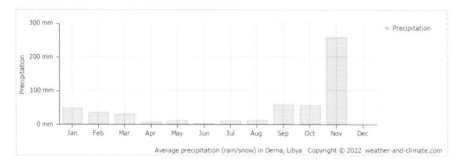

Average precipitation (rain/snow) in Derna, Libya   Copyright © 2022 weather-and-climate.com

- Most rainfall (rainy season) is seen in November.
- Derna has dry periods in April, May, June, July and August.
- On average, November is the wettest month with 256.0 mm (10.08 inch) of precipitation.
- On average, June is the driest month with 1.0 mm (0.04 inch) of precipitation.

Had 'L' Detachment been planning an operation in November at any time over the last decade, concerns would no doubt have been raised around the expected conditions – the contrast in 'normal' November conditions with conditions for the rest of the year is absolutely stark, but in 1941 this does not appear to have been considered a material risk until too late. The area was otherwise hot, humid and subject to sea mists. Daytime temperatures could rise as high as 30° Celsius but at night could drop into single figures. Landing in the dark in this terrain would be hazardous in the best of conditions – November in a good year could clearly be risky but November in 1941 would prove to have been a perilous, and arguably, reckless roll of the dice.

The airfields were thought to be bases for various enemy aircraft, in particular Messerschmitt Bf 109s. These fighters had outclassed the Hurricanes and Tomahawks of the RAF, and by putting them out of action the SAS would help to prevent further damage being inflicted upon supply lines as the Eighth Army advanced into Libya. Other aircraft that were to be targeted as secondary objectives included the ME110s, HE111s, Stuka JU87s and JU88s.

It was a perfect opportunity for the new Brigade to prove its worth and make an important contribution to the war effort – the destruction of enemy aircraft at these airfields could be critical to the success of the Eighth Army's Operation Crusader. In acknowledgement of this, the SAS had been given an unprecedented five Bristol Bombays from 216 Squadron RAF with which to carry out the raid.

On the night of 16 November the Bombays would hug the coast at 8,000ft, then wheel south over the Gulf of Bomba. They would pass over the target area and drop the five sticks about 20 miles west-south-west of their objectives. The sticks would then move into LUPs (lying-up places) overlooking their targets that same night. They would remain hidden throughout the day of 17 November before going into action, destroying all the Bf 109s, and then withdraw across the desert on foot to an RV point called Rotunda Segnale, on an ancient caravan route known as Trig al-Abd or 'Slaves Road'. Here they would be picked up by an LRDG Patrol. Trig al-Abd ran parallel to the coast road, about 40 miles inland.

A Bristol Bombay transport aircraft built by Short & Harland in Belfast, capable of carrying up to twenty-four armed troops (when not modified)

Wadi Derna, 1941. (*Australian War Memorial*)

At the same time, several members of 11 Commando and others led by Blair's 'old friend' Lieutenant Colonel Keyes were to attack Rommel's presumed HQ near Beda Littoria at midnight on 17 November (Operation Flipper).

The raids were scheduled to take place ahead of General Auchinleck's first major offensive (Operation Crusader), scheduled to begin at dawn on 18 November. According to British intelligence, Rommel was expected to launch his own offensive on 20 November in an attempt to end the stubborn resistance of the Tobruk garrison.

The aims of the Eighth Army's offensive were to retake the eastern coastal regions of Libya (Cyrenaica) and seize the Libyan airfields from the enemy, thereby enabling the RAF to increase their supplies to Malta, the island of such strategic importance to the British.

With reference to Stirling's preparatory orders of 9 November, the RAF's (Fairey) Albacores (three-man, single-engine reconnaissance bombers) would drop flares to assist identification of the proposed landing grounds for Operation Squatter, while the RAF's (Bristol) Blenheims (light bomber aircraft) would aim to provide a distraction through so-called 'continued desultory bombing' during the night of 16 November. Stirling and the officers commanding the Bombays, Albacores and Blenheims would meet at Ma'aten Bagush airfield at 1300 on 16 November to coordinate plans.

15 November 1941

On 15 November 1941 Stirling turned twenty-six. His reputation as a 'gentleman commando' was not inspiring, and his experience of battle was limited, given the repeated cancellation of Layforce operations since arriving in the Middle East. In fact, the closest he had come to combat was as part of a planned operation to attack the North African coast from the sea – the aim was to land on enemy beaches and move up to destroy airfields and lines of communication. Two attempts were made, but on both occasions the ship he was on was spotted by Axis aircraft, forcing her to take shelter and return to base. British ships were needed desperately in the Mediterranean, and the Navy had been instructed not to take on any risks. There had been no opportunity to engage the enemy, and the expeditions were not repeated. Nevertheless, Stirling was now about to take a decision that could have the most serious of consequences for the lives of all his men and the future of his new Brigade.

Stirling and the fifty-four men selected for the raid were transported from Khanka to Bagush airfield, west of Alexandria and about 300 miles west of their camp. There, the sealed Operational Orders were opened and the men studied them until each knew exactly what was expected of him. There was also a lot of work to be done preparing explosives, weapons and rations. Ominously, the RAF then treated them to a splendid meal – fit for condemned men – believing that they were on a suicide mission and deserved to go out with a feast. Never before had the pilots been asked to take a 'human cargo' into enemy-occupied territory and cast it off into space. As DuVivier noted in his diary, 'The officers' mess was put at our disposal and we kicked off with a first-rate meal after which there were books, games, wireless and a bottle of beer each, all to keep our minds off the coming event.'

However, after their meal, perhaps taking advantage of the way they had been treated, the men broke into the liquor store of the Officer Commanding the airfield and stole his supplies, becoming 'ingloriously drunk'. The following morning, they were dealt with severely by Jock Lewes, who described them (with a degree of well-disguised pride) as 'either habitual criminals or congenital idiots!' This was no way to prepare for such a pivotal operation, and they sobered up quickly.

16 November 1941

On the day of the operation Stirling was at HQ RAF Western Desert near Bagush when the first weather reports came in – the forecast was alarming. Rain could be expected, along with high winds that in turn could whip up a sand storm or *khamsin*. As ever, the nights were expected to be bitterly cold, but the winds, which were already strong, were expected to be especially ferocious by the time of the drop later that night. The Met Office was tracking a storm that would break over the target area with rain and winds of 30–35 knots. Stirling was stunned; winds of just 15 knots would be enough to justify cancelling an operation. Under normal circumstances, the drop would certainly not have proceeded – if war could ever qualify as 'normal circumstances'. If the forecasts were accurate, the area would experience heavy rains and gale-force winds of more than twice the speed recommended for safe parachuting – let alone at night.

The Brigadier General Staff coordinator, Sandy Galloway, took the view that the mission should not proceed – there would be no moon, the men would be scattered and there would be casualties. Nevertheless, he offered Stirling the choice, saying, 'There will be other opportunities. However, the decision will rest with you.'

Stirling was loath to scrap the mission; after all, when might they get another chance to show what they could do and in conjunction with such a major offensive? When briefed the day before, the men had been raring to go. The atmosphere had been charged with anticipation – here at last was a chance to wipe out a significant number of Messerschmitt Bf 109s. What a difference they could make! After all those false starts and last-minute cancellations with the Commando and Layforce, Stirling wanted to give his officers and men the final say. Were the SAS really going to be put off by some bad weather? Not likely.

Stirling first called his officers together. He informed them that the weather reports indicated a fierce storm was brewing over the target area, with winds of 30+ knots. He also explained that MEHQ in Cairo and the Brigadier General Staff coordinator were of the opinion that the mission should be aborted. Dropping by parachute in those wind speeds, on a moonless night, would be hazardous in the extreme; they would almost certainly sustain casualties on landing.

They also discussed the importance to the Brigade of being able to take this opportunity. 'L' Detachment was a fledgling, secret and irregular new unit, they feared potential disbandment unless they could prove their worth, and quickly, and this was a chance to play an important role in paving the way for the success of the Eighth Army offensive. The five officers and Captain Thomson listened to what Stirling had to say and without hesitation all voted to go ahead despite the obvious risks.

Jock Lewes is reported to have responded, 'I'm with you. Conditions are never perfect. If we sit around waiting for the ideal moment, we'll spend the duration on our backsides' – a sentiment almost certainly born of the Commando experience with Layforce. The difference here was that this was not a choice between proceeding or waiting for perfect conditions, but just meant waiting for even moderately acceptable weather (a conclusion subsequently underlined by Blair Mayne's post-operation assessment of the chances of success in even moderate conditions). However, given the need to coincide with the Eighth Army's Operation Crusader, the officers clearly felt their hand was forced and waiting was out of the question.

Eoin and Blair said very little – there was no real doubt in their minds. It was plain to them there was little choice but to proceed. This was why they had joined, and while conditions may have been far from ideal, Operation Squatter represented the ideal opportunity, with Operation Crusader planned for two days later, to show the top brass what they could do. Was any other outcome of such a vote likely, given that those voting were impatient young men with limited experience of war?

Surprising as it may seem today, the journey from the creation of 'L' Detachment/the SAS Brigade in the summer of 1941 through to their achieving regimental status in September 1942 and the recognition they have achieved today was not preordained. Stirling and his 'originals' had to overcome significant opposition from the military establishment, especially those in MEHQ who viewed their unorthodox methods and informal structure as anathema. In short, there wasn't sufficient oversight of either the Brigade or its members for their liking. However, Stirling had picked his men precisely because they didn't always follow the rules – they had been trained to exercise initiative and judgement under pressure. He had wanted individuals who had already proved their courage under fire, who could think for themselves and take calculated risks. They were highly trained, young and impatient, and he did not want to prescribe to them what they should do. He wanted them for their resourcefulness and determination to get the job done, come what may.

Still, the question needs to be asked: would or should wiser heads with greater wartime experience have prevailed? Given the level of opposition encountered by Stirling in establishing 'L' Detachment, were there perhaps some at MEHQ who wanted them to fail? And did this contribute to Stirling and his officers feeling they could not postpone or abort?

The officers clearly felt they were in a no-win situation: cancel or postpone and risk both further undermining the men's morale and more importantly, disbandment; or proceed and put lives at risk – not through enemy action but because of hostile weather conditions.

Was Stirling, a young officer with limited experience of war and presumably desperate to retain control of his fledgling new Brigade, the right man to make this call? Bear in mind that just prior to Stirling obtaining Auchinleck's stamp of approval, he and other officers from 8 Commando had been requested to return to London. 'L' Detachment had provided him with a promotion, a Brigade and most importantly, an opportunity to remain in theatre.

Were the other young officers ever likely to say anything (in an open group) other than, 'We've come this far, we're not turning back now'? The thought that they might have said, 'It's a bit windy, Captain – probably better to try another time', is not realistic. Postponement would not work – the operation had to take place as planned so as to coincide with Operation Crusader – so they were faced with either going ahead or giving up (although the fallacy of this argument was betrayed by the very fact of their subsequent successes in the month following Operation Squatter).

Galloway may have said there would be other opportunities – the war would not end soon – but he did not insist. However, had Eoin, Blair and all of the fifty-five who went on Operation Squatter not been the type who were prepared to take on something despite the odds, it is possible the SAS would have never got off the ground (even if that is where their feet remained firmly planted for all of the desert operations to come).

Moreover, General Claude Auchinleck was now the man in charge of the Eighth Army offensive – they simply had to try and repay the faith he had personally shown in them. It may have seemed a hopeless cause, but it was a necessary statement of intent which would have important ramifications for the future of the Brigade: it would be quite literally a leap of faith into the dark, but they believed in themselves and had to try.

Stirling confirmed to MEHQ that all of his officers had voted to proceed, but famously they wanted to give the same opportunity to the men under their command. The men were called in and the situation was explained by Lewes. According to Johnny Cooper, Stirling then said something along the lines of 'We'll go because we've got to go. The job is important … the whole army depends on us to get in there and knock off as many of those Messerschmitt 109-Fs as possible.' The men were given the option to pull out, but all wholeheartedly agreed to proceed; the job had to be done.

Nevertheless, it has since very recently come to light that there may have been more to the officers' pre-operation meeting than previously known. Sergeant Kenneth 'Joe' Welch was one of three parachute-jump instructors (PJIs) from RAF Ringway sent to Kabrit to help train the men in October 1941. He also went on to act as the dispatcher for flight No. 1 on Operation Squatter – Stirling's plane.

According to the personal recollections of the family of Sergeant Joe Welch, he attended the pre-operation meeting called by Stirling. In addition to the officers, he recalled that it was also in fact attended by all the dispatchers, and possibly the pilots – in any event, he remembered a group of about fifteen all told. The meeting took place at the same time as the other ORs were having breakfast – much to the dispatchers' annoyance – and lasted approximately 45 minutes.

Stirling reported the latest weather updates and called for views. Jock Lewes thought that, despite the conditions, the men were battle-ready but was concerned the wind was too strong for them all to land safely. Another felt the operation should be postponed and/or that consideration should be given to getting the LRDG (referred to as the 'desert taxi service' by the men) to both drop and pick them up. According to Sergeant Welch, this individual had never been particularly comfortable about jumping and, given the conditions, was especially concerned that the risk of injury on landing would be even more likely.

Although this would be the first time, apart from in training, that Sergeant Welch had been a dispatcher, he considered that the conditions were such that, despite all their training, he was not confident the men would be battle-ready. He was firmly of the view that if the forecast wind speeds were even close to being accurate, not only should the planes not fly in those conditions but the men were certainly not jump-ready. In his opinion, no one, not even the most experienced jumper, could hope to land safely; the parachutes could not be expected to hold up. The discussion became so heated that Welch even expressed the view that they might as well jump without parachutes; that way, at least they would die quickly!

It was at this point that Stirling interrupted, curtly reminding Sergeant Welch that it was not up to him and he would have to follow orders. Stirling told him in no uncertain terms what would happen to him and to any soldier who disobeyed him.

The debate became yet more heated and was beginning to disintegrate, until Blair stepped in to calm things down, allowing everyone in turn an opportunity to have their uninterrupted say without fear of reprisal.

Stirling, and a few of the others, were adamant that postponing the operation was not an option, even for a day. Coordination with the start of Operation Crusader (the Eighth Army offensive) was crucial – it was that day or never, whatever the risk. Casualties were a possibility, but it was worth it.

Blair apparently said very little either way, but felt all would be well so long as they (the team leaders) did not abandon their men or attempt any heroics. This was not a moment for mavericks; it was a question of minimizing the risks involved as best they could. Jock Lewes was one of those who felt the landing risks were too great – he agreed with Welch that there was a real prospect the parachutes could fail in such winds. However, he also agreed with Blair that provided they were in fact able to land safely, all would be well.

There was no discussion regarding mission targets, but a lot of emphasis was placed on the importance of bringing each team together once on the ground and getting them to the RV points safely.

In the end, Stirling said he would put it to the men and allow them to decide. And the rest is history …

However, the reality of what transpired at the meeting according to Sergeant Welch, in contrast to how stoic and uncomplicated the discussion surrounding the weather conditions and associated risks has otherwise been presented, underlines the challenges in retracing events such as these which have long since become unquestioned, legendary moments in the annals of military history.

It is all too easy to look back and find fault or second-guess decisions made in the heat of the moment. It is clear that mistakes were made and competing agendas were in play. However, Welch's recollections serve to underline the questions that have been raised concerning the motives of the more senior people at MEHQ, who in most cases were vastly more experienced and would have known better but were non-committal in their advice and left the final call up to Stirling and his young officers. It adds credence to the view that not only did some of those involved potentially want 'L Detachment' to fail (there was inherent distrust of the concept of an irregular unit) but they took the view that even if it did fail, provided they went ahead and made their presence known to the Germans/Italians through being captured or otherwise, a large part of the mission objective would have been met (i.e. to create the impression that the Allies had a significant force of paratroopers operating in the region).

Stirling and his officers, all the originals, were most unlikely to back down and postpone at such a moment. It was precisely the type of challenge and statement of intent that they had signed up to take on. They had trained hard, were young and fearless and ready to go.

As Bill Fraser put it:

The men were not 'Gung Ho' they just wanted to get on with the job in hand, a job that they had trained so hard to achieve the exacting standards that was demanded of them. It would also help to heal the memories of the two fatalities from the parachute training accident one month previously and make worthwhile all of the injuries that so many of them had sustained. It would also finally put to bed the constant cancellations of operations that they had endured during the brief but troubled existence of Layforce. They were young, fit and well trained. They had no fear, just a belief that they would come through unscathed.

Significantly, given the high likelihood of casualties, it was also understood and agreed by all that should anyone be so seriously injured or incapacitated in the course of the operation that he could not continue, he would be left behind to fend for himself, either to be captured by the enemy or rescued by the LRDG/Allied ground forces. This was to be no Hollywood movie in which the mission was sacrificed to ensure that no man was left behind – for the SAS their objective would come first.

Eoin and Blair had reached a further private agreement – if either was to run into any difficulties and miss the RV, the other would hold off from writing to his family until at least one month had passed, so as not to worry them unnecessarily. They took the view that if the worst came to pass, they could simply lie up, sit tight and wait for British ground forces or the LRDG to arrive. Save for the possibility of becoming a PoW, they did not speak of or contemplate anything worse.

Devastatingly, Operation Squatter saw noble, determined aspiration turn into harsh reality. Of the fifty-five men who set out across the desert on the night of 16 November 1941, only twenty-one returned – the rest were

David Stirling and Jock Lewes. (*SAS, RA*)

either left for dead or became prisoners of war for the next couple of years (which surely helps to put two weeks of quarantine into perspective for our generation!). Eoin was one of the thirty-four not to return, but nobody appeared to know whether he had died slowly and alone in the desert storm, or been found alive by Axis Forces and taken prisoner, or killed.

16 November: 1830 hours

The weather did improve somewhat, and by the time the aircraft were due to take off conditions were recorded as 'clear and still'. However, this was to change quickly and dramatically; it was quite literally the calm before the storm.

The men would jump wearing standard-issue desert shirts and shorts, with skeleton web equipment on their backs containing an entrenching tool (small shovel). Each man also carried a small haversack packed with some grenades, food (dates, raisins, cheese, biscuits, sweets and chocolate), a revolver, maps and a compass. Mechanic's overalls were worn over all of this to ensure none of the equipment would be caught up in the parachute rigging lines during the drop. Some also brought a supply of cigarettes – Stirling packed his beloved Cuban cigars and Eoin his lucky silver cigarette case.

At 1830 hours, thirty minutes before the first aircraft was officially due to take off, a fleet of RAF trucks arrived at the officers' mess to transport the men to the five Bristol Bombays. On arrival at their planes, the men chatted, had a final smoke before take-off and said cheerio to their comrades in the other sticks. They noticed that the wind was starting to change, and Jeff DuVivier in the Jock Lewes stick 'muttered a silent prayer and put myself in God's hands' as he climbed aboard.

The teams targeting the airfields at Gazala took off first. Stirling's plane led the way, followed by Eoin's and then Lewes'. The planes bound for Tmimi came next – first Bonington in the fourth plane and then Blair's stick in the fifth. Each aircraft carried five or six canisters, inside which were two packs containing weapons, spare ammunition, fuses, explosives, blankets and rations. The precise make-up of each stick is not entirely clear. It would seem that because of modifications made to each of the aircraft to accommodate additional fuselage tanks as well as the addition of a Vickers K, GO or VGO gun, space was limited. As a result, two men were switched from Stirling's stick to Eoin's and Bonington's respectively. Lists of all those believed to have participated are at Appendix H. In short, it seems that Eoin and Bonington both took eleven men, Lewes and Blair ten each and Stirling eight.

The eleven men in Eoin's stick were:

Sgt R. Lazenby (Scots Guards)
A/Sgt C. McCormack (Royal Scots)
L/Cpl R.D. Evans (Welsh Guards)
L/Cpl J. Maloney (Somerset Light Infantry)
L/Cpl S. Hildreth (South Lancashire Regiment)
Pct R.D. Mackay (Scots Guards)
Pct W. Morris (Black Watch)
Pct J.P. Robertson (Scots Guards)
Pct J. Blakeney (Coldstream Guards)
Pct R.D. Davies (Welsh Guards)
Pct A. Westwater (Royal Artillery)

The initial plan was to start departing at 1730 hours. This was formally put back to 1900 hours and then on the night delayed a little further; the first aircraft took off from Bagush at 1930 hours, the others at roughly ten-minute intervals thereafter. It was a moonless night with cloud, some rain and the anticipated high winds gradually beginning to make their presence felt. Eoin's plane took off at approximately 1940. Blair's plane was delayed and didn't take off until 2020 – 20 minutes after Bonington's. This was a stroke of good fortune because, as it transpired, the men in the first four planes ended up jumping in the worst of the weather and attracting all of the Italian anti-aircraft fire.

16 November: 2220 hours

With the transit time extended by about thirty minutes as a result of the conditions to 3 hours and 15 minutes, the first of the aircraft banked south over the coast of Cyrenaica at approximately 2220, with the other three following on, and headed straight into a wall of Italian ack-ack. The aircraft were spaced out, with their pilots looking for separate DZs (drop-zones) on the littoral plain about ten minutes away – meanwhile, below them a fierce sandstorm was beginning to rip through the desert.

As David Stirling later recalled:

The night on which [the operation] took place was almost unbelievably unsuitable for a parachute operation. There was no moon and the wind was so strong that in arriving in our Bombay aircraft over the Gazala coastline, the flares dropped by the Wellington bombers were quite insufficient for our navigators to pick up any fixed point on the coast because the Desert sand and dust was obscuring the whole coastline.

Therefore, in effect, the navigators had to take pot luck in their dead reckoning and as far as I know, no party was dropped within 10 miles of the selected DZs.

As it transpired, only Blair's stick were dropped anywhere near their intended DZ – having been delayed in taking off, they jumped unobserved by the Italian anti-aircraft artillery.

Johnny Cooper, one of the men in Jock Lewes' stick in No. 3 flight, recalled that just as they turned inland for the final run to the drop zone, they

were caught in a searchlight beam. At the same instant a firework display comparable with the fifth of November came up from the Italian ground-defences, their streams of tracer seemingly converging on the Bombay. [The pilot took evasive action, trying to avoid the Italian searchlights.] All of us were terrified, imagining that we would plunge to the ground. Bits of kit broke loose and flew about, adding to the confusion.

According to Jimmy Storie, 'The flak was terrible; we were all leaning back against the side and the flak was coming up through the centre. How the hell no one got wounded I don't know.' Jeff DuVivier had evidence of how close it had been; when he returned from the raid, an RAF dispatcher asked him who had been sitting next to the rear left door. DuVivier confirmed it had been him.

The dispatcher laughed: 'We found an unexploded shell embedded under the seat. A couple of inches higher and you'd be talking in a very high voice.' (Gavin Mortimer, *Stirling's Men*)

The ack-ack didn't last long, and they were soon shrouded in darkness again; but then almost as quickly, as they reached the next line of defences, they were lit up by more Italian searchlights – the AA fire resumed and this time, they were hit. The men clipped on their static lines and readied themselves for an emergency jump, however, 'with a final dive we cleared the coastal strip, to the immense relief of all of us.' (Johnny Cooper, *One of the Originals*)

Just ahead of them, Stirling in the lead Bombay was now only six minutes from the jump – they had avoided taking any hits and were unaware that one of the five aircraft hadn't made it through the Italian ground defence.

Bonington's No. 4 flight's pilot, Flight Sergeant Charlie West, had taken his Bombay down to 200ft to try to get a visual fix on the coast. Immediately after the aircraft broke through the clouds it was hit by flak, shattering the instruments and piercing the port engine. West told Bonington that he was aborting the drop and turning back, and they headed back east for fifty minutes until their fuel was almost out. West then set the Bombay down on what he was sure was Allied territory, only to discover his compass had been damaged by shrapnel and they had flown round in a circle!

Using the last of the fuel, West decided to at least try to get the aircraft airborne again and as far away as possible from enemy territory. However, bizarrely, before they could get away, an Italian cook happened upon them

Messerschmitt Bf 109s, Libya, April 1941. (*A.R. Khan*)

and was taken prisoner. The cook was 'invited' to join the flight, but unfortunately their hospitality was short lived as almost as soon as they were back in the sky they then ran into a Messerschmitt that shot them down. No. 4 Flight crash-landed in the desert and broke up. West suffered a fractured skull, ribs and shoulder and a ruptured diaphragm. His wireless operator was badly hurt and the co-pilot was killed.

As for Bonington's stick, they were all, including Captain Thomson, injured and taken prisoner by German troops. Sergeant Stone died three weeks later from his wounds while a PoW. The Italian prisoner survived his short-lived stay in captivity.

16 November: 2330hrs

Blair's stick reached their DZ without attracting the attention of any enemy anti-aircraft batteries. Blair described events in his operational report:

> As the section was descending there were flashes on the ground and reports which I then thought was small-arms fire. But on reaching the ground no enemy was found so I concluded that the report had been caused by detonators exploding in [canister] packs whose parachutes had failed to open.
>
> The landing was unpleasant. I estimated the wind speed at 20–25 miles per hour, and the ground was studded with thorny bushes.
>
> Two men were injured here. Pct Arnold sprained both ankles and Pct Kendall bruised or damaged his leg.
>
> An extensive search was made for the [canister] containers, lasting until 0130 hours 17/11/41, but only four packs and two TSMGs [Thompson sub-machine guns] were located.
>
> I left the two injured men there, instructed them to remain there that night, and in the morning find and bury any containers in the area, and then to make to the RV which I estimated at 15 miles away.
>
> It was too late to carry out my original plan of lying west of Tmimi as I had only five hours of darkness left, so I decided to lie up on the southern side. I then had eight men, 16 bombs, 14 water bottles and food as originally laid for four men, and four blankets.

Dave Kershaw recalled that he

> hit the deck and couldn't get out of my harness, and was dragged along the ground. I was pulling on one side of the chute, then pulling on the other to try and spill the air out of the canopy. I was dragged in the sand,

and it was folding the skin back, the sand was getting underneath, and I was in a shocking state. Eventually the canopy collided with a boulder or something like that, and I got it off.

Pct Johnny Cooper, from Lewes' stick, also recalled the landing:

The wind when you jumped was ferocious and of course you couldn't see the ground coming up. I hit the desert with quite a bump and was then dragged along by the wind at quite a speed. When I came to rest I staggered rather groggily to my feet, feeling sure I would find a few broken bones but to my astonishment I seemed to [have suffered] nothing worse than the wind momentarily knocked out of me. There was a sudden rush of relief but then of course, I looked around me and realised I was all alone and, well, God knows where.

It was a lottery, a tragic farce. Another member of Lewes' stick was found literally hanging from a cactus plant – he had landed right in the middle of it, his skin torn to shreds, and was stuck. Having come to a rather sudden and uncomfortable stop, he was one of the lucky ones.

Reg Seekings, from Blair's stick, remembered how they

hit the deck and the wind took over, and we went at a hell of a lick. We were trapped. You couldn't shake yourself free of the chute. I was struggling to free myself and I thought: 'This is it.' I had one more go, struggled like hell, got over on my stomach, and I just went face first into a thorn bush. I could feel blood running down, and Jesus this got my temper up, and eventually I managed to break free. My hands and arms were completely skinned, and my face was a hell of a mess.

Bob Bennett, also from Blair's stick, experienced the same problems:

We set off, and the next two and a half hours seemed to me a lifetime. It was cold – intensely cold … On hitting the ground I immediately found myself being dragged by the wind … I was dragged for about half a mile – I just couldn't get out of the chute, the wind was blowing that fast … I could not stop myself, but made desperate efforts to release my harness, this being a job for Houdini…but after being used as a human bulldozer for what seemed an age, a lull in the fury of the gale allowed my chute to collapse … Our luck was out: all we found were two out of eleven containers … Three bottles of water were handed to the injured members of the party together with a few rations. We shook hands with them, wished them luck, and set out to find our objective.

Desert terrain, Libya. (*P. Rateau, Shutterstock*)

The reality was that few in any of the groups escaped without injuries of some description. All but one of Stirling's stick were injured; one (Stan Bolland) was blown away and could not be found – he was later reported dead by the Italians – and Stirling himself suffered injuries to his arms and legs. Lewes lost a man (Sergeant Cheyne), and Blair sustained a serious injury to his back that, although he didn't mention at the time, plagued him for the rest of his life. One of his men fractured an arm, and neither of the two men he was forced to leave at the DZ could walk – they were captured by a sole Italian soldier on the 18th after successfully posing as members of a road-building Royal Engineers detachment that had become lost (albeit 200 miles behind enemy lines!). The Italians who held them turned out to be part of a road-building unit themselves and so were happy to accept the men's story.

For the jumpers, hitting the ground would have been like falling from a 20ft wall; this combined with the fact that the men could not see the ground as they fell, and therefore could not anticipate and brace for the impact, made it all the worse. The heavy winds had dragged many of them for long distances across the desert floor, and their bodies were scraped by sharp gravel and rocks as well as the spiky acacia scrub that covered the drop zones. In addition to not being able to activate the quick-release buttons on their harnesses (which were clogged with sand), some of the men's parachute straps became twisted around the handles of the small spades they were carrying in their packs – and so, even if they were able to activate the quick-release buttons, they continued to be dragged across the desert. This problem was not anticipated, as the spades had not been used on any of the practice jumps. It seemed as though anything that could go wrong, did.

As for the Jock Lewes group, they had jumped from No. 3 Flight in a well-drilled stick – the 'Wizard' dropping first, and each successive man instructed to bury his parachute upon landing and wait where he was. Lewes intended to move back along the compass bearing of the aircraft, collecting the second jumper, then the third, and so on – what he called 'rolling up the stick'. But the wind had dragged Jeff DuVivier for 150 yards until finally he snagged on a camel thorn bush, allowing him a chance to take stock of the situation. He wrote in his diary:

> When I finally freed myself, I was bruised and bleeding and there was a sharp pain in my right leg. When I saw the rocky ground I'd travelled over, I thanked my lucky stars that I was alive.

Eventually, DuVivier found the rest of the stick and joined his comrades in searching for the containers. 'We couldn't find most of the containers with our equipment, so Jock Lewes gathered us round and said that we'd still try and carry out the attack if we can find the target,' said Cooper. The plan was to see if they could at least link up with Stirling's and Eoin's sticks and play some part in the attacks. However, Lewes' giant troop sergeant, Jock Cheyne, appeared to have experienced a problem with his chute and/ or landed badly, breaking his spine. It meant only one thing: having agreed in advance that anyone unable to carry on without assistance would have to fend for himself, Cheyne readied himself for a long and hopeful wait. His best chance would be discovery by the enemy. His great pal from 11 Commando days, Jimmy Storie, was loath to leave him, proposing instead that he carry the stricken Cheyne (even though he had damaged his own back); but after much hesitation he was persuaded to leave him. The men shook hands, and Cheyne was left with some blankets, water and a revolver. It was a pretty forlorn situation. Storie was later quoted as recalling:

> Sergeant Jock Cheyne was my best friend and he broke his back. We had to leave him with a bottle of water and a revolver. We had been told that if you broke a leg and couldn't make it, you just had to crawl to the nearest roadside and hope. But there's nothing there in the desert.

And they all knew it. As it was, Sergeant Cheyne was never heard of again. They all took this hard, in particular Sergeant Pat Riley. According to Storie, during the flight, 'Neither had been happy with how his parachute felt, so they'd swapped.' As a result, Riley couldn't stop wondering whether the loss of his good friend was because he had taken Riley's chute. This was all the more poignant given that at the time the men were still responsible for packing their own parachutes.

In some SAS texts Cheyne is referred to as having jumped with Stirling's stick – based on a report by Corporal Bob Tait and a comment by Johnny Cooper from Lewes' stick that all of Lewes' stick had made it back to the RV intact. However, given their very personal nature, it is hard to look beyond the Storie and Riley accounts. Cooper may have been quoted out of context and referring only to the men who set out on the march to the RV, whereas Tait's report, prepared for the purposes of the SAS war diary, may have had consistency in mind, before any thorough post-war investigation into the composition of each stick had been undertaken.

The more likely explanation is that Tait confused Cheyne with the loss of Stanley Bolland, who jumped with Stirling's stick but was lost on landing and never found – Tait does not mention Bolland in his report at all and so in the intervening years must have confused him with Cheyne. Oddly, however, while the Riley account confirms that Cheyne had jumped with them, in contrast to Storie, Riley (in a reported conversation with Jim

Almonds) denied even finding Cheyne on landing. In his conversation with Almonds, Riley is said to have recounted that:

> They all left the 'plane in quick succession. Jock Cheyne was the second to last to go. He was a good bloke, according to Riley, 'full of quaint Scots humour'. But he was never seen again. They thought his chute may have been damaged by the anti-aircraft fire or perhaps it failed to open. Riley was worried about that because he and Cheyne had just swapped chutes for a better fit – he was even bigger than Riley. They had searched for him for a while [but] couldn't find him. (L. Almonds, *Gentleman Jim*)

What is odd about this is that if Lewes and his men never found Cheyne, it is not clear why they would have speculated that his chute was either damaged by AA fire or had failed to open. (Or why Riley should have had such misgivings about swapping harnesses with him.) The suggestion is that in fact they probably did find him and were aware that Cheyne had hit the ground hard because of a malfunctioning chute – not that he had been blown miles off course in the wind and was too far away to be found. Quite naturally, Riley may well just have decided that he didn't want to talk about it with Almonds – the men had just returned to camp and would have obviously hated leaving Cheyne in such a helpess condition. And Riley clearly had misgivings as a result of having swapped harnesses.

17 November, dawn (Mayne)

Blair and his men marched for several miles before lying up in a *wadi*. He estimated they had covered six miles and were approximately five miles from the target. Of the five sticks, Blair's group was the only one to be dropped at the correct DZ. When daylight broke on the 17th, a dawn reconnaissance revealed that they were only four to six miles from Tmimi airfield, and Blair identified seventeen Messerschmitt Bf 109s waiting to be destroyed. There was one tent between them and the airfield but no other signs of activity – it seemed their luck was in. However, there was no sign of Bonington's stick.

Blair planned to lie up in the *wadi* before moving forward and attacking the airfield at 2050 hours. Each of his stick would carry two bombs, while he and Sergeant McDonald would carry the Thompson sub-machine guns. But, as Blair noted later in his report, the weather intervened:

At 1730 hours it commenced to rain heavily. After about half an hour the *wadi* became a river, and as the men were lying concealed in the middle of bushes it took them some time getting to higher ground. It kept on raining and we were unable to find shelter. An hour later I tried two of the time pencils and they did not work. Even if we had been able to keep them dry, it would not, in my opinion, have been practicable to have used them, as during the half-hour delay on the plane the rain would have rendered them useless. I tried the instantaneous fuses and they did not work either.

At first, Blair's stick tried to wait out the cloudburst, until it dawned on them that they were sitting in what was rapidly becoming a fast-flowing river. They scrambled for higher ground and tried to seek cover, but it was raining so hard it was difficult to see. The rain pounded through the *wadi*, pulling with it twigs, branches and other debris as the collecting waters gathered force. Various bits of gear were carried off with the rain, penetrating everything, and as the light began to fade, Blair discovered the instantaneous fuses were soaking wet – having come so close, it looked like they would be leaving empty-handed. They then endured a miserable night in the hope that better weather the following day might dry out the fuses, but although conditions did finally improve, it remained overcast and never warmed up enough. Blair still considered going on regardless – at least with a view to using the few grenades that had been recovered – but with the prospect of swimming across a 25ft *wadi* in spate, he had to accept defeat. (Blair had never been a fan of the swims off Arran to Holy Isle but also recognized that he could not prevent the bombs being soaked.)

Reluctantly, Blair called off the attack. He and his men then endured a pitiful 20-mile hike during the night of the 18th, before lying up the following day and carrying on again in the evening towards the RV point – located about 34 miles inland from both the Gazala and Tmimi airfields. All told, it would take them three nights to make contact with the LRDG. The operation had been a complete failure, but Blair finished his report by concluding that had the weather been normal or even moderate, it would have been entirely successful. It had taken an extraordinary combination of wind and rain to knock them off course.

All told, Blair is reported by the LRDG to have returned with eight men, two having been left behind injured. However, as an illustration of how fallible memory can be, it is interesting to note that when interviewed many years later, at least three members of his stick remembered only six of them making it back to the RV and only one being injured in the jump.

Shallow *wadi*, Libya. (*P. Rateau, Shutterstock*)

Reg Seekings recalled that 'There were six or seven of us left'; Bob Bennett noted, 'So six of us were sitting there with blankets over our heads'; and Dave Kershaw recalled the same arrangement: 'We had a blanket and we spread it over and above us. There were three that side and three this side … Of the sixty-five, apparently there were twenty-two of us left. I still say there were only sixteen.' As for the two men who had to be left, Seekings said, 'One man had a broken ankle and we had to leave him', and Kershaw recalled that they 'discovered Keith [Kendall] with his damaged back, and detailed Corporal Arnold to stay with him.'

In fact, Blair's report to some extent supports this, albeit with the men's names the other way around, saying that while Arnold sprained both ankles, Kendall just bruised his leg.

Perhaps one of the oddest remarks is that attributed to Johnny Cooper, who said in part (spoilers removed):

From then, our lot came in in dribs and drabs … Bob Bennett came in. Paddy came in with his crew – Gunner Gulkis never turned up … Fraser came in, of course – he was all right.

This suggests that Bennett was on his own and not with Mayne's group. There is no record of anyone named 'Gunner Gulkis' in 'L' Detachment, and even the reference to a gunner in relation to Operation Squatter is unusual. Fraser wasn't there – he was injured in training and was instead waiting for the returning men at the second RV point.

It is a clear illustration that at best, reports of these events can only really be taken as a guide to what may have happened. This is a feature that we see repeated when trying to work out what may have happened to some of the other sticks.

Lewes

The Lewes group marched through the night of 16 November and lay up at 0930 hours the next morning. Sergeant Pat Riley was sent forward to reconnoitre the area, only to return reporting that there was no sign of the Gazala airfield or of Stirling's and Eoin's sticks. In his opinion, they had been dropped much further south than planned. Nonetheless, Lewes decided to continue, and at 1400 they departed the *wadi* and headed north for eight miles.

Late that afternoon, 17 November, the weather turned, soaking the men and more importantly, their explosives. 'The lightning was terrific', recalled DuVivier. 'And how it rained! The compass was going round in circles. We were getting nowhere. And we were wallowing up to our knees in water. I remember seeing tortoises swimming about.'

'The water was up to your chest,' recalled Johnny Cooper. *Wadis* were transformed in minutes into torrents of surging water, and they were saturated. Lewes, with the same grudging acceptance as Blair, decided to abort the operation and head south towards the RV. The hours that followed tested the resolve of all the men, even Lewes who, cold, hungry and exhausted like the rest of his section, had to temporarily hand command over to Sergeant Riley, the one man who seemed oblivious to the conditions.

Riley, an Irish-American, was a formidable amateur boxer who had moved from Wisconsin to Cumbria as a seven-year-old and grew up working in the local granite quarry with his father and grandfather – he seemed as impervious as the rock he used to mine. Riley had the men march for forty minutes, rest for twenty if there was any dry ground to be found, march for forty more, and so on. Marching through the night of the 17th in this manner, often wading through chest-high water and in quite unsuitable clothing, Jeff DuVivier – a veteran of 11 Commando's wet and windy winter marches on Arran – had never experienced such cold ('I was shivering, not shaking. All the bones in my body were numbed'.) But he acknowledged Riley's strength, noting, 'I must mention here Pat Riley, an ex-Guardsman and policeman … I shall always be indebted to him for what he did. I'm sure he was for the most part responsible for our return.'

Michel Asher in *The Regiment* describes the scene:

The terrible rainstorm that swept the coast of Cyrenaica on the afternoon and evening of 17 November … has become part of Second World War legend. It came in a shock-wave – a wall of water that crashed out of the sky on the tail of cracking forked lightning and booming thunder. It sizzled across the sand, spreading like electricity into the vast network of clefts and channels, plunging downward with increasing momentum, until *wadis* had become swirling deep rivers hundreds of feet wide. The transformation it brought was breathtaking. The storm was characterized by war correspondents as 'the worst storm in living memory', or 'the worst storm in forty years'. This may have been the case, but the stitchwork of deep *wadis* gouged across the desert was adequate indication of the part water had played in its geological history. It rained frequently in this area at this time of year – Cyrenaica averaged 24 inches annually, and it was by no means rare for nomads to be drowned in flash floods. No one at GHQ had anticipated it, mainly because of the enduring Western belief that

Sgt Pat Riley (Archant/BNPS)

the desert is a hot, dry place that can be cold at night, when in fact it is a landscape of extremes in a constant flux. Not even Lewes, for all his brilliance, had considered the possibility of rain – the fuses and time-pencils weren't waterproofed.

The rainstorm had resulted in a dramatic transformation of the landscape. The area surrounding the drop zones, which had been bone-dry, was suddenly turned into a heaving mass of dark, rushing water; the landscape was unrecognizable.

As Blair and his men had found, the rain and wind did finally ease during the morning of 18 November, allowing some respite. However, even with Sergeant Riley's determined lead, it was not until 0900 on the 19th (over thirty-six hours after they had decided to abort the operation) that Jock Lewes and his men finally reached one of the LRDG's hurricane signal lamps. It was deposited just three-quarters of a mile from the RV camp, so after signalling and being quickly spotted, they were brought in and greeted with bully beef and hot mugs of tea, disguising the presence of some medicinal rum.

This was more than welcome, for the second night's interminable hike in the cold had pushed some to their limit. Jeff DuVivier said:

> The men were used to British winters … [but] none of them had ever experienced such cold before. I couldn't explain how cold it actually was. To believe it one would have to experience it … I couldn't speak, every time I opened my mouth my teeth just cracked against one another.

20 November, dawn

Blair and his men also made it to the RV zone on the 19th, but later in the day. They did not contact the LRDG until the early hours of 20 November, but this was partly born of caution on Blair's part: they had spotted a smoke fire lit by members of the LRDG waiting party but were unsure whether it had been set by the LRDG or by the Germans. They therefore spent part of the 19th lying up and observing, before eventually determining it was safe to make contact. They were collected at dawn on the 20th – just before the 0700 deadline.

Although desperately disheartened that they had not been able to complete the job, Blair was nonetheless pleased with the way his men had conducted themselves in punishing circumstances. 'The whole section,' he reported, 'behaved extremely well and although lacerated and bruised in varying degrees by their landing, and wet and numb with cold, remained cheerful.'

More bully beef and mugs of tea with rum were produced while the groups swapped horror stories – all the while wondering privately how many others would make it back, and when.

Stirling's stick

A few hours earlier, the LRDG had recovered Stirling and Corporal Bob Tait out on the trail, but they were on their own. Things were not looking good – the number of survivors was just twenty-one, and two groups were yet to be heard from at all. Lewes had left Sergeant Cheyne and returned with nine ORs; Blair had left two men and brought in eight ORs; but Stirling was still waiting for the remainder of his stick to appear – it transpired that although one man (Stanley Bolland) had disappeared somewhere in the DZ, the remaining six should have made it back to the RV camp well before Stirling and Tait.

In his operational reports (there are two versions – Appendix G), Tait described how their aircraft was delayed in its approach to Gazala by strong winds and heavy anti-aircraft fire (or as he put it, 'an uncomfortable amount of A.A.'). When eventually they jumped, 'owing to the high wind … estimated … at about 30 miles per hour … we all made very bad landings [resulting in various injuries to all but Tait] … [and] had considerable difficulty in assembling, the wind having scattered us over a wide area.' Finding it hard to breathe as the air was thick with sand and dust, the men struggled to see anything through the black, bellowing night. After several hours of stumbling around in the raging winds and flashing their torches, all but Stan Bolland were found; he was later presumed to have died on landing. Stirling himself had hit the desert floor with such force that he blacked out for several minutes, and he was incredibly fortunate not to have been dragged along unconscious by his parachute. (Tait described Stirling as having sustained injuries about the arms and legs).

Once assembled, they set off towards a meeting point overlooking the Gazala targets to make contact with Jock Lewes and Eoin's parties. However, progress was slow, and while they should have reached the meeting point before daybreak on the 17th, they were still out in the open when the sun rose and had to lie up. Very little enemy activity was observed, but by nightfall Stirling decided to send all of the party to the first withdrawal RV to meet the LRDG, while he and Cpl Tait continued on.

It ran directly contrary to Blair's warning at the officers' pre-operation meeting that given the conditions, it would be important that each leader prioritise ensuring that their respective groups remain together. Nevertheless, unable to find most of the containers, and with most of his men injured by the drop, Stirling decided that he and Corporal Tait, the one man to emerge from the swirling sand and shadows unharmed (he had only sprained an ankle), would at least try to find the airfield, conduct some reconnaissance and possibly even join Lewes' and/or Eoin's sticks in carrying out an attack. In the meantime, bearing in mind their condition and the minimal supplies, he asked the rest of his men, under the command of Sergeant Major Yates, to make their way towards the withdrawal RV. Despite the injuries, there was some unhappiness at this – the decision to cancel was all too familiar and the suggestion that they split up was not popular. Nevertheless, Stirling was keen to try and recover something from the situation, and with future operations in mind presumably felt this would be the best use of resources.

Interestingly, although Tait's reports contain some clear errors in terms of timing and dates, his recollection contradicts that of Stirling, who remembers making the decision to split the group immediately upon assembling after the drop – not sometime after having already marched a good way towards the meeting point.

In any event, whether the decision to split happened at the outset or as seems more likely based on Tait's reports, while en route after they had established more precisely their location, both groups had significant marches ahead of them – *if* dropped in the correct location, the six ORs would have over thirty miles to march while hampered significantly by various sprains and fractures. If they were not in the correct location (as turned out to be the case), the route back would have been considerably longer – estimated by Tait to be as much as 70 miles. Stirling and Tait, by marching in the opposite direction in an attempt to locate the other sticks and/or the target airfield, would potentially be adding a 20–30 mile round trip to their journey to the RV.

There were also a couple of other issues – unless Stirling and Tait found the other two sticks there would be little they could accomplish apart from some reconnaissance. This was because although they had recovered some canisters containing bombs, the accompanying fuses had been packed in separate canisters and could not be found – yet another lesson learnt. In addition, just as Blair and Jock Lewes had discovered, Stirling and Tait were struggling to find a way through the changed landscape; the *wadis* they encountered were unfordable, and after several hours of scrambling through the worst of the weather, they were ultimately forced to abandon the mission in the face of what the noted war correspondent Alexander Clifford called 'the most spectacular thunderstorm within local memory'. Even had they recovered the fuses, they would no doubt have experienced the same problem as Blair and Lewes – drenched fuses do not make good igniters. Stirling had an additional complaint: his beloved Cuban cigars were also wet through. Matters could hardly have been any worse! As Tait reported:

> We were unable to see more than a few yards in front and within fifteen minutes the whole area was under water. Eventually reaching the fork *wadi* we endeavoured to make our way down it on the flat coastal strip, but found this impossible owing to the water which rushed down with great force. From then until long after midnight we moved along the escarpment, attempting to go down the various *wadis* but with no success, so accordingly about 0100 hours [on 18 Nov] Captain Stirling abandoned the attempt and we turned away and marched south.

Almost exactly two days later, Stirling and Tait were spotted and brought into the RV camp just after midnight in the early hours of 20 November after a march of anywhere between 55 and 70 miles, but there was no sign or news of the rest of their stick, let alone Eoin's or Bonington's stick. Something had gone badly wrong.

Stirling and Tait were confused – Stirling had spotted the other six members of their group in front of them, approximately four miles away, when on their way to the RV. They were too far ahead to attract their attention, but it had appeared at that stage that they were heading in the correct direction. They then lost sight of them and didn't see them again. Dave Kershaw from Blair's group apparently also saw them and even tried firing some shots from his revolver to attract their attention, but without success. However, it appeared to him that at that point they were not moving in the right direction:

> After a couple of days and nights, we came to the Makele and Masous track, that cut right across out front, and we saw four or five bodies, which was going completely away from the direction that we were going. I got the glasses on them – I had binoculars with me – and it seemed they were Sergeant Yeats with Tranfield, Bolland, Calhoun, and maybe a couple more. So we whistled and I got my .45 out and fired a few rounds but they took no notice. So we carried on. (Gordon Stevens, *The Originals*)

The reference to Bolland must have been in error, but in any event this was the last anyone from 'L' detachment or the LRDG saw of the six men – but not the last the six men saw of the LRDG; it was later discovered that they had spotted an LRDG patrol but mistakenly taken it to be an enemy vehicle and taken cover. Luck was firmly against them.

Unbeknownst to the six men, the LRDG stayed at the RV camp for eight hours beyond the planned departure time, but to no avail – as discovered later, the six had argued about the correct direction, taken a wrong turn and would have had no chance of reaching the RV even by the extended deadline. In fact, having gone so far astray, even the agreed second RV camp was now beyond them. They were left with no alternative but to strike out towards Tobruk in the hope they might meet Allied forces advancing as part of Operation Crusader.

The group contained some experienced men, including CSM Yates, Lance Sergeant Colquhoun and Lance Corporal Orton, a pre-war regular. Under normal circumstances, they should have been back by now. Stirling and the LRDG wanted to give them as much of a chance as possible but eventually ran out of time and had to move out to the second rallying point.

About thirty miles south-west of the original rendezvous, Bill Fraser and some ORs were waiting at a second RV located at the northern end of the Wadi El Mra – the hope, however unlikely, was that the six men might still get there instead. If they couldn't, the LRDG had left provisions for them (and the other two missing sticks) at the current RV camp, comprising 12 gallons of water and two 4-gallon tins of dates to sustain them for their onward journey.

As events transpired, these arrangements would prove to be to no avail as all six men were captured by the Italians and held as PoWs. But of course, it wouldn't be an account of 'Operation Squatter' without one further curious element worth highlighting.

On one account, after a couple of wrong turns and losing their way, the six men were captured on the afternoon of 20 November. Stirling recalls being told by CSM Yates after the war that 'They had walked all night. Next day they saw what must have been [the LRDG]'s vehicle but had taken cover presuming it to belong to the enemy. After *three days* of wandering about the desert they had been spotted by an enemy patrol and picked up.'

The men had spotted some British vehicles on the horizon and flagged them down only to be greeted by several menacing Italian muzzles. Their time with 'L' Detachment in the desert had come to a premature end.

However, another account would suggest that following some disagreement as to the correct route, the group may have split, with some accompanying

Desert track, Libya. (*P. Rateau, Shutterstock*)

Yates (based on Stirling's account) and some heading in the opposite direction and spending an extraordinary ten more days marching and evading capture in an attempt to make it back. A subsequent recommendation for the award of Mentioned in Despatches to Pct Trenfield indicates that Trenfield was in fact taken prisoner on 30 November (Appendix I – it is not noted whether he was taken alone or had been discovered with anyone else from the group.)

If accurate, this would have represented a mammoth expedition of the type for which the men were woefully unprepared – both in terms of rations and, after the jump, their physical condition. It would have entailed almost two weeks of survival on limited rations with intermittent marching while also taking cover from enemy patrols, aircraft and the sun, before 'the relief' of finally being captured. However, there is a precedent for this given that the following month, after an unsuccessful operation, Bill Fraser and four men survived a 9-day trek across the desert by 'eating lizards, berries and snails'. Also, it is so far wide of what might have been expected it is surprising that, if a typo, it was not corrected, given the nature of the document.

Of course, the accuracy of some of the dates mentioned in the few reports that have been retained – even an MiD award such as in the case of Trenfield – is to say the least suspect. A good example is the dates mentioned in Cpl Tait's report – he both recalls the men taking off in the planes to start Operation Squatter one day after they in fact did (i.e., 17 instead of 16 November), and making it back to the LRDG's RV on 22 as opposed to 20 November (a date corroborated by the LRDG). There are numerous other examples of inconsistencies in his and other reports, and so while the reports are helpful as a guide to what may have happened, it would be a mistake to place too much reliance on them without some further corroboration.

It is a pity that Stirling (and Jock Lewes) does not appear to have ever filed a contemporaneous report on the operation, and his subsequent accounts of various events evidence clear errors in recollection. That being the case, we cannot be sure.

In any event, the twenty-one survivors who had managed to find a way back waited at the RV for a further eight hours in the hope that their missing comrades would eventually be spotted. However, there were no more sightings, and so finally, with grim reluctance, they agreed to depart with the LRDG for the second RV. The next day, 21 November, the LRDG searched an eight-mile front in the hope of picking up the missing sticks, but no one was found.

The men who had jumped in the first groups had landed in what ended up being 35mph winds. Unlike today's parachutes, 'L' Detachment's chutes were designed so that the men would hit their drop zones at some speed before then immediately rolling on impact – this was difficult at the best of times but even more so on a moonless, stormy night, when they could not see what they were landing on. The instinct ingrained through weeks of training to immediately roll upon impact found some men blindly rolling headlong into boulders and rock, propelled along by parachutes they were unable to release. Although some casualties had been anticipated, the losses were much greater than expected. In fact, virtually nobody had walked away unscathed and thirty-four of the original fifty-five had not made it back.

It was not until much later that Stirling discovered that the aircraft carrying Bonington's stick had been shot down and all of the crew and the stick were either dead or taken prisoner. He also discovered much later that the rest of his own stick had been taken prisoner, but he would have been completely unaware that while he and the rest of the 'L' Detachment survivors had moved on to a temporary desert camp where they were already planning their next operation, at least some of the six men from his stick could still have been marching through the desert.

As for Eoin's stick, there was no word of them.

Chapter 22

'Eoin has not yet come back'

When they did not appear at the RV point, the hope was that Eoin's stick were either all lying up, waiting for British ground forces before making their way back, or at worst had been taken prisoner. Put to the back of the survivors' minds was the possibility, given the appalling weather conditions, that if any of Eoin's stick had been injured on landing and forced to fend for themselves, it would have been a monumental struggle to survive. If mobility was an issue and they were lying up in the wrong place, the flash flooding could well have claimed some lives. The same applied to those who had been left behind from the other sticks; they would at least have needed to reach higher ground before either finding a way back or being rescued.

The discovery that his young Irish comrade had not made it back hit Blair hard. Eoin must have been taken prisoner – Blair refused to entertain the thought that anything worse had happened. Even in a worst-case scenario, surely some of the men from Eoin's stick would have survived the jump and made it back to the RV? Blair could only conclude that the fact nobody had made it back must mean they had been taken prisoner; and, in this sense, no news so far was probably good news.

Still, as matters stood on 22 November, there was just the silence of the desert in the aftermath of the storm – no survivors to report back, no means of communication, no modern-day tracking information, nothing at all. What is evident, both from later discussions Blair had with Stirling and from an attempt made some months later by Blair to locate Eoin's body, is that Blair was deeply affected by the absence of his comrade. As a friend of the McGonigal brothers from their rugby-playing days with QUB and the RUR in Ballymena, and Eoin's senior by some years, Blair clearly felt a sense of responsibility towards the young man, still only twenty. The operation had taken place just a couple of weeks before his 21st on 5 December. Having visited the house on Malone Road, Blair knew the McGonigal family well and knew how this news would be received; he agonized over Eoin's disappearance, vowing to take his revenge on the enemy.

1941 Italian reconnaissance photo of Al Jaghbub.

Stirling was also agonizing over matters on his way to the Eighth Army's forward landing ground at Al Jaghbub oasis. Thirty-four of his men were missing, either captured or dead, and yet, so far as he was aware, no one from 'L' Detachment had even fired a shot in anger. Nevertheless, despite the apparently abject failure of the operation, Stirling wasn't totally despondent. They had established that the idea should work in more suitable conditions, and so the foundation for the unit's future success had taken root. Perhaps recalling the suggestion made by one of his officers at their pre-operation meeting, Stirling was already coming to the view that rather than expose themselves to the elements by parachuting, the SAS would in the future be driven in on trucks by the LRDG. He had been impressed by the way in which the LRDG had handled the recovery operation and recognized the sense in taking advantage of their expertise in navigating through the desert. In this way, as Stirling later commented, the LRDG would be 'able to drop us more comfortably and more accurately within striking distance of the target area'. His aim was to maximize the elements he could control and minimize unnecessary risks.

What this also meant was that, after just one mission, it would become unlikely that any future desert-based SAS recruits would earn the right to wear their Parachute Wings on their breast; despite their name, they would be launching their operations from the ground not the air. Johnny Cooper

Two modified Willys MB desert jeeps with mounted Vickers guns, SAS, January 1943. (*Keating, Army Photo Unit/IWM*)

recalled that after Operation Squatter he 'didn't parachute for a long time … [my] next parachute operation was jumping into France for D-Day.' Consequently, Stirling later decided that new recruits would earn their wings after three successful operations instead.

As it was, the remnants of 'L' Detachment eventually reached Al Jaghbub oasis on the afternoon of 25 November 1941. As well as serving as the Eighth Army's forward landing ground it also had a first-aid post set amongst the ruins of a well-known Islamic school. However, it was not a place for some badly-needed R & R, described by the '113 Squadron' website in the following terms:

Jaghbub … an oasis … near the Libyan-Egyptian border approximately 150 mi south of Sollum and the Mediterranean. The nearest other village is Siwa approx 70 miles East across the border in Egypt. [Jaghbub] is literally in the middle of nowhere, with no roads, the only way to get there is a long and dangerous trek following sand tracks through the desert. Looking out from [Jaghbub] the Great Sand Sea stretches away into nothingness as far as one can see to the south of the oasis, and to the North, East and West one looks out over the rock strewn ground of barren craggy valleys and strange ugly wind eroded hills. If it is not the most desolate place on earth it must be high on the

Al Jaghbub Fort and Ma'ten Bagush (113 Squadron).

list, most of those who have been there 'under the adverse conditions of war' considered it a fly-infested hell on earth.

They would not stay long. All had experienced a rough time, and many of the men they had been drinking with just a week or so earlier had either lost their lives or been captured. Saner, less bold individuals would probably not have undertaken the task in the first place. The weather conditions were appalling, on an historic scale, and the idea of jumping in such wind on a moonless night seems insane today. It was a statement of intent, and although unsuccessful, they would be back. The originals were brave, foolhardy and calculating – just the sort of people you wanted for this type of work.

Before giving the wounded into the care of the medics, Stirling assembled his men to tell them that, despite the obvious disappointment of its inaugural operation, 'L' Detachment was far from finished – they had shown that save for the conditions, the concept would work. There would be more and soon. At the RV camp, a photo of the survivors was taken by Lieutenant Colonel Easonsmith of the LRDG. However, having just learnt that Eoin and many others had not made it back, Blair was not happy posing for pictures. This was not a time for self-recognition – all he could think of was going back out.

From Al Jaghbub the group were then taken to Siwa on the 26th and flew back to Kabrit to collect supplies and watch a 'movie' of sorts – the Kabrit airbase cinema showed a two-minute British Pathé News film entitled

Stirling wearing dark glasses with Blair to his left looking down and distinctly unengaged. (*Family of the late Lt-Col 'Jake' Easonsmith*)

Paratroops in the Middle East, shot just three days before Operation Squatter. The men were briefly transported back to their recent demonstration jumps in front of General Auchinleck. Fleeting images of smiling, hopeful men flashed across the screen – a piece of propaganda intended to bolster morale but a painfully poignant reminder of the friends and comrades they had just lost. How quickly things had changed. Despite the benign daylight conditions, the footage of men landing showed some hitting the deck in an explosion of sand and being dragged for several metres before being able to release their chutes. These were ominous images, given what was to come.

As for the film itself, Jim Almonds wrote, 'That's quite a good show, for a unit that's supposed to be "hush, hush".' (Lorna Almonds, *Gentleman Jim*). Of course, bearing in mind that part of the reason why MEHQ had agreed to Stirling's proposal was to deceive the enemy, the newsreel would also have been seen as an effective way of perpetuating the myth that a significant Brigade of British paratroops was operating in North Africa. The men's mere presence in the region, whether through rumour, the newsreel, or the capture of their comrades, had served a valuable purpose, even if the operation itself had been a disaster.

According to Sgt 'Joe' Welch, those days at Kabrit camp were terrible: 'two sticks had not returned and the camp was so silent without the men – those who had survived just sat and waited for news.' So far as Sgt Welch was concerned, 'the sense of what would be described today as 'survivor's guilt' was almost tangible.' He spent most of his time waiting with the LRDG, as they were getting the most up to the minute reports but recalled that 'Paddy refused to accept that any of those classed as missing were dead. Paddy could not let his great friend Eoin go, and because he could not let him go, he could not let any of them go. Paddy was of the view that they were just "lost" until proven otherwise.' Sgt Welch did not know Eoin well – he had got to know him over those two months of training about as well as he knew most of the team but it was clear he and Paddy were best mates: 'They were like chalk and cheese. Eoin was more mellow in his manner, speech and movement, and extremely good at telling "tall tales"' – a skill which tied in well with his role as the camp's letter writer. 'Despite being the youngest officer, he was far more eloquent than Paddy, whereas Paddy was more like Ares, the Greek god of war – it was a dangerous combination; Eoin could talk them into all sorts of trouble and Paddy could get them out of it, a perfect friendship.' 'A few days after the operation, Paddy was brooding saying he was going to have to write a letter home at some point and what the heck was he meant to say. In one of those abrupt moments, quite out of the blue,' Paddy explained to Sgt Welch that 'unlike himself, Eoin was not shy in front of women – he had the charm of the Irish and had a lady at home. But he was a loyal type of man and so what on earth could Paddy write? This was followed by lots of blame ranting.' 'Over the next year or so, Paddy would talk about what Eoin could be doing, guessing he was probably a PoW somewhere far away from the desert, living the life of Riley – he could imagine him spinning some yarn to his guards about being Hitler's long lost brother. Paddy would continue to toast him on his birthday in the years to come.'

In any event, it was at this time while still in Kabrit that Blair received some news which set the alarm bells ringing. An intercepted enemy message made reference to events in the area where Eoin's stick were thought to have landed. It appeared that a party of Germans had been wiped out and an important dump destroyed. However, there was also reference to one British parachutist having been killed. No mention was made of the fate of any others. Immediately after arriving at Kabrit, Blair quickly wrote to Ambrose. His letter, sent from 'SAS Bde, MEF' and dated 27 November 1941, is revealing both in its content and timing:

> McGonigal,
> As I think you know, your brother and I have for some time been in this parachute unit. On Sunday the 16th we dropped in to Cyrenaica. Eoin has not yet come back.
>
> We had decided, before we went in, that if one of us did not get back to the rendezvous, the other would not worry or write home until at least a month had elapsed as we reckoned that if the worst came we could lie up and wait until our ground forces reached us; but I think now I can do little harm in telling you what has happened.
>
> Eoin had with him 8 ORs & all I know of him is by an intercepted enemy message in which they said that one of his party had been killed, but that they had wiped out a large party of Germans and had blown up an important dump. If I get any more news I shall write or wire you, but I am certain that barring bad luck that it will be from your brother you will be hearing next.
>
> I have not written to your family as I would not like to worry them unduly.

It would seem that Blair's reference to eight ORs may have been a mistaken reference to the number of ORs in Stirling's stick (or perhaps numbers based on early pre-operation plans); there were eleven in Eoin's.

Plainly, Blair was sufficiently concerned to partly break his agreement with Eoin to wait for at least one month before writing (albeit that he did not at this point write to Eoin's parents). While there was a possibility that the members of Eoin's stick who had not been killed had gone into hiding and were waiting for ground forces to arrive before making their way back, he feared it was equally possible that after attacking the Germans and blowing the dump, Eoin and his men had either been captured or killed.

Blair's thinking was reflected in two early 'L' Detachment Nominal Rolls dated August and September 1941 and then subsequently updated with abbreviations indicating what was thought to have happened to the original members (see Appendices B and C). Against Eoin's name it is initially indicated that he had been taken prisoner, but later it would seem that a view had been formed that he must have died in the desert, as the notation is changed from 'P.O.W.' to 'killed'. When this was changed is not clear – plainly, the dates marked on these documents cannot reflect the dates on which they were created or amended, and it could be that they were edited long after the events in question and by persons not directly connected to the original 'L' Detachment members.

The Casualty Notices issued by the War Office in 1941/2 (see Appendix L) show the same change. While the notice dated 17 December 1941 reports Eoin as 'missing', a second report issued on 3 August 1942 records that he 'died of wounds' on either 17 or 18 November 1941. This change in his status must have been based on reports from PoWs received at some point in mid-1942, perhaps via the Red Cross channels, although no report appears to have been retained in the files.

This assumption is based on the fact that as it later transpired, apart from Eoin and L/Cpl Hildreth, all of his stick had survived the jump only to be taken as PoWs. They were the only ones who might have been able to explain what had happened to him and get a message back to Stirling and Blair. However, in an intriguing turn of events, it seems from later reports that they were captured at Tmimi airfield by the Italians – they were the only stick to have reached their target! Perhaps the intercepted enemy communication reported by Blair was accurate? Nevertheless, they all remained PoWs, unavailable for interview until July/August 1944 following their eventual escape after the armistice with Italy in September 1943. Even then, only the most summary and inconsistent of statements were ever recorded.

By the end of 1941 it was still a complete mystery what could have happened to Eoin's stick, and the intercepted enemy message did little to ease the sense of despair felt by the survivors of Operation Squatter. There was a growing acceptance that their comrades would not be returning; they had either died or been taken prisoner. Still, speculation continued to grow and Blair continued to brood on the loss of so many men and in particular his fellow Ulsterman. Writing to his sister Babs on 24 January 1942 from 'SAS Bde, CTC', Blair explained:

> I had a letter from Mrs McGonigal yesterday asking for news of Eoin. She is a fine woman, she didn't tell his brother Ambrose who was getting married until after his honeymoon. I had already written to her & I still believe that the odds are he is a prisoner. I wish I knew.

While it was heartening to think that Operation Squatter may not have been a total failure, the absence of any hard information was exasperating. Some felt Eoin could have foreseen the problems the rain would cause for the fuses (he was the officer in charge of the Brigade's weapons training, and the range doubled as a testing ground when Jock Lewes was experimenting with different versions of his bomb) and might therefore have decided to wait out the rain and attack the airfield once the fuses had dried out. It would probably have meant risking not getting back to the RV point in time – they would then either have had to find British ground forces or, failing that, surrender. Nobody knew what to think – the intercepted enemy message could not be corroborated unless further related messages or reports on or from the PoWs were received. It became a waiting game, and in the information vacuum Blair focused his anger and desire for vengeance on subsequent missions.

Chapter 23

Subsequent Missions

As important as it had been to proceed with Operation Squatter despite the atrocious weather, the survival of the SAS as a unit had taken a severe hit – they needed some validated success, and quickly. What remained of 'L' Detachment, and Blair in particular, set about this task with relish. The surviving members had many demons to exorcise and, using this motivation, they went on to achieve astonishing success. Due in no small part to Blair personally, the SAS was essentially 'saved' through the operations he led in the Sahara, an environment to which the unit's skills and mindset were uniquely suited. As Reg Seekings said, 'We'd lost two thirds of our men on the first job, all good men, lost them through no fault of their own, and I think we all felt that we owed it to them to really make something of it.'

From December 1941 to the end of 1942 'L' Detachment conducted a series of night raids deep behind enemy lines, wreaking havoc by destroying significant numbers of enemy aircraft on the ground. They pioneered the use of military jeeps – the US Willys with a pair (and more) of twin-mounted Vickers K machine guns firing modified Buckingham incendiary bullets to target aircraft fuel tanks – in making repeated hit-and-run raids on Axis airfields. By the end, it was claimed that Blair had personally destroyed well over 100 aircraft. His first successful raid occurred just three and a half weeks after Squatter. By 5 December Stirling and his much-depleted Brigade had left Kabrit. They flew to Ma'ten Bagush and then went on to Jalo oasis with the aim of achieving some success before reporting back to MEHQ in Cairo. Jalo oasis is 150 miles south-east of the Gulf of Sirte and west of the Great Sand Sea and at the time comprised a white wooden fort, mud houses, a few Berbers and their camels, and a plague-like population of flies. It was distinctly inhospitable, with a well that was salty and almost undrinkable. However, as the only source of water for many miles, it was strategically located and had just been captured from the Italians on 24 November 1941 during Operation Crusader. It was the ideal temporary base – a perfect launch pad for the targets Stirling had in mind and located far enough away from Cairo to minimize the risk of any repercussions following Squatter. It is no exaggeration to say that Stirling viewed their position as tantamount to an existential crisis – they desperately needed some success before returning to their main camp at Kabrit.

Once reorganized at Jalo, Stirling and Lewes drew up further attack plans, and on 14/15 December 1941 Blair led a small raiding force against Wadi Tamet airfield. Approximately twenty-four aircraft, plus ammo and petrol dumps, were destroyed or put out of action (the total included ten whose flight instrument panels were destroyed, at least one of which reportedly was torn out by Blair with his bare hands). During the same operation a hut containing about thirty Italian pilots and soldiers was attacked using sub-machine guns, pistols and bombs, causing an unknown number of casualties. Ten days later, Mayne led a second raid on the same Tamet airstrip, destroying a further twenty-seven aircraft and petrol dumps – a combined total, therefore of over fifty planes. In between these raids, on 21 December a further thirty-seven planes were destroyed by a group led by Bill Fraser at Agedabia, bringing the combined total up to almost ninety enemy aircraft destroyed. The future of the Brigade had been comprehensively secured.

Stirling and his concept of the SAS were vindicated. For his part in the December Tamet raids, Blair was awarded the DSO. His official report on the first raid notes:

> The following damage was done on or in the vicinity of the aerodrome: (a) Bombs were placed on 14 aircraft. (b) 10 aircraft were damaged by having instrument panels destroyed. (c) Bomb and petrol dumps were blown up. (d) Reconnaissance was made down to the seafront but only empty huts were found. (e) Several telephone poles were blown up. (f) Some Italians were followed, and the hut they came out of was attacked by sub-machine gun and pistol fire and bombs were placed on and around it. There appeared to be roughly thirty inhabitants. Damage inflicted unknown.

Blair was both praised and criticized for these actions, with some (including Stirling) considering his approach too ruthless (Stirling notes that he felt it necessary to rebuke Blair for 'over-callous execution in cold blood of the enemy'). However, without the success achieved on these raids, it is uncertain whether the SAS would have survived. Whether it was a question of luck or instinct or a combination of the two, it was Blair who almost alone amongst the officers had repeated success on the raids that took place in the months following Operation Squatter. Blair was a man possessed, and he had only just begun.

Further significant raids took place in March, June and July, all notably successful. For example, between 8 March and 13 June 1942 the SAS conducted a series of attacks on five airfields (Benina, Berka, Agedabia, Sirte and Agheila) plus Benghazi Harbour to which the men were again transported by the LRDG. They destroyed between sixty-one and seventy-five aircraft without losing any men.

Interestingly, while making their escape at the end of one of these raids, at Benina airfield in June, Stirling threw a grenade into a guardhouse containing several German soldiers and an officer. The casualties inflicted were unknown, but he is reported to have regretted doing it. Save that Blair had used a sub-machine gun at Tamet, it was otherwise a remarkably similar incident to the one for which Blair had received so much criticism.

One of the single most successful SAS raids of the Desert War was carried out by a combined force of fifty British and French SAS troops, when on the night of 26 July 1942 Blair and Stirling led eighteen armed jeeps in a raid on the Sidi Haneish airfield. They avoided detection, destroyed up to forty German aircraft and escaped with the loss of only three Jeeps and two men killed. The success of the SAS was continuing to keep their critics at bay.

Despite this, many of their achievements actually went unheralded at the time. On 18 September 1940, one of the RAF's greatest days during the Battle of Britain, England's renowned legless Wing Commander Douglas Bader and his squadrons had quite rightly attracted international headlines when they downed thirty German planes. By comparison, Blair and his marauders destroyed thirty-seven planes in just one night at Bagush airfield in July 1942. It was an example of both the unit's effectiveness and its resourcefulness; as a result of discovering that over half of their bombs had not detonated, Blair and Stirling decided to go in using the LRDG's jeeps, driving them between the rows of parked planes and firing at them with machine guns and grenades. A group led by Blair then followed this up by destroying another thirty-six planes over two nights at the Fuka and El Daba airfields on 7 and 9 July, contributing to the Eighth Army's victory at El Alamein in October. Ultimately, the SAS archive shows that Blair personally accounted for the destruction of more enemy planes than any pilot. Yet outside the immediate area, very few were aware of these achievements.

The clinical detachment, unselfishness and determination with which Blair approached his duty are typified by his encounter with Major General David Lloyd Owen of the LRDG, after the raid on the German airfield at Fuka in July.

'How were things tonight?' asked Owen.

'A bit trickier tonight,' replied Blair. 'They had posted a sentry on nearly every bloody plane. I had to knife the sentries before I could place the bombs.'

When Owen asked how many of these guards had Blair killed that night, the casual reply was, 'Seventeen'. Far from demanding recognition and reward for this mass throat-cutting, he never mentioned it again. Had Owen not asked, the incident would have been recorded as just another night's work for the SAS. It is possible nobody but Blair would have ever known about it. (Kelly Bell, *Ireland's Wolf of the Desert*)

Blair Mayne.

Research sponsored by the US Air Force into the success of the SAS in North Africa has concluded that the SAS destroyed at least 367 aircraft and possibly more than 400 – with Blair personally responsible for at least a quarter of this number.

Chapter 24

The VC: 'a signal act of valour'

After Africa Blair worked hard to ensure the survival of the SAS, which he achieved despite a changing environment, structure and formation. Soon after Eoin disappeared, Jock Lewes was killed on 30 December 1941 (on only his second operation after Operation Squatter), and the Germans captured David Stirling in January 1943, eventually imprisoning him in Colditz. Not long afterwards, the SAS was reorganized into two separate parts: the Special Raiding Squadron (SRS) over which Blair was given command (he was by then a major); and the Special Boat Squadron, a forerunner of the Special Boat Service (SBS) under the command of Lieutenant Colonel (as he then was) Jellicoe, and a group into which Eoin's brother Ambrose was expressly recruited the following year. Blair adapted the Squadron's methods to suit their changing environment as they left Africa and engaged in further operations in Europe; the unit fought in Sicily and Italy through to the end of 1943 and then as the reformed 1st SAS Regiment in France, the Netherlands, Belgium, Germany and Norway. They continued to be extremely effective, and by the end of the war Blair had become one of the British Army's most decorated soldiers. This included the initial award of a Victoria Cross which remains the subject of some controversy following its subsequent withdrawal by a person or persons unknown. It led to, amongst other things, an unsuccessful Early Day Motion put before Parliament in June 2005 calling for the reinstatement of the VC and stating:

> This House recognises the grave injustice meted out to … Mayne … who won the Victoria Cross at Oldenburg in North West Germany on 9th April 1945; notes that this was subsequently downgraded, some six months later, to a third bar DSO, that the citation had been clearly altered and that David Stirling, founder of the SAS has confirmed that there was considerable prejudice towards Mayne and that King George VI enquired why the Victoria Cross had 'so strangely eluded him'.

In 2020 Lord Ashcroft presented a documentary and related article on the topic which concluded:

Did his valour deserve the VC? Absolutely, in my opinion. Should the powers that be now go back and reassess whether he is entitled to receive the award 75 years on? Probably not, simply because it is impractical to review such gallantry awards decades on, especially when the witnesses are dead.

However, there is another way of looking at this. Whatever the reason behind the decision to downgrade the award, the VC was definitely earned. Contemporary witness evidence was obtained, the citation was given and approved, and Blair was informed. It is not therefore a question of whether Blair's actions merited the VC – his citation was approved at the highest of levels at the time (including Brigadier J.M. Calvert and Field Marshal Montgomery); indeed, the award was acknowledged by King George VI. What needs to be explained is how such a high-ranking citation could have been downgraded without explanation six months later. In short, the evidence which needs to be examined relates not to the act of gallantry in question but to the administrative decision to downgrade the award. This is an important distinction as there could well be army records which might explain how it came to pass.

Such an investigation would be not dissimilar to the role of an appeal court in reviewing a tribunal's award – it would not try to second guess the tribunal's findings of fact but rather to focus on whether the relevant laws and rules of procedure were applied correctly. In this instance, the only review necessary is whether any application of the requirements for awarding a VC could possibly have warranted overturning the original decision to award it.

One argument for the idea that it was an administrative oversight or mistake concerns the requirement under the original 1856 Royal Warrant:

It is ordained that the Cross shall only be awarded to those officers and men who have served Us in the presence of the enemy, and shall have then performed some *signal act of valour* or devotion to their country.

It has been suggested that the word 'signal' was misread or misunderstood to mean 'single', and that as Blair did not act alone, his gallantry did not qualify. It is doubtful whether the downgrading of such an important award and one recommended by such high-ranking individuals, including the 'Senior Military Officer Commanding the Force' (paragraph 8 of the Royal Warrant), could have been the result of such an obvious error. Nevertheless, it is worth mentioning a letter written by Brigadier J.R.C. Gannon, Deputy Military Secretary (HQ, 21 Army Group) to Colonel J.W. McLain, Deputy

Military Secretary (HQ, First Canadian Army) dated 3 July 1945, which is quoted in part by Hugh Halliday in *Valour Reconsidered*:

> You will remember putting up Lieutenant-Colonel R.B. Mayne for a VC, and while I myself thought it was a magnificent act of heroism, *there was a certain flaw* in it that made me doubtful as to advising the Chief to recommend it without further advice. I therefore sent it to the Military Secretary at home who deals with the VC Committee.
>
> He has replied saying that he has discussed this case without actually taking it up and he is afraid that the VC Committee would not regard Mayne's case as quite up to VC standard. *It was not a single-handed act of heroism*, rescuing the wounded, as another officer was present in the jeep giving covering fire. Nevertheless, it was a magnificent performance and it is suggested that the rare distinction of a third Bar to the DSO would be the appropriate award.
>
> Would you please be so good as to put this letter before General [H.D.G.] Crerar before making his final recommendation. [Italics added]

As Halliday notes, '"A certain flaw" is a weak, weasel phrase', and it is hard to disagree with this assessment. As for the apparent justification, 'It was not a single-handed act of heroism', clearly this is both an incorrect reading of the requirements as well as evidence of a wholly inconsistent approach when previous VC awards are taken into account – a prime example being the award of a VC to Blair's one-time nemesis, Lieutenant Colonel Geoffrey Keyes, in connection with the attempt to assassinate Rommel in 1941. Taking nothing away from the courage displayed by Keyes, the fact is that he did not act alone – he was accompanied by several comrades, a point underlined by the conclusion that he was in fact shot not by the enemy but by one of his own men. (The operation led by Keyes took place on the same night as 'L' Detachment's ill-fated Operation Squatter, 17 November 1941.)

In any event, the Royal Warrant was amended in 1920 and again in 1931 to consolidate all previous amendments and read as follows:

> It is ordained that the Cross shall only be awarded for most conspicuous bravery or some daring or pre-eminent act of valour or self-sacrifice or extreme devotion to duty in the presence of the enemy.

Thus the qualifying words, 'conspicuous' and/or 'daring' or 'pre-eminent' took the place of 'signal'. The 1920 Royal Warrant went on to confirm that 'It is ordained that the Cross may be awarded posthumously.'

The requirement that there be a 'signal' act of valour was therefore no longer relevant in 1945, and even if it was it should not have gone beyond a requirement for evidence of a noticeable, unusual or significant act – a threshold which Blair's actions clearly exceeded. Similarly, the requirement that there be a single-handed act does not appear in any previous iteration of the various Royal Warrants. Indeed, provision is in any event made to cover situations in which candidates for an award act collectively – up to two individuals from any one group may be nominated by secret ballot.

In short, it seems clear that the VC should not have been downgraded and that the reasons so far available to explain why this was done do not bear even cursory scrutiny. The decision was based on a clear and incontrovertible error, as suggested by the best available record (Brigadier Gannon's letter).

Moreover, there appears to be no reason why the error cannot now be remedied and the award made posthumously – this is expressly contemplated by the Royal Warrant and indeed happened as recently as December 2020, when Ordinary Seaman Teddy Sheean of the Royal Australian Navy was awarded a VC in recognition of his actions on board HMAS *Armidale* (I). In a response to requests from the Blair Mayne Research Society, the Ministry of Defence explained that it would not be possible to make a belated award to Mayne because 'all postwar Governments have upheld the decision not to make retrospective awards.' Clearly, that policy directly contradicted the express terms of the Royal Warrant as confirmed by Her Majesty

Perhaps a more obvious testament to the SAS and Blair's achievements; a 1974 *Victor* cover.

Queen Elizabeth II's approval of a posthumous award of the Victoria Cross to Sheean.

Other reasons that have been suggested to explain the decision to downgrade include: Blair's non-conformist spirit, his record of dissent with superior officers and unorthodox methods; a desire to avoid mythologizing either Blair or the 'irregular' SAS (apparently described by a general from the War Office as 'gangsters in the British Army' upon their temporary disbandment in 1945); and the fact that the war was by then over and the government had no more need for further heroes.

Who knows, and does it really matter? It will not change how people who know about Blair and what he did really think of him, and it will obviously make little difference to him personally or his contemporaries, few (if any) of whom remain alive. In fact, Blair himself described the experience of being publicly honoured as 'embarrassing' (Hamish Ross, *Paddy Mayne*). However, for that group of men and those times, as represented in this instance by Blair, there is clearly a more persuasive case to be made 'for the honour of the regiment'. Ultimately, as the well-known expert on Blair's life, Peter Forbes has noted, 'Perhaps Blair Mayne is destined to go down in history as one of the bravest men never to have been awarded the VC.'

Chapter 25

Ambrose

As Blair and his comrades were wreaking havoc in the desert and then in Europe, another Irish soldier seeking vengeance was doing likewise in multiple Commando raids in coastal France, the Channel Islands, the Aegean and Yugoslavia. Ambrose McGonigal joined 12 Commando before being selected by Fitzroy Maclean for the SBS (Special Boat Service, or Special Boat Squadron as it was then formally known), formed (after a number of earlier iterations) in April 1943 with a combination of men from 1st SAS and the Small Scale Raiding Force (SSRF, also known as 62 Commando).

Ambrose's war service commenced in earnest with the TA in September 1939 alongside his continuing legal studies. He was commissioned in January 1940 and trained with the RUR from 1940 to August 1942 in 'gas, messing and motor contact', as well as taking a parachute course in July and August 1942. He spent several months recuperating from motorcycling injuries in early 1941 before being posted to 8 RUR in September 1941 and then to the 1st Battalion RUR in March 1942. Having spent longer at university than Eoin, Ambrose decided against joining Eoin and Blair when they left on secondment with the Cameronians. There was also the small matter of having just met his wife to be, Patricia ('Paddy') Taylor, a Wren from Belfast; his priorities at that point were different to those of his younger brother. However, he was very soon doing all he could to make up for lost time.

Everything changed for Ambrose when he married, and not for the usual reasons. In December 1941, just a few days before the wedding, his parents received notice that Eoin was missing in action. The War Office issued a Casualty Notice on 17 December 1941, but the information was limited – it was not known if he had been taken prisoner or killed. Just a vacuum – your son is missing; we do not know what has happened to him; the show must go on. Ambrose had also been informed of what had happened by Blair and he was devastated. Both brothers knew the risks of war but both had assumed they would be among the survivors. However, the reality of war hit Ambrose when his younger brother disappeared in North Africa while he was at home in Belfast preparing to celebrate his marriage. The fact that Eoin would have turned twenty-one exactly two weeks before Ambrose's wedding only made it more poignant. The war had just become personal for Ambrose.

The exchange between Ambrose and his mother which opens this memoir is fictional, but not so far from the truth that it cannot shine a light on some of the unspoken emotions that overwhelm communication within families in times of war. Whatever could you say, and what would constitute the 'right time' at which to hear such news? Eoin, the adored youngest son and brother, would not be coming home.

Ambrose had met his wife to be while Eoin and he were training with the RUR in Ballymena. Her father, (Robert) John Taylor, was a telegraphist with the civil service in Belfast, and her mother, Molly Smith, came from Co. Cavan. The Smiths were a well-known 'Fenian' family (an umbrella term covering groups in both Ireland and America dedicated to Irish independence but also to the complete separation of church and state). Paddy's grandfather,

Molly Smith and her father, Philip Smith.

Philip Smith (who was active in various organizations representing the interests of farmers and town tenants), was a friend of John Redmond, John Dillon and Joe Devlin. Redmond was also ex-Clongowes and King's Inns, and an Irish Nationalist MP – not to mention, a leader of the (paramilitary) Irish National Volunteers. In fact, all three were MPs and leaders of the Irish Parliamentary Party.

In any case, the marriage of a member of the British special forces to the daughter of a well-known Fenian family would have made for some unusual family dinners at Christmas in Cavan and Belfast. But the circumstances of this Christmas would mean that dinner was the last thing on anyone's mind.

Ambrose and Paddy were to marry on 19 December 1941, and so neither Margaret McGonigal nor Ambrose told each other or anyone else what they knew. Their concerns

Ambrose McGonigal and Patricia ('Paddy') Taylor.

would remain unspoken – nothing was known for sure.

Margaret was in a terrible dilemma – Ambrose had to be told but she feared what it might do to him. The brothers had always been close, having grown up together after most of their siblings had long since left home; Ambrose and Eoin were almost like a second family and stuck together as a result. At school in Ireland, although respected and popular amongst their peers, they had been treated a little like outsiders in that, although born in Dublin, they were raised in Belfast and therefore considered to be Northerners – they were different, and they still felt it was them against everyone else. Ambrose, having grown up with Eoin always snapping at his heels and pushing him at school, had rarely felt the need to be the protective big brother. However, this was very diffcrent and it appeared that it was now too late.

After discussing the news of Eoin's disappearance, John and Margaret decided to say nothing for the time being. Margaret later confided as much in Blair, who confirmed it in his letter to his sister Babs of 24 January 1942.

Ambrose was in two minds whether to go ahead with the wedding – it wasn't a question of not wanting to get married, it was simply a matter of timing. Paddy shared his concerns – after all, nobody knew how long the war would last, whether it could be won, or who would come back from it. In some ways it was his brother's disappearance that helped make up Ambrose's mind. He had been wavering, and Eoin had picked up on it in his letters, but it seemed ridiculous to be carrying on with such things while the world was falling apart and the Nazis were knocking on Britain's door. He should have been out there with Eoin. Why not postpone the wedding? But marriage would add a little hope to their lives as well as underline what he was fighting for and give him something to return to. The concern over what may

Major Sir Ambrose Joseph McGonigal KBE, MC [113419]: Royal Ulster Rifles; No. 12 Commando; No. 10 (IA) Commando (attached); SOE and SBS.

have happened to Eoin just strengthened his resolve. The wedding would go ahead, but the celebrations would be muted; the newspaper notice stated, 'A marriage has been arranged and will take place very quietly this month.' Plainly, this was not a time for unbridled joy and celebration but it still deserved to be marked.

Ambrose felt an unbearable sense of guilt for having remained at home while his younger brother was lost in the desert. Matters were not entirely within his control – amongst other things, having applied to join the Commando he had broken his leg in training and so missed the opportunity to follow Eoin and Blair. However, he vowed not to miss any more opportunities; he was determined to seek revenge for his brother's death.

Chapter 26

Raiding across the Channel: a 'bare-knuckled fighting opponent'

Ambrose found this time particularly testing. Paddy was expecting their first child in late 1942. With responsibilities at home and under no obligation to get involved, he did not need to accelerate his involvement, but Eoin was gone and that changed everything. He was becoming angrier and more frustrated by the day – drinking more than he should and getting into fights. Finally, after extended periods of training and convalescence as a result of training-related injuries but little real action, Ambrose joined 12 Commando on 21 May 1943.

At the time, Sir Frederick Lawton, a fellow subaltern with Ambrose in the RUR but with responsibility as assistant adjutant for putting Ambrose's name on a list of volunteers for the Commando, recalled being reprimanded for doing so by his commanding officer, who said, 'You have deprived the Regiment of one of its best young officers.' Still, there wasn't much Sir Frederick could have done to talk Ambrose out of signing up.

No. 12 Commando – the 'Irish' Commando as it was known – was a

Ambrose McGonigal.

unit formed in 1940 in Northern Ireland. About the size of half a Battalion, it carried out a large number of small-scale raids in Norway and France between 1941 and 1943 before being disbanded in December 1943 and its personnel dispersed to other Commando units. In joining the Commando Ambrose was following a similar route to his brother.

Ambrose was primarily involved in high-risk, small-force raids and sabotage operations across the Channel, with teams from 12 Commando as well as leading teams from No. 10 Inter-Allied Commando. The consequences of failure in these raids were heightened simply by virtue of being a member of the British special forces. Incensed by the actions of the special forces in North Africa and Europe (specifically on Sark), Hitler had issued a secret order on 18 October 1942 that any Commando soldier caught alive was to be shot, regardless of the circumstances. The stakes, already high in operations of this type, were now even greater. 'The Commando Order', as it became known, was deemed to be illegal by the Allied forces and later recognized as such by the war crimes tribunal at Nuremberg. Twelve copies of the 'Kommandobefehl' were given to Hitler's most senior commanders:

> The attitude of the so-called Commandos, who are recruited in part among common criminals released from prison, is particularly brutal and underhanded … For this reason … the German troops will exterminate them without mercy wherever they find them. Therefore, I command that: henceforth all enemy troops encountered by German troops during so-called Commando operations, in Europe or in Africa, though they appear to be soldiers in uniform … armed or unarmed, are to be exterminated to the last man, either in combat or in pursuit … If such men appear to be about to surrender, no quarter should be given them – on general principle … I will summon before the tribunal of war, all leaders and officers who fail to carry out these instructions – either by failure to inform their men or by their disobedience of this order in action.
>
> Adolf Hitler

> All members of … saboteur bands, including (on general principle) all parachutists encountered outside the immediate combat zone, are to be executed.
>
> [Supplement to Commando Order, 18 October 1942]

It appeared that Hitler had taken exception to the Commando not sticking to pre-assigned combat zones – the very idea that they might instead take boats or parachute in behind the lines was unacceptable.

In response to what was clearly an illegal order, Blair issued the following recommendation:

I am of the opinion that any personnel who may take part in future SAS operations should be fully informed of the risk they are running and be given the opportunity of refusing … I feel very strongly that no small party operations should be proposed unless they are absolutely essential, also any person concerned with the planning of any such operation must be fully aware of the risks the men taking part in the operation are running.

Undeterred, Ambrose led many successful small raiding parties along the French coast and in the Channel Islands (Sark) for which he was awarded his first Military Cross. One of the men he fought with at this time, Ian Smith, recalled some of these events in his memoir:

[We were stationed with 12 Commando at Freshwater Bay, Isle of Wight] … mounting raids on occupied Europe, via the cliffs of Normandy, and the odd excursion to the Channel Islands. Our other task was to train others in the art of landing on rocky shores from small craft, and to climb cliffs.

Fynn Force was a lovely bunch of officers and men … Ambrose McGonigal, fed up with the routine of the Ulster Rifles, came for a spot of fun, he was totally without fear, and had an insatiable thirst, and really loved a fist fight, all of which went to make him my very best mate, and strangely to him becoming a Judge in Northern Ireland. Jock Blackie was Ambrose's bare-knuckled fighting opponent. After a horrible drunken bout in a respectable Eastbourne B&B, I had to take them both to hospital for serious injuries, all had to be kept from HQ, and I had to spend the rest of the night clearing up the bloody mess. Afterwards they seemed mysteriously pleased with their activities.

Fynn Force

The objective of Fynn Force was to conduct a series of small-scale raids on the north coast of France between Fécamp and the Dutch/Belgian border. Code-named 'Forfar', these raids were linked to GHQ Home Force's preparation for the invasion of Europe and the need to persuade the Germans that at a landing in Pas-de-Calais was likely. The raids were therefore designed both to convince the enemy that they were a precursor to an imminent much larger landing, and to make life as uncomfortable as possible for the Germans, take prisoners and conduct reconnaissance. Unlike the usual orders to get in and out without a trace, commanders were instructed to leave evidence of their presence. Essentially, as noted pithily by Evelyn Waugh, the aim was 'to raid for raiding's sake'.

These raids mostly involved men from 12 Commando organized into three groups under three different commanders. Ambrose was with the recently promoted Major Francis West 'Ted' Fynn, Fynn Force's eponymous leader. Also involved was Pierre Boccador, who was attached to No. 12 Commando from 1 (French) Troop as an interpreter and was soon afterwards involved in the raids on Sark under Ambrose's command.

The Forfar raids took place during the dark of the moon between July and September 1943. The methods of operation differed depending on circumstances but in most cases a Motor Torpedo Boat (MTB), sometimes with a Motor Gun Boat (MGB) or aircraft escort, ferried raiding parties of one or two officers and eight to ten men across the Channel. About a mile offshore, the raiding party would transfer to a dory and then, for the final approach, they would switch to an RAF dinghy tethered to the dory by a floating line with a telephone cable, and paddle into land.

Eleven raids were mounted and seven were landed with varying results. Barbed-wire defences, unscalable cliffs, German E-boat (fast attack craft) patrols and poor sea conditions hampered many of them. Nevertheless, by remaining concealed on land during the day and taking advantage of opportunistic encounters with German patrols, some modest progress was made. While no prisoners were taken, telephone wires were cut, barbed wire removed and an optical sight removed from a searchlight. Contact was made with French fishermen and, while avoiding a burst of fire from a Spandau machine gun, intelligence was gathered in the form of photographs and information concerning German security arrangements and numbers in the area. So nothing exceptional was achieved, but the primary aim was met – to make their presence known and contribute to efforts to deceive the Germans as to the likely location of the Allied invasion.

Attempts were made to send reports of their findings back to England by 'airmail' – but not quite in the way that one might imagine. This was bird mail, and reports were inserted into canisters attached to two homing pigeons. However, almost as soon as they were released, the pigeons were attacked by five (German?) peregrine falcons; one pigeon was killed, and while the other got away it failed to make it back to England. Perhaps harshly, neither was mentioned in dispatches.

In one of the Forfar raids that did not involve Ambrose, a dory waiting for the return of raiding commandos became trapped in heavy surf and sent careering towards the shore, where it grounded. Its engine was damaged beyond repair and it developed a leak. The commandos tried hauling it back into deeper waters against the surf but were losing the race against the rising sun. As soon as it became light, everyone stripped naked to avoid detection by German snipers stationed at various coastal watchpoints! Baring all for their country, the men eventually made it through the surf, but by then the leak had worsened and they had to jettison all their equipment and kit. Paddling furiously and bailing out even more furiously, the naked commandos eventually arrived back alongside the MTB and returned to Newhaven, to be revived with rum, tea and blankets. While it cannot be confirmed, it was rumoured the Germans were laughing so much they couldn't hold their guns straight!

Chapter 27

Sark

'We did carry out some varied operations and I think it was in this period that Ambrose McGonigal and a small band tried to take the small German garrison prisoner on the Isle of Sark. Unfortunately the approach to the target was mined, one of the party detonated an anti personnel mine, and typically, Ambrose went to the help of the wounded man, in the process detonating several more small mines, though wounded, [he] managed to get back to the boat and safety.

Ambrose was in hospital in Weymouth where I visited him, it was [as] though he had been crucified, shrapnel had gone through the palms of both hands and both feet. Luckily, there was no major damage and Ambrose (he was known as Mac to us) soon rejoined the merry gang.'

(Ian Smith, unpublished memoir)

With the disbandment of 12 Commando, Ambrose's next posting was to Layforce II. During December 1943 reconnaissance operations were stepped up for Operation Overlord, the codename for the D-Day landings. An enormous amount of intelligence had already been gathered from aerial photographs and from the French Resistance. However, it was often still necessary to put men ashore to examine the physical characteristics of the intended landing beaches. Sometimes the operations were conducted in complete secrecy. On other occasions the Commandos were employed in small raiding parties with the aim of confusing the enemy as to the Allies' real intentions, taking one or two prisoners as well as discovering the lie of the land.

A series of raids were planned, codenamed Hardtack and Menacle, in late 1943 under the command of newly promoted Lieutenant Colonel Peter Laycock (the deputy CO of 10 [IA] Commando under Lieutenant Colonel Dudley Lister). The force involved, essentially an ad hoc formation of Commandos, was named 'Layforce II' – harking back to his brother, Major General Robert Laycock's original Layforce, which had ceased as of the summer of 1941, shortly after having pulled in Eoin and the rest of 11 Commando (C Battalion) for the Litani River Battle. The overall operation would not be confined to the intended landing beaches – that

MTB No. 344, one of the boats used by Ambrose on coastal raids.

would have made it too obvious where the invasion was to happen. Instead, raids took place along the French coast and included the Channel Islands. The operations were conducted primarily by men from No. 10 (Inter-Allied) Commando, along with some from the now disbanded No. 12 Commando, 4 Commando and the Special Boat Section (SBS). (The SBS were also known as No. 2 SBS and tended to focus on covert beach surveys, in contrast to Jellicoe's Special Boat Squadron, which tended to conduct raids and reconnaissance *above* the high-water mark.) Most of the raiding parties consisted of ten men of various ranks carried by MTBs, MGBs and dories, except for one airborne landing. MTBs were used because of their relatively small size, which made detection by radar more difficult. Their armaments comprised two Vickers machine guns either side of the bridge and Lewis guns aft of the crew's quarters. Depending on size, they carried a crew of between eight and ten men.

In the Channel Islands, raids were planned against Sark, Jersey and Herm. The Herm raid was cancelled at the planning stage, but the raids on Sark

Derrible Bay, Hog's Back, Sark Island.

and Jersey went ahead. Both were planned for the night of 25/26 December with the aims of reconnaissance and capturing prisoners. The Jersey raid was not successful. While the raiding force landed safely at Petit Port, after climbing the cliff they failed to locate any German soldiers. On returning to the beach a mine was set off, seriously injuring Captain Ayton; he was returned to England but died of his wounds.

Ambrose led the raids on Sark, but these also ran into difficulties. As on Jersey, the raiding force used men primarily from No. 1 (French) Troop of 10 (IA) Commando, although some such as Ambrose were temporarily attached from 12 Commando and the SBS. The Commando Veterans website notes that those temporarily attached 'included highly experienced and courageous individuals like McGonigal, IDC Smith, Brodison, Nash and Barry, all veterans of many cross-Channel raids.'

Sark is a royal fief which forms part of the Bailiwick of Guernsey, with its own set of laws based on Norman law and its own parliament. It has a population of about 600 and, apart from tractors, no mechanized transport of any kind. The island was occupied by German forces from July 1940 until liberation in May 1945. It is essentially a plateau rising to 375ft with a scenic coast encircled by precipitous granite cliffs – daunting natural defences which make access difficult. A failed attempt – not involving Ambrose – was made to liberate Sark in October 1942. The Commandos never again penetrated Sark's defences, although Ambrose's four-man team, three of whom were French, did try at Christmas in 1943.

Sark 25/26 December 1943: Operation Hardtack 7

The first raid was attempted on Christmas Day, late at night. However, having landed by dory from MGB (ML) 292 at Derrible Point at approximately 2355 hours, the Commandos were unable to scale the cliff. The party was commanded by Ambrose and comprised ten men from No. 1 Troop, 10 (IA) Commando as well as two from the SBS. As the dory's capacity was just eight, two men from 10 (IA) remained on board the MGB while the others went ashore.

Local Sergeant Andre Dignac (nicknamed 'Tarzan' for his climbing ability) led the climb but was unable to make the final ascent and at 0200 was forced to admit defeat. Back on the dory, Ambrose and Sergeant Pierre-Charles Boccador (translator) decided to survey the beach at Derrible Bay and the cliff along Hog's Back, where despite the presence of a German sentry patrolling the cliff head overlooking the bay, they encountered and brought back a mine. They got back to the MGB at 0425 and returned to

Dartmouth. On arrival they were given permission to try again and planned another raid for 27/28 December, but this time from the other side of Hog's Back at Dixcart Bay, where they felt there might be easier access to the top. Ambrose's report noted:

> The passage entailed a series of climbs up and down and it was not until 0100 hours that the last ridge connecting the point to the mainland was reached; this consisted of a knife ledge. On one side there was a sheer drop to Petite Derrible Bay, and on the other side a similar drop to Derrible Bay. An attempt to cross this ridge proved unsuccessful. The ridge itself was about 30 feet in length with no footholds, and the edge itself was too sharp to provide a hand grip. The patrol therefore attempted to descend and bypass this ridge. As the rope had been left at the initial climb, toggle ropes were used and the crossing was accomplished in a series of stages governed by the length of the toggle ropes. At the other end of the knife ledge, a sheer climb of about thirty feet to the mainland plateau was encountered and was found impossible to climb. Below this there was a sheer drop to the sea.

Sark 27/28 December 1943: Operation Hardtack 7

Using MGB (ML) 322 for the raid, they left Dartmouth at 1600. Ambrose and his force landed from Dixcart Bay on to Hog's Back at 2220, with the same men going ashore. Dignac led the climb and paid out a rope for the others to use in following him up. When they reached the top of the cliff, Ambrose assumed the lead. They would have to move slowly and carefully – when he and Boccador surveyed the area on Boxing Day, it was clear that mines had been planted; they had recovered one from the area below the cliffs, and there were likely to be more. Their rudimentary map indicated the general presence of a minefield but not its precise location or how extensive it might be. However, there was really only one route that they were able to take – a narrow coastal pathway splitting the Hog's Back and bordered on each side by rocks and thick gorse. They were concerned that if they tried to force their way along either side of the path they would attract the attention of the Germans. The rocks and gorse provided good cover, but it would mean crawling cautiously along what turned out to be a heavily mined path. They cut their way through a thick copper-wire boundary fence and reached the path. Ambrose led the way carefully, checking for mines and indicating the safest route. Suddenly, after about 15 yards, two mines exploded to the rear of the raiding party, killing Corporal Robert Bellamy

View of the path looking back towards the Hog's Back. (*Sark Branch British Royal Legion*)

almost immediately and badly wounding Dignac – somebody must have strayed slightly off the route. Ambrose immediately went to Dignac's aid, trying to bring him back part of the way, but then another mine went off injuring both of them. Dignac was now seriously wounded, and Ambrose had been hit by shrapnel in both hands and feet. Boccador attempted to inject Dignac with morphine, but just as the injection went in, Dignac died. They left the two bodies behind, and more mines then exploded as the men tried to retrace their steps back towards the edge of the cliff and make their escape. Debris from the exploding mines triggered neighbouring mines and like collapsing dominoes set off a chain of explosions. Matelot Maurice Le Floch was hit in the chest but was still able to walk. Matelot Joseph Nicot was also injured but remained mobile. Boccador was the only one not wounded and was able to help the others in getting down the cliff using the rope. They got back on board the dory by 0230 and were on the MGB by 0300. Corporal Pierre Vinat (a medical orderly who had remained on the MGB) treated the wounded during the journey, and on arrival they were immediately taken to hospital.

Ambrose's report on the patrol states:

The force landed at point 599021 and, after climbing a 200-foot sheer rock face met a further very steep slope about 100 feet in height with a shingle, slate, and stone surface. The force followed the eastern edge of this slope and encountered a wire fence consisting of three strands of very thick copper wire and two thinner strands or ordinary wire. This wire was cut and the force proceeded along the top of the Hogs Back, continually searching for mines as it progressed. Plentiful cover was afforded by rock and gorse.

At point 599024, a path approximately six feet wide was encountered, on either side of which the ground, which was thickly covered with gorse, fell away very steeply. We found that it was impossible to walk through this gorse without making considerable noise and we therefore continued along the path.

I was leading the patrol and had gone forward some fifteen yards, feeling for mines as I did so, when two mines went off behind the patrol, wounding Corporal Bellamy and Private Dignac. Corporal Bellamy died about two minutes later and Private Dignac received very severe wounds in the body.

The first mine had exploded about two feet behind Corporal Bellamy, the last member of the patrol, and the second mine about five feet to the left of it. (The empty container was taken from the first hole and brought back with the force.)

The force then started to carry Corporal Bellamy and Private Dignac out of the minefield. I took the lead, still feeling for fresh mines, and had taken only a few steps when two more mines went up in quick succession in front and to the side of me. (Lieutenant McGonigal himself was injured as a result.) After these explosions, Sergeant Boccador was the only member of the force who remained unwounded. Private Dignac was wounded still further by these explosions and Sergeant Boccador told me that he was dead.

In view of the fact that my force had sustained such casualties. I decided to leave the two bodies, retrace my steps and return to the boat. No sooner had we started to move, however than more mines went up all around us. I cannot say how many there were but at the time we had the impression of being under fire from a heavy calibre machine gun. We continued our withdrawal to the dory.

On our way up we had hidden a wireless set No. 536 under a rock but we were unable to find it on our return journey and so were obliged to abandon it. It was also impossible for us to get down the last sheer twenty feet of rock and to bring the rope with us. Repeated attempts were made to pull it down after we had got to the bottom but it had stuck firmly, and so, cutting it as high as we could, we left it and returned to the MGB …

The first two mines that exploded were behind the patrol and, although we moved about continuously in advance of the two craters, no further mines were exploded. It would therefore appear that we had reached the edge of the minefield and had been unfortunate enough to explode perhaps the last two mines in the field. It is interesting to note that although Sergeant Boccador and myself were feeling our way very carefully, we felt no contact points nor other signs of mines.

All the injuries caused by the exploding mines were sustained by those members of the force who were either standing or kneeling. A person lying flat seemed to be immune from them. Despite these explosions, no signs of Germans were seen or heard.

Shortly after this the Commando operations were discontinued in order to avoid alerting the Germans to Allied interest in the area.

Ambrose, by now promoted to Captain, was awarded a Military Cross in recognition of his actions and leadership on this and earlier such operations. The award of an MC was recommended by Laycock as follows:

On the night of 27th December 1943 the above named officer was ordered to land on the Island of SARK with a small force to carry out a reconnaissance, obtain certain information, and if possible capture a prisoner. Very shortly after landing, the patrol penetrated into an unsuspected minefield. Two mines went up in quick succession, killing one of the force and badly wounding another. Surprise having been lost Lt McGonigal ordered the patrol to withdraw to the beach with the dead and wounded men, having first examined the hole made by one of the mines and obtained the metal container left in it. Almost immediately after the patrol commenced its withdrawal a further four mines went up, killing the already badly injured man and wounding Lt McGonigal and a further two other ranks. In spite of his injuries Lt McGonigal continued personally to direct the difficult withdrawal down the cliff and by refusing all offers of assistance allowed greater aid to be given to the other injured members of the patrol. This officer personally signalled in the dory, superintended the embarkation of the wounded, and retained his command until the M.T.B was reached where for the first time he received medical attention. Lt McGonigal showed great powers of leadership and devotion to duty throughout all phases of the operation, and by his courage and gallantry extricated his force from its extremely hazardous position. He has on several previous occasions taken part in similar operations and has shown throughout a high sense of duty, disregard for personal danger and superior powers of leadership.

Indeed, even after the war and upon demobilization, Peter Laycock saw fit to provide a reference noting that he had found Ambrose 'to be an officer of very considerable ability. He had a strong personality and the men under his command both liked and respected him. I do not wish to be served by a better officer.'

Ambrose's leadership was also acknowledged by the men in this raiding force. Sergeant Pierre-Charles Boccador, the force's translator, sent him New Year wishes in January 1944 and finished with sentiments most probably echoing those felt by Ambrose:

> The remainder of the Section … send to you their best souvenirs and respects … they all hope to see you again as our commander … Again I tell you all my sincere thoughts and wishes of the best time for new year, I knew that you are a better man, but I hope soon you will be my C.O. again, because I am not afraid to go everywhere with you! …
>
> I will remember the [sacrifice] of Bellamy and Dignac … I am the only one of our patrol again ready to fight but I will fight for six and I will revenge those friends as I will revenge my father.
>
> … I will forget not a minute of those hours the 27/28/12/43.

(Sark Branch British Royal Legion)

Chapter 28

'Hiltforce'

During the end of '43 and the first part of '44 myself, Ambrose McGonigal and about ten men were in what can best be described as limbo. We seem to have got detached from 10 Commando in that we left Eastbourne and based ourselves in Newhaven at the Louis Napoleon pub by the bridge across the harbour, we had our own armament and a limitless supply of ammunition, and became really expert shots with the Sten gun. One of the exercises at which we became expert was to roll an empty bean tin down the face of a quarry, and then with single shots keep the tin in the air.

(Ian Smith, unpublished memoir)

The Dover Tarbrush Raids

In May 1944 Ambrose became involved with what were known as the Dover 'Tarbrush' raids. In April 1944, Bomber Command attacked a number of

Bridge Hotel and Inn, Newhaven (of Louis Napoleon fame).

German coastal batteries (dug-in concrete pillboxes) at Houlgate. One plane dropped a bomb short of its target which exploded when it hit the water and caused sympathetic explosions all along the foreshore, just beneath the water's surface. Scientists attached to Combined Operations HQ (COHQ) later examined images taken of the raid and expressed concern that the explosions might have been caused by the Germans using a new type of mine, triggered acoustically or through vibration. This greatly worried the D-Day planners, and so Admiral Ramsay and General Montgomery requested that investigations be carried out urgently. Consequently, about ten different raiding missions were planned. Four of these were commanded by Captain Hilton-Jones, based in Dover – he planned for them to take place simultaneously during the next period of dark nights (14–19 May 1944), with targets well away from the planned D-Day landing beaches. The four places chosen were Bray Dunes, Les Hemmes, Quend Plage and Onival, and the operation was codenamed 'Tarbrush'. The men chosen for the operation were the most experienced Captain Hilton-Jones could find within the SS Group, and they were concentrated at Dover and codenamed 'Hiltforce'. Ambrose (who had by then recovered from the injuries sustained during Hardtack 7) led one group, Tarbrush 5 (Les Hemmes), while Tarbrush 3 (Bray Dunes) was commanded by Lieutenant Ian Smith.

All Hiltforce members were either part of 10 Inter-Allied Commando or, as in Ambrose's case, temporarily attached to it. The method of landing, perfected during the Hardtack raids, was by powered dory, which took the

A Small Scale Raiding Force crew with a dory of the type used by Ambrose.

A German
Tellermine.

raiding party from an MTB close to the shore before they transferred to a rubber dinghy.

In total, eight raids were launched during the three nights, 15/16, 16/17, and 17/18 May 1944.

On the first night Tarbrush 3 and 5 did not land – either because the sea was too rough or because of insufficient time due to enemy sea patrols. However, on the 16th, having been taken by MTB and dropped into their dories about a mile offshore, both Ambrose's and Ian's forces managed to land by dinghy. Both forces confirmed that, despite the concerns, all mines discovered appeared to be ordinary Tellermines – no new types were found.

Ian Smith recounted his experience of the evening's entertainment:

Armed with a Sten gun and accompanied by a sapper, I crawled up the beach. The smell of cigarette smoke alerted [us] to the presence of a sentry. Then [we] heard German spoken. The guard was being changed. The sapper groped his way up one of the stakes and found an anti-tank Tellermine nailed to the top. Having decided not to remove it because the sentry would be sure to hear the noise, we returned to the dory, slid over the side and paddled until we were far enough from the beach to start the engine. We then transmitted our call sign by 'S' phone, an early 'walkie-talkie', but received no answer from the MTB. A ship approached us and, turning on its searchlight, scanned the sea. The Germans permitted no fishing at night, and I feared that it was one of their armed naval trawlers. We flattened themselves on the bottom of the dory. The vessel sailed past only a few yards away. How it did not see us, I shall never know. However, I spoke too soon because some minutes later it turned about and, directed by its radar or shore radar, loosed off some heavy gunfire in our direction. Just as it was getting very close there came a sudden ringing of bells and shouted orders and, having apparently become stuck on a sand bank, it stopped. We eventually then found the MTB, which had moved out to sea to avoid the trawler.

Ambrose's raid went off without any particular hitches and with the same results – the Germans were still using Tellermines. It was a similar story with the other raids; the evidence was conclusive that the sympathetic explosions spotted by the British bomber had been caused by Tellermines tied to underwater posts but without adequate waterproofing. As a result, seawater had corroded the firing pins and made them extra-sensitive.

Afterwards, Ambrose and Smith celebrated the success of the raids in a series of Dover hostelries and Smith became so inebriated that Ambrose had to get Smith's batman to take him home in a wheelbarrow. Both were awarded a bar to their Military Cross, with the citation in Ambrose's case by Hilton-Jones:

This officer was the commander of a military force which landed to the East of Calais on the North coast of France on the night of 16/17 May 1944, to carry out a reconnaisance of enemy beach obstacles. The operation was of the highest importance and was of an extremely hazardous nature, involving as it did a three mile approach to a heavily defended enemy coastline, by night in an 18 foot Dory, and the carrying out of a minute examination of beach mines and obstacles of unknown potentialities. During the run in, and the return passage to the parent M.T.B., Lt. McGonigal was forced to alter course on two occasions to avoid a single enemy vessel and a convoy of seven vessels proceeding towards Calais a mile offshore. Despite such interference he so navigated his craft as to reach the selected landing point without error thus greatly facilitating the task of the landing party. Throughout the entire operation his skill, courage, and level headedness inspired his force to the maximum of effort and resulted in the obtaining of vital information.

Chapter 29

The SBS: 'urgently required for operations in Yugoslavia'

May 1944 brought a distinct change in direction for Ambrose. His recent exploits along the French coast had brought him to the attention of Brigadier Fitzroy Maclean, a Scottish soldier, writer and politician. Maclean was one of only two men to enlist as a private and rise to the rank of Brigadier (the other being his future fellow Conservative MP Enoch Powell). He is also believed to have been one of Ian Fleming's inspirations for 007. Maclean had been chosen by Churchill to lead a mission to Yugoslavia where, as Churchill told him personally, he was not to concern himself with how the country was to be run after the war, but 'simply to find out who was killing the most Germans and suggest means by which we could help them to kill more'. This was a task to which Maclean, on the advice of Peter Laycock (brother of soon to be Major General Robert Laycock of 'Layforce' fame) thought Ambrose was ideally suited. Therefore, at Maclean's express request, Ambrose switched to the SBS, at the time made up of men from 1st SAS, comprising men from four British squadrons, one Free French, one Greek and the Folbot Section (using two-man canoes or 'folding boats' for reconnaissance purposes and small raiding operations) as well as the Small Scale Raiding Force (SSRF). The balance of 1st SAS remained under Blair Mayne's command with a new name, 'Special Raiding Squadron'.

Using a small force and working with the local partisans, Ambrose conducted a series of successful operations inside Yugoslavia, blowing up trains, killing Germans and earning a Mention in Dispatches 'in recognition of gallant and distinguished services in the Mediterranean Theatre during operations in the Aegean with the Special Boat Service'.

Ian Smith recalled the start of this:

> Everywhere preparations were going ahead for the invasion of Europe and we began to feel out of it, our efforts seemed puny and useless. Ambrose and I were discussing our position in the Rising Sun Inn at Warsash when a dispatch rider burst in – 'Lts Smith and McGonigal?'

We admitted to who we were. 'Right, sir, been searching for you everywhere. Sign for this,' and handed an envelope to me marked 'Top Secret'.

[We were] 'Lts' – we could not become Captains as we really had no units – a problem particular to those operating in special or covert groups.

In fact, Ambrose had already been promoted to Captain before March 1944, but it was a 'temporary' rank, reflecting the fact that he was not a regular soldier and therefore unlikely to remain with the army following the war. Ambrose went on to be promoted to Major (again 'temporary') by the end of the war, a title he retained on an honorary basis after demobilization.

Smith continued:

At about this time, we had news of a different sort. Apparently our activities had been noticed and to all our astonishment we received medals, Ambrose and I got MCs ... It was a great honour but we had achieved little and apart from the odd fright we had enjoyed it very much.

The Rising Sun Inn, Warsash, River Hamble, south of Southampton.

It also happened that Fitzroy Mclean, then a brigadier, was in London, he was in charge of the mission to help Tito's partisans who were harassing the Germans in Yugoslavia and he wanted agents to drop into various partisan units. Laycock recommended Ambrose and myself writing that 'they are very good officers, but bloody independent' … and so we were included into the Special Operations Executive, the Official Secrets Act was signed, finger prints were taken and we were told on pain of something awful happening not to breath [sic] a word to anyone. All the signing etc was done in the old Marks and Spencer building in Baker St.

At McLean's request, Ambrose's transfer from 12 Commando into the SOE (MI5)/the SBS happened at the end of May 1944, shortly before D-Day (6 June 1944). The application form states that Ambrose had been 'selected by Brgd. McLean' and he was 'urgently required for operations in Yugoslavia' with 'immediate effect'. Ambrose left on 2 June 1944.

Chapter 30

Into the Balkans: 'an aggressive, independent Irishman'

August/September 1944

None of the Special Boat Squadron patrols inserted into Yugoslavia during this period met with much success, or received much help from the locals. According to one SBS member, 'Yugoslavia was a difficult place to operate and bridges were about the only things we could attack … The Yugoslavs didn't want us there, Tito didn't, and they were uncooperative and suspicious.' There was another factor that mitigated against SBS operations: they were no longer fighting an enemy from island to island but were engaged in a war on a continent. As a result, lines of re-supply were more difficult and securing a means of escape presented a greater challenge.

However, the SBS officer who adapted most quickly to this more demanding environment was Ambrose, as John Lodwick's *The Filibusters* confirms:

> If anyone overcame those difficulties on that occasion it was Lieutenant Ambrose McGonigal who with Sergeant Flavell and his patrol operated for over two months in southern Jugoslavia. This McGonigal was a real Irishman inasmuch as he actually lived in Ireland and did not base his claim, like so many people, upon a hypothetical Hibernian grandmother. McGonigal, with his mucker, Ian Smith, a regular soldier, had just come out from England, where they had taken part in many pre-invasion excursions from Newhaven to the French coast. Both were vastly experienced men who felt no shame at being, in Lady Astor's too-famous phrase, 'D-Day Dodgers'. 'France', Ian Smith would exclaim contemptuously, 'why, we got tired of France last year.' As armies mass for stupendous offensives, the value of raiding men, who have done so much of the groundwork, declines.

However, with the SBS Ambrose was back in his element, and the raids continued. He landed in southern Yugoslavia, close to the border with

Albania, towards the end of August, in charge of an eight-strong patrol and with orders to harass and delay the Germans as they retreated north from Greece. Ambrose made not the slightest attempt to inform the local partisans of his plans – he very quickly realized that the best method of establishing a working relationship with them was 'to tell them absolutely nothing'. That way there would be no interference and no room for suspicious partisans to get in the way. And, 'if the partisans had harboured any doubts as to the British commitment to kill Germans they were completely dispelled by [Ambrose].'

His methods seemed to enjoy marked success. He and his men spent their time taking largely independent action against German rail and road convoys. Allowing the local partisans to tag along if they wished, he never made the details of his plans known to them. Maybe they thought that this 'aggressive Irishman' only found targets of opportunity (as they themselves usually did); in fact, Ambrose's first-rate interpreter (Captain Eden) had much to do with smoothing the path for this small patrol, negotiating their way through an environment of mistrust and risk.

As a result, the partisans got used to trailing along behind Ambrose's raiding force on long night marches. And his intentions rapidly became clear, as throughout September 1944 he waged a vicious war on the enemy, ambushing convoys, blowing up a railway tunnel and wrecking nearby installations.

The tunnel in question was guarded by fifteen Chetniks (nationalist rivals of Tito's partisans), whom Ambrose and his men dispersed with Bren gunfire. They then laid charges in a manhole inside the tunnel, at the points to three sidings, in a nearby station and on a large water-tank. As they were doing this, shots were heard in the distance. Investigation revealed trigger-happy partisans shooting at bushes. 'This whole area,' wrote Ambrose, 'was very thoroughly controlled by Milhailovitch Chetniks on behalf of the Germans. Movement by day was impossible.' The Chetniks made several daylight attacks on the British party, but were driven off on each occasion with such severe casualties that soon they left Ambrose and his patrol in peace.

Ambrose then had further successes. He attacked and destroyed a number of trucks laden with Germans, one of them in full view of an enemy-held village. A battery from this village opened fire on the SBS as they scrambled among the truck's cargo of cigarettes and chocolate. Ambrose was unable to get all the chocolate away, but he removed a great amount and found time to attack and kill the occupants of a second truck which had come to the aid of the first.

He then made contact with an Austrian driver of the local German Commander, and 'in return for a consideration' the driver offered to drive the Commander into an ambush. Unfortunately, the Gestapo heard of the arrangements and managed to foil the attack; Ambrose was almost captured and shot in the process. The driver was arrested and tortured, and the residents of three villages were ordered to move into a single one, to make it easier to monitor them and prevent the passing of any further information to the SBS.

Ambrose was not put off by this close shave and instead saw it as an opportunity. He assumed correctly that the Germans would need to send patrols to these villages to enforce their orders. Therefore, with the eight men under his command, he ambushed forty-five of the enemy in a steep, narrow gorge, killing about twenty of them without loss to his force. 'The remainder,' Ambrose said, 'threw arms, ammunition, even water-bottles away, and ran as hard as possible.'

Ambrose then learned of a German troop train that would be passing along a stretch of remote railway in a couple of days. In a joint attack with the partisans, and using machine guns, the SBS ambushed and derailed the train. Wagons containing hay, cement and flour were set on fire. 'The enemy evacuated the train and we pursued them down the railway line where they took cover in a wood at the side of the line,' remembered Captain Eden, 'and it was now hand-to-hand fighting.' The Germans were trapped in the wood, losing thirty-seven killed or wounded. One of Ambrose's men, Private Howells of the SBS, was killed, and the entire local population attended his funeral as a mark of respect. The achievements of Ambrose and his force of just eight men had illuminated an otherwise bleak period for the SBS.

Ambrose's party then moved further inland and spent the next two weeks ambushing more German patrols – and when more and larger patrols were sent out to investigate the disturbances, ambushing them too. His sense of timing would seem to have been impeccable, for when he eventually withdrew – leaving behind several thoroughly exasperated partisan commissars – he and his men had killed or wounded well over seventy German soldiers and an unknown number of Chetniks. They had also derailed a train, left the local German command in complete disorder and destroyed the railway tunnel, their original target. By the end, Ambrose's interpreter, Captain Eden, was receiving daily applications to desert through a local intermediary. And they had lost just one man in two months of regular action.

So ended Ambrose's first adventures with the SBS. They had not been without result. When he arrived, a well-disciplined enemy had faced him. When he left, German officers were no longer able to control their men, who were desperate and selling all they possessed. The local garrison for the area was kept ready to move out at an hour's notice. The German force in the area was in utter disarray.

Ian Smith recalled:

Ambrose McGonigal had also been in Jugland where he had the great pleasure in blowing up a train, which he was told was full of Home Guard troops but it was in fact full of fearsome Bulgarians who gave him a wild chase … Ambrose got out before me and had chummed up with David Sutherland who at the time was O/C Special Boat Service. Ambrose joined his unit and asked me to also join which I did, as I was not enamoured of the politicking of Jugland, in any case I was in the Partisans very bad books.

At this time we heard that Ambrose and I had been awarded bars to our MCs in other words we got two of them. It was for the Dover operation, which I suppose is the only really important thing I did in the whole damned war … There were quite a few officers with three MCs but two was sufficient for me, and when I think of the ordinary regimental officers (and soldiers) who endured the set piece battles with all their blood and mayhem and above all noise, I think I had an easy time, usually sleeping dry and warm and getting regular food. The only difference is that if an ordinary soldier had been caught he would have been a PoW whereas if we had been nabbed then the consequences would have been very unpleasant [a reference to Hitler's infamous Commando Order].

The war was drawing quite quickly to its close, there was no possible alternative to a complete Allied victory and abject surrender of Germany. The SBS mess at that time seemed to be split between those who wanted to have one last go and those that took the view that they had been at very considerable risk for

BUCKINGHAM PALACE.

I greatly regret that I am unable to give you personally the award which you have so well earned.
I now send it to you with my congratulations and my best wishes for your future happiness.

George R.I.

Captain A. J. Mc Gonigal, M.C.,
The Royal Ulster Rifles.

the last four years and we had survived more or less intact, why risk it all on one more operation which could not possibly be essential for victory? The Bravo boys, who were my friends, had their eyes on some very big prizes. The Germans were retreating from Northern Italy to Austria, and there was a lot of talk about a force being dropped in the Klagenfurt area to take the German surrender. Need I add that there were equally strong rumours that with the retreating Germans there was much gold, where the gold came from I am not sure, but seemed reasonable to assume that from the time they achieved complete control of their part of Italy any gold there would be taken with them. Ambrose McGonigal was as usual all for a fight, and talked about the enormous possibilities a drop near Klagenfurt held. I, having a new wife with whom I had enjoyed but a four-day honeymoon before joining the Yugoslav Partisans and having been lucky enough to survive quite a number of adventures during the last four years without being shot, blown up or captured, was disinclined to chance my luck any further and hoped that we would be left alone to appreciate the quiet of our Manopoli camp site.

It goes without saying that, although also recently married and father to a baby daughter, Ambrose was not yet quite ready to call it a day. The SBS were now about to resume operations in their traditional island-hopping manner, but this time in the Eastern Adriatic.

The following month, Peter Lessing, the war correspondent in Athens for the *Daily Sketch*, described the liberation of the city on 13 October 1944 (Operation Manna – a joint British-Greek action). In particular, Lessing described the earlier actions of the SBS at Patras when, greatly outnumbered, 'L' Squadron of the SBS bluffed a German garrison force of 1,200 men into evacuating and escaping by boat into the Gulf of Corinth. Describing the handful of SBS 'daredevils' as 'a small unit unlike any other in the British Army … a cross between parachutists and boat service commandos', Lessing reported this audacious raid and then explained how they

Lived By Their Wits

JELLICOE'S unit comprises specially selected volunteers – men trained to shoot in the dark, march long distances and carry heavy loads. They are also expert Parachutists and all are trained sailors. This year they have ranged the Adriatic and the Aegean Islands, and though they have dealt the Germans severe blows their casualties have been negligible. The reason they give for this is that they know how to look after themselves and that they specialise in outwitting rather than outfighting the enemy. After their raids they leave behind their beret and badge to let the Germans know who was responsible and so prevent reprisals against the local population.

Men of 'L' Squadron SBS investigating the Acropolis, 13–14 Oct 1944, three carrying US M1 Carbines, and one possibly a British Bren gun. (*Sgt Johnson, No.2 Army Film & Photo Section, IWM*)

Chapter 31

Croatia – Unie, Cherso, Lussino, Istria: 'Kill the f——ing lot of them'

T
he winter of 1944 was not kind to the SBS. A series of misfortunes befell the squadron, including the death in separate air accidents of Dick Morris, who had been with the unit for nearly two years, and Major Ian Patterson. Patterson's loss was felt keenly by Lieutenant Colonel Jellicoe (as he then was, the Commander of the Special Boat Squadron), although he too was soon to depart the squadron for a staff college at Haifa. T/Lieutenant Colonel David Sutherland replaced Jellicoe as commanding officer of the SBS, and despite being a 'mere' temporary Captain, Ambrose took over 'L' Squadron in place of the deeply mourned Patterson. A nominal roll for 'L' Squadron can be found at Appendix K – it contained within its ranks Captain John Lodwick, soon to be the author of *The Filibusters*, a 1947 book recounting the wartime exploits of the SBS. In it Lodwick comments on the choice of Ambrose as the Squadron's new leader: 'No better choice could have been made.'

At this time, Ambrose's experience was formally noted in the SOE and MI5 records as including 'amphibious warfare, guerilla warfare, counter-espionage and working in enemy-occupied territory' with 'knowledge of map-reading and pilotage (special coast marine)'. He had been busy since joining 12 Commando. However, promotions were difficult for officers in the special forces because of the clandestine nature of their work and the nature of the units to which they were at any one time attached – this was particularly so in Ambrose's case, given that his parent unit, 12 Commando, had by now been disbanded.

Nevertheless, with signs emerging that an end to the war was approaching, much of this period was spent monitoring the activities of the remaining German troops in Crete, where there was little or no aggression by either side. It was essentially a peacekeeping role. However, from late February 1945 Ambrose's attention shifted to various jagged splinters of land off the Croatian coastline.

On 24 February Ambrose and three men landed on Unie, to the north-west of Olib, with the objective of using it as a vantage point from which to observe the neighbouring islands of Cherso and Lussino to the east. Information concerning the islands was scarce and for the most part inaccurate. It was therefore decided to carry out thorough reconnaissance of each before mounting any attack, and to this end an Intelligence Officer was sent to the small island of Olib with instructions to collect data concerning Lussino and Cherso, which at the time were reported to be strongly held by the enemy. But on the second day of his reconnaissance, rather than depend on the Intelligence Officer alone, Ambrose decided to cross-check this information for himself from the larger island of Unie. Exceeding his instructions 'in the interests of accuracy', he managed to take advantage of a cooperative partisan group and rowed the couple of miles to Lussino. Landing on the northern part of the island, Ambrose spent an hour climbing to the top of a hill covered in thorn bushes and low scrub. It was worth the effort. From the peak, he was able 'to obtain a good view of the bridge and the town of Ossero'. He spent two hours on his observation point before moving on to investigate the village of Neresine. His report, economical as ever, noted that he had 'watched a somewhat slovenly parade outside a house occupied by Germans, but otherwise saw very little'.

Intrigued by Ambrose's intelligence, Sutherland planned a bigger and less impromptu reconnaissance targeting Lussino, Neresine and Ossero. Lieutenant Gallagher and Sergeant Holmes were given Ossero to see if they could add to Ambrose's report, but there was some trepidation on both men's part, with Holmes, who was in his third year of guerrilla warfare,

> wondering how much longer his luck could last. The war, in Europe at least, was all but won but would his luck hold? In the Balkans there was little we could do to influence the war and we wanted now just one thing: to survive. Yet I had to go on reconnaissances right up to the end of the war and that was no joke. (Gavin Mortimer, *The SBS in WWII*)

Nevertheless, all groups survived, and acting on the information obtained, a large party (including Ambrose's Sergeant Flavell from the raids in southern Yugoslavia) was sent in to take a small post on Cherso reputedly manned by Italian fascists. Fire was exchanged, but the occupants, numbering twelve in all, surrendered after minimal resistance. The SBS recovered a radio transmitter and a significant number of code books.

Villa Punta: 'Kill the f——ing lot of them'. March/April 1945

Next up was a German post on Lussino (or Losinj). At Zara (or Zadar) on the Croatian coast, following the capture of two Italian deserters, plans were made to dispatch a much larger patrol north to Lussino. The intelligence was not comprehensive, but the captured Italians had informed Ambrose that their unit at a German post called 'Villa Punta' would surrender en masse if they received a guarantee of lenient treatment. Ambrose therefore decided to send a small force to deal with the Italians. Ideally, he would have sent one of his experienced officers, but as they were mostly out on operations, he ordered an inexperienced lieutenant to lead the mission ('It was a rushed job with a new officer on his first raid'). And when Ambrose issued his operational orders, it was clear that encouraging surrender was not a priority. The task was to 'attack and destroy the occupants of Villa Punta and bring away any prisoners and equipment captured'. Corporal Ken Smith remembered standing on the jetty in Zara waiting to board the motor launch with one of the Italian guides close by. Ambrose and his lieutenant appeared and began a discussion. 'I heard the senior officer say "Kill the f——ng lot of them"', recalled Smith. 'This Eyetie heard this and immediately ran forward and said "No need to kill".' He need not have worried, as plans quickly fell apart – as well as problems during the operation between Smith and the new lieutenant, their Italian guide managed to lead them astray. It was eventually decided to abort.

A few days later, on 9 March, they decided to try again – only this time, Ambrose would lead the operation armed with a revised plan. Instead of simply accepting the surrender of Italian deserters, a much more difficult and uncertain objective was now decided on. Shortly after arriving on

Villa Punta. (© *The SAS and LRDG Roll of Honour*)

Lussino, Ambrose had received intelligence that the garrison at Villa Punta had been reinforced with German troops and that four two-man patrols had been posted in the village guarding the approaches to the villa.

The intelligence revealed that Villa Punta was in fact a strongly held post housing no fewer than forty-five Germans – a very different prospect to a handful of unenthusiastic Italians. Originally a rambling old villa with a large garden and outbuildings overlooking the beach, the Germans appeared to have introduced various modifications such as reinforcing its cellars as air raid shelters.

To counter the patrols, Ambrose issued instructions for two approaches to be made – a smaller one from the rear to attract attention and a bigger one, the main approach, from the front. He planned to clear the building by drawing the Germans to the back (seaward) side, while his main body – a slightly optimistic description of his force of some seventeen men – broke in through the front door.

Ambrose's expedition sailed as a strike force of twenty-one men in total. They landed unobserved and then, with locals acting as guides, approached the target area from about two miles out.

One of the three lieutenants led a unit along the beach, but trying to clear a barrier enforced with barbed wire they were heard by an alert German sentry, who challenged them and opened fire. All possibility of surprise had now been lost, and Ambrose was left with no alternative but to order a general attack.

At the same time, instead of waiting for an attack, the Germans sent out a small fighting patrol to try to seize the initiative. However, the SBS were ready for them, and as they ran out they were met by fire from Bren gunners on the walls of the garden and quickly driven back into the house.

'Fire returned,' wrote Ambrose in his report. 'Enemy driven back into house and house surrounded.' The enemy may have been surrounded but they were in no way inclined to surrender. A call from Ambrose to lay down their arms was met with a burst of machine-gun fire. The SBS replied in kind and a fierce firefight developed lasting 20 minutes, as Ambrose gauged the strength and disposition of the enemy inside the villa. He then ordered the storming of the building and led his men into the attack. They broke into the front of the house while SBS Bren gunners kept the Germans from firing back through the windows or lobbing grenades from them. In pairs, the SBS then began clearing the house passage-by-passage, room-by-room, and going through the outbuildings. This would have been a difficult job in daylight, working to a timetable so that covering fire from outside would not strike the rooms being cleared; but at night (it was 0230) and with an improvised plan of action, the job was verging on the suicidal. Fire had broken out, and the men were faced with trying to keep the Germans at bay while also avoiding friendly fire as the building was cleared.

Nevertheless, all resistance soon appeared subdued; it seemed unlikely that many of the garrison could have survived. 'By 0300 hours all resistance ceased,' wrote Ambrose. 'The house was a complete wreck inside from the Lewes bombs used by ourselves and from blast bombs used by the enemy in house fighting.'

Ambrose counted seven enemy dead and estimated at least twice as many again were buried under the 'rubble covering the floors and the stairs blown away from one flight'. However, it had come at a price. The SBS had suffered two dead and another eight men more or less severely wounded. Therefore, as Ambrose had only eleven fit men remaining, he withdrew the patrols. The two-mile march back to their motor launch was a punishing journey for the walking wounded, some of whom were badly hurt.

This action at Villa Punta showed the difficulty of dislodging determined men from a reinforced defensive position. Despite their bravery, the SBS had been unable to win a conclusive victory, for it was later discovered that approximately twenty of the original forty-five or more Germans had survived undetected in the reinforced cellars. The Italian fascists were not so determined, however, and as anticipated, several later surrendered to recce parties.

In reality it is particularly difficult to deploy more than fifteen men, under night conditions, against a fixed objective when the element of surprise has been lost and you are working to an improvised plan. Sutherland was nevertheless undeterred by the casualties incurred during the attack on the villa. It had achieved its objective and so, a few days later, the SBS was instructed to launch a similar raid on a bridge at Ossero which linked the islands of Cherso and Lussino and was of such strategic importance to the maintenance of the enemy's communications that they guarded it with eighty men and several light anti-aircraft and machine guns.

Ossero Bridge

The Balkan Air Force had already tried to destroy the bridge, as had the Royal Navy; now the task was placed in the hands of the SBS. The prospects of success were not good, and the operation was not well received by the veterans of the squadron. If a navy and an air force could not destroy it, then what chance did a small force of soldiers have (about thirty-eight relatively

The current day bridge at Ossero (Osor) in Cres Island, a rotating bridge linking Cherso (Cres) with Lussino (Losinj).

fit SBS troops remained available)? Nevertheless, Ambrose was instructed to try.

Ossero was awkward. Heavy casualties were expected, and the inclusion of no fewer than three medical orderlies in the party as they sailed from Zara did not pass unnoticed. The men were left with a distinct sense of foreboding.

Ambrose had given a lot of thought to what had happened at Villa Punta and was determined that on this occasion there should be no cases of mistaken identity, no confusion and, above all, no early and disastrous alerting of outlying sentries. His plan involved the approach of numerous patrols in such a manner that they could not possibly come into conflict with each other. From the moment of disembarkation of the main party, no enemy forces, however small, were to be allowed to remain alive behind the advance towards the target.

The expedition left Zara at dusk on 18 March in two MLs. The main force then landed approximately 10km from their objective and began a three-hour march towards Ossero. At the same time, a two-man 'Folbot party' landed just south of the bridge to ensure that any German reinforcements

Reconnaissance photo of Ossero Bridge.

would not arrive unexpectedly from that direction. Their instructions were to maintain a watch before joining the main party at a rendezvous point nearer to the bridge.

Ambrose's plan was to assign different SBS units to the tasks of neutralizing the outer defences one by one, using stealth rather than open engagement. It was anticipated there would be a number of minor encounters with German patrols, but with luck (and with Ambrose's order to leave no German alive behind the line of attack), no encounter should amount to anything more than a skirmish. Regrettably, however, one of these encounters resulted in a general alarm being sounded throughout the German positions. A patrol under Sergeant Wright observed a party of five Germans approaching them from the north and opened fire. Four of the Germans were killed, but the fifth escaped; once again, the element of surprise had been lost, and Ambrose was obliged to launch an assault before his troops were properly in position.

He ordered his men to advance, but they found their way blocked by massive coils of barbed wire which they struggled to break through. They were still trying to force a passage when the Germans opened up with two 20mm Oerlikon cannons, wounding three SBS soldiers with the first salvo.

An intense engagement now developed, in which the only thing in the SBS' favour was that the enemy were sometimes forced to break cover in order to deliver fresh supplies of ammunition to their gunners. At this point, just nine Germans had been killed and two wounded.

With at least eight German machine guns covering any final approach to the bridge, it became clear that a way through could not be secured without the intervention of much heavier ordnance. Accordingly, Ambrose contacted the MLs and requested that they use their 20mm cannons on the target area. A bombardment commenced, but the Germans continued to resist, it has to be acknowledged, with some determination.

Ultimately, having to attack from an exposed position and carrying only light weapons and limited supplies of ammunition, there was little to be gained from continuing to engage with an enemy that outnumbered them two to one, was well entrenched and equipped with heavier munitions. Therefore, with their ammunition running low, and realizing that the attempt to destroy the bridge by direct assault would have to be abandoned, Ambrose concentrated his force's efforts on sniping, with a view to causing the maximum number of casualties. As Lodwick put it, 'Even a man of McGonigal's bellicosity now realized that to press the attack was unwise; at 0350 hours he ordered his men to withdraw.'

It was the right decision. In the end, the German positions had held, despite almost half of the garrison becoming casualties (twenty-seven were killed). They held the bridge with great courage, and not one German soldier surrendered. Ambrose had lost one man, and another three were wounded. The men were despondent – it had been an almost impossible objective, and coming at the end of the war, it was a sour note on which to finish.

David Sutherland shared the men's disquiet and now intervened:

In view of the strong precautionary measures being taken by the Germans almost everywhere, I decided that raids of this nature could only produce diminishing results. In future, attacks would be made exclusively upon road transport and, in particular, upon the Cherso–Lussin Road.

There was little point in risking more men in operations against a fleeing and desperate enemy. Defeat was inevitable for the Germans but they were still clinging tenaciously to their garrisons on islands such as Pag, Rab, Losinj, Cherso and Krk. As such, it was decided to establish a small Combined Operations HQ at Zara, a town on the Croatian coast 200 miles north of Dubrovnik, with the focus turning towards infrastructure, the enemy's means of transport and disrupting his movements. In this latter regard, Ambrose's experience of dealing with (or ignoring, as it transpired) the partisans the previous year when leading a small raiding force in a series of attacks against the Germans in southern Yugoslavia proved invaluable, as is evident from an intelligence report produced at the end of April 1945 (Appendix K). In it he describes the tensions that existed between the civilian population and the partisans when it came to cooperating with British troops:

> Civilians in Eastern ISTRIA do not appear whole-hearted in their support of the Partisans. The Partisans have lived off the country for long periods without producing concrete results … vociferous civilian complaints … the Partisans show that while outwardly submissive, many feel the presence of Partisans in their neighbourhood to be a burden. A large proportion of Istrians have been sailors, many working for years with the Cunard Line. They were disposed to be most friendly to British troops with whom they came in contact. This friendliness was openly discouraged by the Partisans. Incidents ranging from the Partisans forbidding civilians from accepting cigarettes from troops, to the arrest of a girl whom they considered over-friendly, illustrate Partisan insistence on aloofness vis-à-vis the British … which resulted in the Partisans at one stage forbidding the civilians to help the British in any way … [however] … much help was given unofficially, local villagers furnished troops with eggs, and other food, although the Partisans had ordered that the British should be fed only through Partisan channels – local guides helped in reconnaissance entirely on a good will basis – donkeys were produced by villagers when the Partisans claimed that none were available. These and other examples show that the views of civilians with regard to the desirability of the presence of British troops by no means coincided with those of the Partisans. Expressions of regret on our evacuation appeared genuine.

Little could Ambrose have envisaged that twenty-odd years later, as a judge in his home town of Belfast, he would be dealing with perhaps more inflamed but not dissimilar tensions between rival communities of civilians, paramilitaries and British troops.

Chapter 32

King Farouk and the Charismatic Company Commander

O ne month later, having flown home from Lüneburg Heath near Hamburg in May 1945, the 1st Battalion the Royal Ulster Rifles was preparing for service in South-East Asia, when Japan announced its surrender on 15 August 1945. The Battalion was therefore deployed instead to Palestine, stationed first at Gaza, then deployed to defend Lydda Airport, before moving to Tel Aviv after riots had broken out. Typically, operations consisted of constant patrolling, curfew enforcement and endeavouring to keep the 'King's Peace' in what was still territory mandated to the British Crown. Ambrose had left the SBS and returned to the RUR as Commander of C Company in Tel Aviv. A fellow RUR officer, Colonel W.R.H. Charley, recalled meeting him in Palestine at the end of that year:

I first met Ambrose in December 1945 when both regular battalions of the Royal Ulster Rifles were stationed in the British Protectorate of Palestine, keeping the peace between Jews and Arabs. I was with 2 RUR, about 20 miles north of 1 RUR, in Camp 87 Pardes Hannah between Tel-a-Viv and Haifa. 1 RUR were just south of Tel-a-Viv in

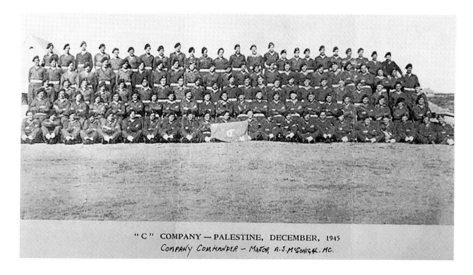

"C" COMPANY — PALESTINE, DECEMBER, 1945
Company Commander – Major A.J. McGonigal. MC.

Camp 22 Nethanya. Both camps were mainly tented surrounded by barbed wire. I was then a lieutenant in 2 RUR and was the Battalion Intelligence Officer. My duties included getting to know the country and I had the opportunity of often visiting my friends in 1 RUR.

One of the main North/South roads in Palestine went right past the front entrance of Camp 22, and C Company 1 RUR, in their red berets and airborne shoulder flashes, were responsible for maintaining a road block opposite the Camp checking all movement North and South. Major McGonigal was C Company's charismatic company commander and there were numerous stories of what went on at that road block!

Just after Christmas 1945 I received orders to attend a Regular Army Commissions Board at Mahdi Camp, Cairo. I discovered Ambrose was also ordered to attend, as well as a boisterous Scottish Major friend of Ambrose from the local Airlanding Brigade. I soon formed the impression that Ambrose had no intention of applying for a regular commission but was looking forward to a trip to Cairo. We travelled across the Sinai Desert by train, one had to be careful because the Arabs were known to climb on to the roof of the railway carriages and if your

One of King Farouk's red Rolls-Royces, 1939.

window was open a hand would come in and lift anything, especially weapons.

When we got to the railway station in Cairo we discovered that all the central streets in Cairo were closed while King Ibn Saud of Saudi Arabia and King Farouk proceeded through the centre of Cairo in two bright red Rolls Royces for an official Royal Visit. This did not stop the two British Majors. They grabbed two … jaunting cars, and challenged each other to a race down the [main procession route from the station towards the Nile]. The crowds cheered the two men who were followed by hordes of Egyptian policemen. However, the two red Rolls Royces suddenly appeared. Ambrose and his friend disappeared into the crowd near the bridge over the Nile to Gezira Island which was our destination. Ambrose soon sailed home on demobilisation leave and nothing more was heard of the incident in Cairo. Incidentally, I lost my wrist watch in that excited crowd!

Looking back at old Pathé newsreels of the day's events, it seems that while the red Rolls Royces may have been part of King Farouk's procession, both he and King Ibn Saud actually travelled in an open-air carriage pulled by mounted guards. Strangely, there is no footage of the two British Majors in their jaunting cars …

And so, with Ambrose and his Scottish racing friend's whistle-stop tour of the streets Cairo, the war for Ambrose finally came to an end.

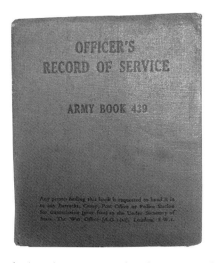
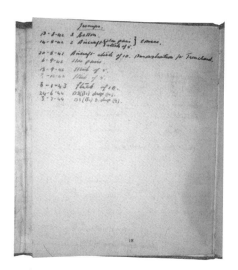

Ambrose's service record with an extract showing his jumps.

Chapter 33

Eoin: 'A Huge Character of a Guy'

Before leaving North Africa, Blair returned to Cyrenaica some time in the spring of 1943. The timing was dictated by the Eighth Army's recapture of Gazala after the Second Battle of El Alamein under Montgomery in November 1942. Shortly afterwards, Tobruk and Benghazi were retaken, and by 23 November the British were back at El Agheila. By March 1943 the Allies had taken Tripoli and crossed into Tunisia. This afforded Blair the opportunity of conducting a private search for evidence of what might have happened to Eoin. Throughout this period he had continued to brood over the fate of his friend from back home, and he continued to write to Babs about it, in February ('I haven't heard anything yet of McGonigal. But his people may have, apparently they are advised by the Red Cross first.') and then again in April 1942 ('Still no news out here of McGonigal, it is about time we heard of him').

However, given the change in status recorded by the War Office Casualty Notice of August 1942, he must by then (or soon thereafter) have learned that Eoin was not among those members of 'L' Detachment who were being held as PoWs in Italy. But there were still many unanswered questions about his disappearance, and Blair decided to investigate for himself.

Approximately 15–17 months after Operation Squatter, Blair returned to Gazala to conduct his search. We know that in late March 1943 the unit moved to Azzib (Palestine) and later to the Gulf of Aqaba to commence a period of intensive training following reorganization of the unit into the Special Raiding Squadron (SRS) under Blair and the SBS under Jellicoe, prior to the start of their work in Europe. The SAS were preparing to leave the desert. The new Commander-in-Chief, General Alexander (who had replaced Auchinleck), visited the training camps on 12 April 1943, and Blair would have been there to meet him. This means that Blair must have returned to Tmimi either in early March or during a period of weekend leave in late March or early April.

In either case, it is not clear how much Blair can have found out at this stage. It is unlikely that any further enemy messages of relevance were intercepted, because even if a body had been discovered, Eoin did not carry identification discs. It is more likely that Blair heard back from one of the surviving members of Eoin's stick who were still being held as PoWs. We know from correspondence with Eoin's mother that Blair had tracked down where some of the men from Eoin's stick were being held and had written to one of them, Pct Robert McKay. On 10 May 1942, Blair wrote:

Dear Mrs McGonigal,

I am sorry for the delay in answering your letter written on the 5th March, but I have been away and when I came back to-day I found it was here. Thanks you for your congratulations, I was lucky.

The people whose names you saw as being prisoners were all with Eoin. Here are their numbers and regiments

2698040 Pct Mackay R. Scots Gds
2756712 Morris W. Black Watch
5672160 Maloney J. Somerset Lt. Inf.
30618334 McCormick C. Royal Scots
811911 Robertson J. Scots Gds.

Mackay was the only one I knew was a prisoner and I got his address –

Pct Robert Mackay
Piani Di Corriglia
Chiaoari Genova
Italy.

I have written to him and I think you should also in case my letter goes astray. He should be able to tell you what happened.

I sent you what photographs I had of Eoin. I kept the negatives so if you don't get them soon please let me know and I can send them again.

I will send a cap badge and the parachute badge by letter. The badge is worn on the left side of our tunics and is given after completing the training jumps and having done an operation by parachute in the enemy country. The English one is a different pattern and is worn on the shoulder after completing the training jumps.

I need not tell you how much I miss Eoin, it would be impossible to have lived with a person of his character for nearly two years without getting to like and admire him tremendously. Also although I am several years older than Eoin I depended on him greatly when I had any serious decisions to make.

More important now than the personal loss which I feel it is the loss which the Unit has suffered. Eoin worked very hard here and was entirely responsible for all the Weapon Training and much of the night training and we would not have been nearly as successful as we have been had it not been for him.

The men too liked and admired him tremendously, my batman tells me that whenever he sees any of our old Commando they are always asking about him.

Please accept my sympathies for Justice McGonigal, yourself and your family.

Yours very sincerely, R.B. Mayne

As Blair's letter confirms, Eoin's disappearance was both a professional and personal loss – emphasized when he wrote to his sister Frances, 'I am getting very tired of this country, especially since Eoin landed a loser, it was all right when there was someone you could talk to about home with.' They may have come from different religious and political traditions in a divided Ulster but the two shared a common bond and understanding. His fellow Ulster Rifles man was missing, and Blair was still trying to find out what had happened and bring some closure to the McGonigal family.

Indeed, despite the fact that the War Office had issued a Casualty List referring to Eoin as 'Missing', it is clear that nobody (outside of a PoW camp in Italy) had any idea what might have actually happened. Therefore, about ten months or so after writing his letter, Blair requisitioned a truck and, much as Eoin had done when he went off hunting for his 'Desert Rat' and to get away from uniforms for a few days, headed out into the desert on his own. He would have known that after so much time it was most probably a hopeless cause, but with the SAS soon to leave their desert home, he felt he couldn't just abandon his friend – he needed to find out what had happened, as well as do what he could on behalf of the McGonigals.

In any event, it seems clear that at this point Blair was acting on the basis that Eoin had not been captured. The understanding accepted by all those who took part in Operation Squatter was that the mission objective took priority, and as with Sergeant Cheyne and Lance Corporals Arnold and Kendall, anyone who was unable to continue would have been left to fend for himself. Putting aside the intercepted enemy message that Blair reported to Ambrose, Eoin must have either been dead or too badly injured to make the long march to the RV without help and so had decided to lie up until he could find some British ground forces. There was a possibility that Eoin had either died on landing, or during the skirmish reported in the intercepted enemy message, or shortly after landing, being too injured to escape the worst of the flash flooding.

The difficulty was that whenever any further reports were received, they tended to raise as many questions as they answered. In October 1944 more snippets were obtained when two survivors from Eoin's stick, Pcts James (Jim) Blakeney and Roy David Davies, arrived in Britain having been released from an Italian PoW camp in September 1943 and spending a year in Switzerland.

The report of Pct Davies is the more detailed of the two – Pct Blakeney's account is short and essentially mirrors that of Davies (see Appendix I), which states:

> This soldier proceeded on operations in the Western Desert on 16th November, 1941, and was dropped in a gale over the DZ. After a rough landing he lay up until daylight when he met some other members of the operational party, which included Lt. MacGoneagle [*sic*], Sgt. Lazenby, Cpl. Westwater, Cpl. Evans, Pcts. McKay, MacCormick, Malone, Morris, Robertson, and Haldreth. The last-named member died later. Lt. MacGoneagle [*sic*], who was badly injured, died the same day. Members of the party commenced to make their way to the L.R.D.G. RV, but got lost in the desert.
>
> They had no supplies, as all their containers were lost. On making their way to the coastal sector, they were picked up by Italian Guards on the edge of TMIMI airfield.

No indication is given that Eoin (or Hildreth) was buried – the understanding being that he would have been left to fend for himself, and having never been heard from again, was presumed to have died shortly afterwards.

Sadly, despite various inconsistencies, their accounts were never developed further – back in action for the first time since their release, both men were killed early the following year while on their first operation in northern Germany with the SAS to support the Allied advance. They died on 8 April 1945 during Operation Archway, part of a force of 300 under the command of Lieutenant Colonel Brian Franks.

Another report that raised more questions than it answered was the hearsay account of a discussion between former members of 11 (Scottish) Commando in 1941, reported in 2003. Jim Gornall, a former member of 11 Commando (but not of 'L' Detachment), recalled that after being captured by the Italians following Operation Flipper and held at a PoW temporary holding station, he came across Billy Morris – a member of Eoin's stick who had been captured by the Italians. Both men were veterans of the Litani River operation. Gornall said:

It was Billy Morris, who had been with me on the Litani job. He'd left 11 Commando for the SAS, and had been on the practice jump when two of them had been killed – [Billy was] the next one in line. The storm that had jiggered up our operation had jiggered up the SAS operation as well. Billy Morris had been with Eoin McGonigal, an 11 Commando officer, on the Tmimi raid, and they had jumped into the storm and were scattered all over the place. Billy Morris told me that he'd last seen McGonigal in his parachute harness, dead, with his body up against a wrecked Messerschmitt 109. He'd landed, but had been dragged by the storm and killed.

This contradicts Davies and Blakeney, who both reported finding Eoin alive the following day with other members of the stick and made no mention of any Messerschmitt. It is also not clear how at the time they came together the men would have been anywhere near an airfield – unless this was a plane which they had happened upon in the desert. Also notable is the reference to how Morris had last seen Eoin lying against the plane, again not buried.

Yet further accounts assert that Eoin had been captured and died while a prisoner of war. Patrick Marrinan in his book on Blair Mayne (*Colonel Paddy*) and Richard Doherty in *In the Ranks of Death* wrote: 'Paddy's friend, McGonigal, was missing and it was hoped that at worst he might be a prisoner. In fact, he died, only a few days after his capture, from injuries received when landing.'

So we have one account indicating that although at least initially alive, Eoin was left behind either dead (but not buried) or possibly with injuries too severe to allow him to continue; another that he was seen lying back against an old Messerschmitt – dead or, as he was not buried, perhaps dying and taking cover from the approaching storm; and a third which asserted that he had been taken prisoner and died in a PoW camp.

These raise several questions. It is said that no supply canisters were recovered, but no mention is made of how the men may have ended up in the same place if two men had died on landing or soon thereafter (Pct Hildreth and Eoin). Were they found and brought together? Or was any consideration given to continuing in some way with the operation (e.g. conducting reconnaissance or linking up with one of the other two sticks in their area)? Bear in mind that although the gale-force winds had caused havoc the previous night, the torrential rains and flash flooding did not arrive in the area until about 1730. Quite how, on landing, Eoin would have been anywhere near any planes (whether wrecked or functioning) is not known, let alone how, despite his injuries, he could have managed to rejoin his men following the jump. Did he manage to release his parachute or had it caught on something (the plane) and collapsed, bringing him to a stop?

What we can say is that Eoin was probably left in the desert, possibly sitting back against a wrecked Messerschmitt taking cover from the advancing weather. Whether or not he was assisted in getting there from where he had landed (and freed from his parachute), it seems that he had been badly injured and was either unable or refused to go on with the remaining members of his stick, as to do so would only have slowed them down. Perhaps he had insisted on staying behind to see if he could salvage something of the operation and take his chances sitting out the approaching storm in the hope that he would be found later by Allied ground forces or the LRDG.

In reality, this would have been putting a brave face on things. At the very least, Eoin must have been badly weakened and had limited mobility after the drop – he had probably been dragged across the rocks by his parachute and if alive, was lucky. Johnny Cooper, a member of Blair's stick who jumped in the later and slightly better conditions, recalls hitting the ground hard, without warning, in the dark and then being dragged at 30mph across the rock-strewn desert floor. He only came to a stop when his chute snagged on a camel thorn bush – the game of dodgems would otherwise have carried on. Survival in these circumstances was a lottery. If hurt on impact, it is unlikely Eoin could have escaped from his parachute. His men all knew the chances of his getting out of the desert without them were slim at best. However, they had all agreed that any injured members of the stick would be left behind. As their leader, Eoin would himself have emphasized this, but we shall never now know for sure what happened. The few contemporary accounts are contradictory and/or incomplete, and the opportunities to clear them up appear to be long gone.

However, a further two interview statements have emerged, one of which directly contradicts the reports of Blakeney and Davies – and what is particularly surprising is that one of the two is actually by Davies. These are PoW statements marked 'Top Secret' taken from Pct John Robertson and Pct Davies in July and August 1944 respectively (extracts at Appendix G). The statements pre-date the Davies and Blakeney reports (which are believed to have been prepared for the purposes of the SAS War Diary in 1945) but only by at most several months – which makes the inconsistencies in the accounts by Davies all the harder to comprehend.

Robertson's PoW statement essentially mirrors the Blakeney and Davies reports but clarifies that the men were captured at Tmimi on 21 November 1941:

> Dropped by parachute 16.11.41, 20 miles south of Tmimi Aerodrome without Arms (except revolver) ammunition ar[sic] food or water. Officer i/c party killed on landing. Forced to go to Tmimi after five days without water.

This suggests that the men remained in the vicinity of the drop zone, potentially waiting for (although no reason is given) Allied ground support, before leaving for Tmimi, a march of 20 miles. It was not quite a 'journey' in the original sense of the word, and one the men could well have accomplished within a day's walk (unless incapacitated through injury or lack of rations).

However, Davies' PoW statement contradicts both Robertson's and his own later report in a number of seemingly inexplicable ways:

> Date and Place of Capture: 23.11.41 South West of Tobruk … Dropped from the air, by plane, wrong place, no supplies, marched six days, and picked up by the Germans, South West of Tobruk.

This indicates that Davies left the drop zone on the 18th (the weather conditions eased that morning), marched for six days towards Tobruk (presumably with the intention of connecting with Eighth Army forces) but was captured on the 23rd by the Germans (who would have been in the midst of trying to mount an assault on Allied-held Tobruk).

Notably, Davies makes no reference to Hildreth or Eoin, or indeed to the fate of the remainder of the stick.

If it is correct that the men were dropped just 20 miles from Tmimi, but some (at least Davies) were then captured near Tobruk, it suggests a relatively circuitous route – bypassing Gazala – although still one which could have been achieved over a six-day march (albeit without rations).

It has been suggested that the inconsistencies in these accounts are down to human error and the frailties of memory, especially after two years spent as prisoners of war. Nevertheless, the errors are glaring, and while it is easily understood how mistakes can be made over dates (Italian hospital admission dates would suggest there were some timing-related errors), it is more difficult to understand how one might confuse the following: having marched for six days, instead of one, from the DZ to Tmimi; being captured near Tobruk as opposed to Tmimi (which lie in opposite directions); and facing German rather than Italian gun muzzles – the last thing Davies would have experienced before spending the next two years thinking about it in an Italian prison. It is notable also that in his later report Davies makes specific reference to having being captured on the edge of Tmimi airfield – again, a detail that he is not likely to have confused with being captured somewhere nondescript south-west of Tobruk.

In fact, looking again at Davies' report, it is also noticeable that in referring to the capture at Tmimi airfield, he distances himself from what is reported by saying 'they' and not 'we' – although this might also be the result of his comments being transcribed by the author of the diary and not recorded in the first person:

> *They* had no supplies, as all their containers were lost. On making *their* way to the coastal sector, *they* were picked up by Italian Guards on the edge of TMIMI airfield.

Like a Libyan oasis after November rains, these accounts provide fertile ground for conspiracies to bloom in the normally arid army bureaucracy. The reports which exist are exasperatingly short and lacking in detail (possibly deliberately so); they are inconsistent and contradictory (and oddly, even more so when by the same person); the two senior officers on the Gazala operation (Stirling and Lewes) appear not to have prepared any reports at all (and one of them was in the habit of otherwise writing profusely); and there is a suggestion that when the War Diary was being compiled, an effort was made to fill certain gaps and introduce an element of uniformity. Even if we put to one side the questions which could be asked about what happened to the members of Stirling's stick, when the available evidence relating to Eoin's stick is looked at in the context of an operation which went so badly wrong, one could easily be forgiven for thinking that, perhaps quite understandably, this was an event that those involved wished to forget. To borrow a quote from the film *Desert Fox*, while 'Victory has a hundred fathers, defeat is an orphan.'

There is plenty of material on which to base speculation – perhaps too much, which is why so little has ever been said. However, it would seem reasonable to conclude that like Stirling's stick (albeit for quite different reasons), Eoin's also failed to remain together and ended up going in two quite different directions. The Davies 'group' (although it may have just been Davies alone) would appear to have waited until the conditions eased on 18 November before marching past Gazala towards Tobruk, to try to find the RV, the other sticks and/or the LRDG or Eighth Army forces. The Robertson group would appear to have lain up at the drop zone for five days, before being forced through lack of rations to march towards the coast on 21 November, becoming lost and then being captured at Tmimi airfield.

It is not clear why the latter group waited at the drop zone for so long – especially if they were fit and mobile enough to make it to Tmimi, despite having had no water or food for five days. It is most unlikely that the Davies group would have been tasked with arranging a rescue – it had been firmly agreed that those who were less mobile would have to fend for themselves.

Moreover, if Eoin had in fact been found dead at some point, why would he not have been buried? The operation would appear to have been abandoned, the men seem to have waited for several days at the drop zone and they were equipped with small shovels. While one author has indicated that Eoin was quietly buried in the sand before the men then struck out for the RV point, there is no evidence for this and similarly no mention whatsoever of what was done with Lance Corporal Hildreth. Had there been a burial (or burials), and had it happened in the vicinity of an old Messerschmitt Bf 109, one would expect that coordinates (just 20 miles from Tmimi) would have been recorded.

So the speculation continues. Given the absence of any reference to a burial, we can speculate that Eoin may well have been alive but badly injured and/or not sufficiently mobile to continue. Quite why some of his men would have stayed in the area rather than setting off at the first opportunity is not clear. It is also possible that at least part of the stick may never have located their comrades and, becoming lost, ended up marching towards Tobruk. In any event, it is possible that part of the stick may have waited until the 21st before striking out towards the coast and the track to the RV, leaving Eoin sheltering under the wing of an old Messerschmitt and perhaps slowly lighting up a final smoke from his ever-present silver cigarette case.

Alone in the desert, but not alone. A surreal situation. We do not know if Hildreth's loss was made known to him, but Eoin was not to know that men from the other sticks had also been left to fend for themselves in the desert – while he was sitting up against the Messerschmitt, others were scattered to the wind and/or still marching, trying to find a way home. Imagine a bird's-eye view of the scene: 'We are all sitting in the middle of wrecked hope and broken dreams.' (Kipling)

What could he have been thinking, maintaining a lonely vigil in the desert? Just a couple of weeks shy of his twenty-first birthday, he must have wondered what was happening at that moment back home in Malone Road. It was a Monday and his father would have been at work. Perhaps his mother was in touch with Ambrose and Paddy, making plans for their wedding and wondering whether Eoin would ever be allowed any leave. He would miss the wedding and he would not be home for Christmas. The family would have known nothing about what he was doing or where he was. We know from his letters how he would have loved to have been back in the Adair Arms having a thick pint of Guinness with Ambrose and the rest of the Ulster Rifles. In fact, it was Ambrose's birthday at the weekend (Saturday the 22nd), and no doubt, a few beers would be downed. But Eoin was also proud to have been selected for 'L' Detachment and of his new title of Parachute-Lieutenant – he was the unit's youngest officer and responsible for a lot of its training. He had wished that Ambrose and some of the other Rifles could have joined him, for he had ended up in command of some of the best men he had served with. Still, this wasn't what he'd had in mind – he had always been one of the best at whatever he'd done – how could he be sitting here in this state? Was he scared? If alive, it can't have been much fun watching his men march off. He'd have wondered how Blair and the others had got on – only five of the eleven men in Eoin's stick were reported as surviving the jump and they were later captured; one had died and the others were unaccounted for until nearly the end of the war. The other sticks would have probably experienced similar casualties. Who else was sitting out there alone in this godforsaken desert? His thoughts may also have turned to his stories; for all his imagination and creativity, there appeared to be no escape open to him on this occasion – although that did not mean he couldn't light up a final smoke, just as the hero in his story 'Escape' had done when walking away from his old life.

It had not been so long since Eoin had left the Rifles in Ballymena, but it must have felt like an age in his young life – the Cameronians in Aberdeen, Arran, Sierra Leone, Cape Town, Alexandria, Port Said, Palestine, Litani, Cyprus, Kabrit and finally Libya, in the desert, alone, sheltering somewhat surprisingly from wind and rain and perhaps reminded of a very poor day in Ballygally. How did he get to the Messerschmitt? How long did he stay under its shelter? Could he move at all? Was he armed? With recovery or escape unlikely, did he decide to use whatever means he had at his disposal to inflict at least some damage on the enemy? It would have appealed to him given his love at school of Cuchulainn's 'one against many' mythological exploits in Ulster. Could there really have been something to the intercepted enemy message reported by Blair? Or did he just drift off after one final smoke from his lucky cigarette case, thinking well, at least the bloody 'Eyeties' and 'Jerries' never got me.

Intriguingly, Eoin's men (or at least some of them) were the only unit to have made it to an intended target, Tmimi airfield – albeit apparently by mistake. While it might have made sense to head towards the coast in order to link up with the ancient Trig al-Abd caravan route towards the RV point, the fact they tried to do so only after the initial deadline of 0700 on 20 November suggests they may have concluded that capture by the Italians represented their best prospect of survival. It simply cannot be that they were taken prisoner having wandered into Tmimi airfield by mistake. Nevertheless, there is no mention in the sparse interview notes of any intention to gather surveillance material or perhaps do some damage with their revolvers and whatever else came to hand. As recorded by Blair in

Plane wreckage, Tobruk, Libya. (*Moussar*)

his report, it appears that Tmimi was very lightly guarded; apart from one tent, there were few signs of activity. There is very little information as to what exactly happened, and there seemed for many years little prospect of anything further emerging from the limited records that were kept.

Yet, many years after the war, David Stirling highlighted one further theory of what might have happened to Eoin. It would seem that even if Eoin had been badly injured in the drop, he was neither entirely finished nor would he have lost the determination to leave one final mark on the war. David Stirling, knowing Eoin as he did, believed there might well be significantly more to discover. In an interview recorded in 1987 (long after the reports from Davies and Blakeney had come to light) and retained on a digital file by the Imperial War Museum, Stirling had the following to say in response to a question about the men who hadn't made it back from Operation Squatter:

Yes, but McGonigal, who was a huge character of a guy and Paddy's greatest friend. There was a theory that he got onto his landing ground and had enough bombs to get ahead with it because the one that he was attacking … when … [the Italians/Germans] retired from this particular landing ground … [the one which] McGonigal was responsible for covering, there were about 18 aircraft all with holes in them and the petrol systems buggered up and looking as if [McGonigal] didn't have the explosives necessary but [he must have] got in there, yes, to put them out of operation because [subsequently] when we attacked (which involved an advance period of about two days reconnaissance from an escarpment overlooking the airbase that gave us the opportunity to familiarise ourselves with the layout/goings on, etc.) … [the men in my troop] put it to me that it was his [McGonigal's] work; that it was consistent; that [McGonigal] wouldn't have been able to function [in the wet on that night]; that [McGonigal] had a limited amount of stuff … and probably no explosive. But … it was something which was never fully explained … we [then] forgot about it … But I think, in fairness to McGonigal, if any research could be done into it …

This theory was mentioned earlier, in 1958, in Virginia Coles, *The Phantom Major*:

There was no trace of McGonigal's group until the Eighth Army went into Gazala in January. Then a story gained currency that a British raiding party had attacked one of the Gazala landing grounds in November and destroyed a number of planes. Stirling believes this must have been McGonigal's party, although he has never been able to track down or confirm the report.

It is an extraordinary revelation but one which to some extent ties in with the intercepted enemy message that Blair referred to in his letter to Ambrose written on his return to camp immediately after Operation Squatter, 'that one of [Eoin's] party had been killed, but that they had wiped out a large party of Germans and had blown up an important dump'.

The only other explanation later suggested for why so many planes had been 'buggered up' in the makeshift way described by Stirling is that the Germans had done it themselves rather than leave them to the advancing Allied forces. However, such a theory is unlikely for a number of reasons. First, even though it is now clear that a small number of enemy aircraft were in fact sabotaged by retreating Axis troops, an Independent Report on 'Damage caused to planes and Luftwaffe Airfields in Libya and Egypt between 1935 and 1945' (H.L. deZeng IV, extracts at Appendix G) confirms that only four planes were recorded as having been destroyed at Tmimi airfield in this way. However, the Independent Report records that twenty-three aircraft in total were found damaged in a makeshift fashion at Tmimi when the advancing Allied forces arrived in January 1942.

Also interesting is the reference in the Independent Report to the ignition of a fuel dump at Tmimi on 20 November – again echoing the contents of the intercepted message referred to by Blair in his letter to Ambrose of 27 November (albeit that it may have been connected with a low-level RAF attack carried out the same evening).

As for the Gazala airfields, the Independent Report notes that seventy-one abandoned Axis aircraft were found on the three Gazala landing grounds when they were overrun by British forces in December 1941; and no record is noted of any planes that may have been sabotaged by retreating troops.

Moreover, although we know that a small number of other planes were bombed by Allied aircraft in the weeks leading up to the enemy's withdrawal, the numbers still fall a long way short of the total number of aircraft discovered by Stirling to have been put out of action 'with holes in them and the petrol systems buggered up'. For example, although the Independent Report does not specify the condition in which the seventy-one planes were left abandoned at the Gazala airfields, it does state that only fourteen planes were damaged as a result of Allied bombing raids between 16 November and the arrival of British forces in December.

Besides, this type of damage would not necessarily have been done at close quarters, but it could not have been caused by Allied aircraft dropping bombs. For example, with only four aircraft at Tmimi confirmed as having been sabotaged by the retreating troops (described as having been 'demolished to prevent capture'), it is far from clear how the remaining nineteen could have been put out of action in the much more makeshift manner described by Stirling ('with holes in them and the petrol systems buggered up … and looking as if [McGonigal] didn't have the explosives necessary').

The one inconsistency concerns the airfield in question. In his interview Stirling implies it was Gazala – presumably because these were the airfields that the first three sticks were targeting. However, as a result of being blown off course by gale-force winds on the 16th, Eoin's stick appears to have been dropped closer to Tmimi than Gazala. The reference in Stirling's much earlier biography also connects the speculation surrounding the discovery of these planes with the arrival of Allied forces at Gazala, but crucially clarifies that this discovery occurred in January 1942 – not December 1941. While Allied forces had taken control of the area from December 1941, the Independent Report is quite specific in recording that although abandoned planes were discovered at Gazala in December 1941, the discovery by advancing Allied troops of damaged planes at Tmimi took place in January 1942.

The references to the destruction of a fuel dump in Blair's letter to Ambrose, as well as in the Independent Report which gives a date of the evening of 20 November (i.e. the evening before Eoin's stick was captured at Tmimi); the fact that only four out of twenty-three planes are recorded in the Independent Report as having been sabotaged by retreating troops; the implausibility that Allied bombers could have caused damage of the improvised/makeshift type described by Stirling; and the fact that 'buggered-up' aircraft were discovered by advancing Allied troops in January 1942, a date which correlates with the same reference in the Independent Report: all these factors point to Tmimi as having been the landing ground that led to the rumours about Eoin's stick that were circulating amongst the SAS in January 1942 and were then repeated by Stirling in his biography in 1958 and interview in 1987.

Chapter 34

An Unknown Soldier

As for Blair, it is still not known what information he may have been working with or what he could have hoped to find – SAS records contain no information other than some of the incomplete reports mentioned above. He may have heard back from Pct MacKay, the PoW from Eoin's stick who was being held in Genova and who he said he had written to – but no correspondence has surfaced from Blair's 'War Chest' of personal papers. However, we do know that he never forgot his Ulster comrade; indeed, the unit's first padre, Fraser McLuskey, confirmed that 'Paddy often spoke of McGonigal (and himself sent a copy of Malcolm James' book to Eoin's mother, Margaret in May 1946 ('Born of the Desert') 'With the compliments of the Officers and Men of 1 S.A.S. Regiment).' It seems there may also have been a sense of responsibility or duty on Blair's part to the McGonigal family – in a letter to his mother dated 27 September

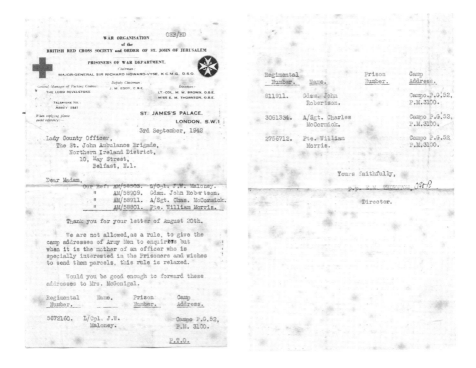

1942, Blair makes a passing but telling reference to Eoin's mother: 'I had a letter from Mrs McGonigal. I am awfully sorry for her but she is very plucky [, it will] soon be a year now since Eoin was killed.'

Blair's use of the word 'killed' instead of 'died' or 'went missing' is intriguing – it indicates that he must by then have heard back from one of the PoWs. This is precisely what Margaret had been trying to achieve – she was still working with minimal information about what could have happened to her son and so acting on Blair's suggestion in his letter of May 1942, she contacted the Red Cross. She wanted to send care parcels to the men in Eoin's stick who had been captured as well as find out if they had any information regarding Eoin.

Blair did eventually make it back to the Gazala/Tmimi region towards the end of the SAS' time in the desert, but without success – whether anything was recovered is not known, but Eoin's body was not found. Blair wrote to Eoin's mother to express his regret at this, and on 2 June 1943 Margaret replied:

My Dear Blair

I have just got your very kind letter & really feel I can't thank you enough for all your great kindness. It was terribly good of you to have gone to Gazala & taken so much trouble to try to find Eoin's grave. I know he did not have an identity disk, I think he just wanted to be an unknown soldier, but I had hoped he had been found and buried as I meant to go to Gazala after the war – however, you know how much he hated a fuss so it is perhaps <u>better</u> as it is – just as he wanted. I miss him so much – more in fact every day, but I know he is safe & happy & terribly interested in what you are all doing. I am sure he has been with you in your operations since he died. I always feel he is very near me – it helps me to carry on until we meet again …

Ambrose has moved to the seaside & can't get letters from me for a bit – he is very fit & very keen on his work – his leg is holding up well although I can't imagine how he ever was passed for parachute work!

There is a little book just published 'Combined Operations' which tells a good deal about the 11th Scottish Commando, & also about the Rommel show, there is a little paragraph of two lines which I fancy refers to Eoin's thing.

His kit has come home, but not the dagger. I suppose it was lost at […].

Thank you very much for all your goodness – it has made such a difference.

Yours very sincerely
Margaret McGonigal.

Margaret's reference to Ambrose relates to the fact that, having recovered from training-related injuries, he was then based on the south coast for Commando operations along the French coast.

Like so many other mothers, Margaret was clearly struggling to come to terms with the fact that all she had of her youngest son were the regimental badges (never worn), some photos sent by Blair with Eoin's kit (but no dagger or cigarette case) and the briefest of references to the Litani River operation in some wartime propaganda. The absence of any clear information about what had actually happened to Eoin must have been impossible to bear – although the knowledge that Blair, a family friend, was

The pamphlet referred to by Margaret in her letter to Blair.

searching for Eoin and had not given up on him must have meant a great deal to her. Eoin may have been an unknown soldier in the desert but he still had a friend out there looking for him.

As is also clear from Margaret's letter, whether because of something that Blair wrote or what she had inferred from the army's notification, she clearly believed that Eoin's body had not been buried. As it is to be presumed that his men would probably have buried him in a shallow grave if he had died before they set out for the RV, the only conclusion is that, being too injured to make the RV unaided, he must have been left (most probably at his own insistence) to fend for himself while his men attempted to reach the RV before the storm hit. It should be noted that Jock Lewes had instructed the men that, as a matter of operational practice, they should not waste time with burials when a mission remained to be completed – the distinction in this instance is that it would seem Eoin's men had decided to abort the mission, remaining at the DZ a number of days before eventually attempting to make their way to the RV instead.

Implicitly acknowledging the mystery surrounding what happened, the Commando Veterans archive notes Eoin's death as follows:

EOIN MCGONIGAL
Rank: Lieutenant
Unit/Base: 11 Commando
Regiment/Corps: Royal Ulster Rifles
Service: Army
Service number: 97290
Died: Tuesday, November 18, 1941
Killed in action or died of wounds
Age: 20
Cemetery/Memorial: Alamein Memorial

Last ever photo of Eoin, taken by Blair at Kabrit.

Chapter 35

Ambrose after Demob: 'The Black Prince'

After demobilization, and following an accelerated completion of his legal studies at Queen's University, Belfast, Ambrose was called to the Belfast Bar in 1948. Unlike the more mixed response, if any, that a returning British soldier (even a decorated one) would have received in Ireland, Ambrose in going north was granted a dispensation from the requirement for a 'long-form' degree in the light of his war service. However, in the same way as being a senior Catholic lawyer in the North had complicated his father's career, Ambrose's place of birth, education, religious background and, in particular, service with the British special forces made life less than straightforward for him and his family in Belfast.

Ambrose became senior crown prosecutor for Co. Down in 1964 before being appointed a judge of the High Court in March 1968 – at the beginning of some of the worst times during the Troubles in the North, underlined

Ambrose on inspection at the Assizes with the High Sheriff.

by a request in August 1969 from Ireland's Taoiseach, Jack Lynch, for a UN peacekeeping force to be sent to Northern Ireland. The Royal Ulster Constabulary was no longer seen as an impartial police force, and the Irish Government did not consider the deployment of British troops to be acceptable, let alone capable of restoring sustainable peace.

Michael McRitchie, who began his career in journalism with the *Belfast Telegraph*, later joining the *News Letter*, returned to Belfast as a teenager in the 1950s having grown up overseas, attending various secular schools in England. McRitchie was 'totally baffled by the fundamentalist bigotry permeating the two communities' and recalls

> the complicated background against which [Ambrose] sought to establish his legal career. At the time, Unionism or Orangeism dominated society, such that the City was required to close down on Sundays, and even playgrounds and park swings would be chained up well into the 1970s. When [I] began reporting, [I] observed that such divisions were notable across countless aspects of life, such as the job advertisements which called for: 'Young man (R.C.) required for van deliveries' or 'Experienced mechanic (Prot.) requires employment'. More subtle discrimination permeated other areas such as the gerrymandering of public housing and the award of local building contracts, etc.

It is not clear whether any of this necessarily affected barristers, but McRitchie observed that even lower court clients would favour solicitors of their own religious persuasion.

Also relevant was the fact that even when compared to England in the mid-50s, there was great respect for servicemen within the community. For example, McRitchie's father was surprised to find bus conductors refusing to take airmen's fares when in uniform and on their way to the RAF's station at Aldergrove, north-west of Belfast. McRitchie noted:

> Many people would have been aware of Ambrose's war record, if only through his association with Blair Mayne. However, it was never something he cared to discuss, even though approached to do so by Jack Sayers, the highly renowned liberal editor of the *Belfast Telegraph*. Sayers was himself a former Lt Cdr RNVR who survived when HMS *Courageous* was torpedoed by a German U-boat west of Mizen Head, Ireland in 1939, with the loss of 518 men. He asked to do a piece on Ambrose's time in the army but Ambrose was unwilling to talk to him.

Worth noting in this context is that during the 1950s and 60s the professions were forbidden to advertise in any way. Even to allow one's name to appear with a quote in a general news story could bring down the wrath of the Bar Council. As such, it was not until the 1960s that counsel even began to be identified in newspaper reports, with references otherwise generally limited to the appearances paragraph at the end of a report as the only opportunity of getting one's name into the public eye and establishing your reputation.

Nevertheless, there was a strong belief that justice should literally be seen to be done, and therefore the papers included column after column of detailed court reports, which necessitated that reports were accurate in all respects. While court reports still appear in some papers today, they are generally limited to the headline-grabbing cases of the day – not the shoplifting and other petty crime cases that were reported in the past. Part of the reason for this is that newspapers were very much the primary source of news for people in the Province. There was no mains electricity in many rural areas until the early 1960s and even then, the BBC Home and Light entertainment programmes would not reach those vast areas which remained out of range of the BBC transmitter near Lisburn. As such, counsel and journalists regularly worked together in mutual interest.

In 1975 Ambrose was appointed to the Court of Appeal and the Privy Council, at which time he was also knighted. Regrettably, because of Ambrose's position in the judiciary, the McGonigals were forced to spend this time under constant surveillance and protection. Indeed, Ambrose himself, nicknamed 'The Black Prince' during his time on the Bench, carried a handgun under his robes at all times and slept with one close by because of the threat presented by (not exclusively) Republican paramilitaries.

The threat was highlighted in an article by Kevin Myers for the *Independent* newspaper. 'Some questions we should never have to ask' listed the following Catholic judges in Northern Ireland at the time of the Sunningdale (power-sharing) Agreement in 1973: William Staunton, Ambrose McGonigal, Michael Nicholson, Turlough O'Donnell, Garret McGrath, William Travers, William Doyle and Rory Conaghan. Myers went on to query how it could be that 'the PIRA murdered judges Conaghan, Doyle, Staunton and Travers [a factual error: Judge Travers survived, but his daughter was murdered], tried to murder judges O'Donnell, McGrath and McGonigal and that it then declared the absence of Catholic judges was proof of a biased judiciary.'

Others who could have been added to this list included Martin McBirney QC, a magistrate who was shot at home in 1974, and in later years, Lord

Chief Justice Sir Maurice Gibson (blown up in 1987), Sir Eoin Higgins and Lord Justice Sir Donald Murray, whose homes were attacked. The shooting of magistrate Martin McBirney and Judge Rory Conaghan in 1974 prompted comments echoing those of Myers, that 'they were killed because liberal Catholic judges and magistrates' were 'more dangerous to the IRA cause than Protestant bigots.' (Roisin Ingle: 'This idea that victims shouldn't speak … it's moral blackmail', *The Irish Times*). Author Tony Geraghty notes in *The Irish War: The Hidden Conflict Between the IRA and British Intelligence*, 'A barrister who was intimidated into the comparatively safe anonymity of the English bar' confided that life in Northern Ireland

> becomes a living nightmare, looking around your shoulder each moment, considering, 'Should I do this? Go there? Are the wife and children safe to take that picnic on the beach this afternoon?' You get tense, knowing the moment you relax and don't take simple precautions, like looking underneath your car before getting into it, could be fatal. In the end some, like myself, say life's just not worth living like that.

Ambrose's nickname, 'The Black Prince', was conferred on him by colleagues at the NI Bar because of his intimidating demeanour and special forces background. It has been described as an 'astonishing compliment' – despite the 'brutal reputation' of the original holder of the name – since few at the NI Bar were given nicknames. In this regard, the late Richard 'Dick' Ferguson QC described Ambrose as having an undefinable quality such that one often wondered if he might pull an Uzi (submachine gun) out from under the bench if you annoyed him and gun you down. Sir Donnell Deeny, former Lord Justice of Appeal in Northern Ireland, has described it as a somewhat 'terrifying quality' and recalls observing one senior silk literally shaking in anticipation of going before Ambrose for a hearing.

'The Black Prince'.

Chapter 36

The First Death Sentence
since the Troubles Began

Ambrose was not always the distant, detached judge that his reputation might have suggested, and despite his experience of war (or perhaps because of it), there were some cases in particular which we know he found difficult to preside over. Notable in this regard was the case of Albert Edward Browne, a 28-year-old member of the Ulster Defence Association (UDA), the Unionist paramilitary group. Browne was accused of the capital murder of an RUC officer, Gordon Harran, on 15 February 1973. Under the Criminal Justice Act (NI) 1966, capital murder was defined as the murder of any constable or person acting in the service of the Crown, and although capital punishment for murder had been abolished in the rest of Great Britain in 1969, it remained the law in Northern Ireland. In short, if found guilty of a capital murder by a jury in Northern Ireland at that time, death by hanging was a mandatory sentence.

It was reported by the *Belfast Telegraph* that Constable Harran died in a hail of bullets when he and his colleague stopped a hi-jacked car containing four armed members of the UDA in October 1972. Browne had emptied all thirteen rounds of his 9mm Browning semi-automatic handgun, hitting both constables, Harran fatally in the head. Browne denied all charges, pleading in defence that in fear for his own life he had 'fired in a blind panic'. The men in the car were heavily armed and, following subsequent searches, further arms and explosives were discovered at Browne's home. It was particularly tragic since in addition to having a two-year-old son, Constable Harran's widow was pregnant at the time. Ambrose was the presiding judge, and after a three-day hearing at the Belfast City Commission (as the crown court was then known), the jury took a little over two hours to return a verdict of guilty.

Reporting for the *News Letter*, Michael McRitchie was the only journalist present at the time and recalls that as the case had been running for a few days before the jury retired, and it was by then late on a Thursday afternoon, it seemed unlikely a verdict would be returned that day. Consequently, the other reporters had gone off to the pub, but he had decided to stay; he didn't know why.

It proved fortuitous because Ambrose returned to the courtroom and there followed some discussion with counsel. It appeared procedural in nature and so, still expecting the case to be adjourned, McRitchie began to gather his things and was in the process of standing up to present the customary 'excuse me' nod to the bench. However, just at that moment, Ambrose

> glanced directly into my eyes while giving no sign of recognition – it was a look of no more than half a second yet I understood as clearly as if he had pushed me in the chest. I hastily sat down and within perhaps 15 minutes, Justice McGonigal said that the defendant had been found guilty of the capital murder of a police officer. He did not don the traditional black cap and speaking in low but clear tones, with his eyes fixed downwards apparently on the front edge of the Bench, stated: 'The sentence of this Court is that you will suffer death in the manner authorised by the law.'
>
> I do not recall if Browne showed any reaction, but everyone was stunned, and apart from a gasp from a relative you could have heard a pin drop. The sentence was chilling to hear even though we knew it was coming.
>
> Defence counsel then gave notice of appeal, which was allowed and within seconds, Justice McGonigal had gathered up his papers, and looking neither right nor left, walked briskly from his courtroom.

This accords with what is known about how Ambrose dealt with this matter beyond the courtroom – he did not speak to anyone, and was not seen for the remainder of the day having retired to his study at home, not to be disturbed. He never spoke about it, and others knew well enough not to raise it with him.

It was the first death sentence handed down since the Troubles had begun and would turn out to be the second last death sentence ever handed down in the UK – the last coming just two months later in the same court room, a controversial conviction which many years later was overturned in the case of William Holden presided over by the then Chief Justice, Lord Lowry. Holden was convicted of the shooting of a soldier based on an admission of guilt found later to have been obtained following the use of a range of torture techniques (including water-boarding) and with a gun to his head. Holden was eventually released in 1989 but his conviction, which remained active and barred him from employment, was only quashed following a review in 2012: he was fifty-eight, having been imprisoned at nineteen. His case served to illustrate perfectly why Ambrose was so clearly uncomfortable with his role in administering such a sentence. There is a suggestion it was expected that although Browne might have been convicted of manslaughter, he would be acquitted of murder, and the jury would not have sent a member of the UDA to his death. Nevertheless, Ambrose had ordered the killing of and had killed men during the war – regardless of any misgivings he may have felt with regard to capital punishment, he would have recognized the original rationale behind the sentence for murder of a member of the RUC. As he demonstrated throughout his career, irrespective of any personal reservations and despite the fact that capital punishment had already been abolished elsewhere in Britain and abolition would inevitably follow in Northern Ireland, he was bound to apply the law in the manner prescribed. He did so unceremoniously and left.

Just two months later (April 1973), under pressure, the British Secretary of State for Northern Ireland, Willie Whitelaw, commuted Browne's death sentence to life imprisonment. Three months later, capital punishment in Northern Ireland was finally abolished under the NI (Emergency Provisions) Act 1973.

McRitchie does not recall encountering Ambrose again, since he later moved to the paper's features department. However, he was not sorry to have left the courts behind, as he returned a few months later to find a very different atmosphere, 'with Troubles cases dominating the lists and my friends on the Bench and court staff clearly showing the strain of those terrible times, with worse to come'. As for Ambrose, McRitchie noted that his overall impression was of a man who was 'icily reserved yet willing and perhaps even wishing to help young people such as myself. Above all, he had the most commanding if indeed forbidding presence of any man I have met, and I shall never forget him.'

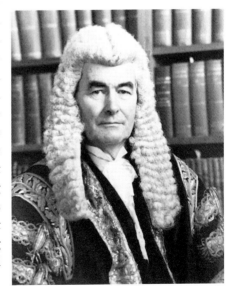

Chapter 37

McElhone: 'shot in the back'

Despite the contradictions of Ambrose's position, he was known for taking positions contrary to those advocated by the Government in a number of notable cases. One example was his dissenting judgment in the Court of Appeal on 'the McElhone case' in 1975.

Mr McElhone had been shot in the back and killed, while unarmed, after he refused to stop when ordered to by a soldier on patrol in South Armagh. It was acknowledged that the soldier knew he was unarmed, but he shot him because he honestly believed him to be a member of the IRA. The soldier was acquitted on the grounds that he did not intend to kill or seriously injure McElhone, he only wanted to apprehend him. The decision was referred to the Court of Appeal to determine whether, even if he had intended to kill or seriously wound an individual believed to be a member of the IRA, the soldier could have committed a crime. The majority concluded the soldier's actions could be reasonable. Ambrose did not agree.

Ambrose took the view that as there was no evidence the soldier feared for his or his comrades' lives if McElhone escaped, the decision to shoot him was clearly unreasonable. McElhone's only crime, if any – that of failing to stop and answer questions – carried a maximum penalty of six months and/or a £400 fine; not death or serious injury as determined by an individual soldier.

Ambrose was in particular unhappy that *suspected* membership of the IRA could warrant being shot at by the army, commenting:

> Does that mean that the man who is a known sympathiser but not a member of the Provisional IRA may also be shot and killed if he runs away because in the future his sympathies may crystallise and he may become a card-carrying member and be required for questioning and arrest?

The case later went before the House of Lords, but they declined to intervene on the basis that the question of reasonableness should always be a matter for a jury. Of course, the fact that it was a report by one of their members, Lord Diplock, that led to trial without jury in Northern Ireland – the so-called 'Diplock Courts' which permitted judges to draw inferences from the silence of defendants – did not help to ease concerns. Indeed, Lord Diplock took the view that one could not rule out the possibility that a suspected member of the IRA could get away, alert 'fellow' IRA members 'lurking in the neighbourhood' and then ambush the soldiers. Lord Diplock went very close to giving credence to Ambrose's fear that the shooting of suspected members of the IRA was being licensed when he commented:

> In the other scale of the balance it would be open to the jury to take the view that it would not be unreasonable to assess the kind of harm to be averted by preventing the accused's escape as even greater – the killing or wounding of members of the patrol by terrorists in ambush, and the effect of this success by members of the Provisional IRA in encouraging the continuance of the armed insurrection and all the misery and destruction of life and property that terrorist activity in Northern Ireland has entailed.

Diplock's concluding comments making clear which way the balance appeared to him to tilt.

Another case from 1975 was reported by the *Belfast Telegraph* as evidence of Ambrose's willingness to 'impose the full rigours of the law on Protestant and Roman Catholics alike who appeared before him on charges arising out of the troubles':

> [Ambrose] denounced the Ulster Defence Association at the old Belfast City Commission as a 'vicious and brutalizing organisation'. This came on the day that he sentenced two girls to be detained during the pleasure of the Secretary of State for the murder of 31-year-old Ann Ogilby, who was hooded, bound and 'rompered' and battered to death in Sandy Row UDA hall. Nine other women and a man were also given sentences. Passing sentence, he said: 'What appears before me under the name of the UDA is gun law, a vicious and brutalizing organization of persons who take the law into their own hands and who, by kangaroo courts and the infliction of physical brutality, terrorise a neighbourhood through intimidation, and rule an area of this city.'

Similarly, on 4 February 1977, in a case which has continuing resonance today, Ambrose sentenced five members of a notorious unit from the Black Watch regiment for planting ammunition in cars belonging to innocent civilians during the course of 'searches' they were conducting in Andersonstown, West Belfast in September and October 1975. Some of the soldiers who were jailed were separately implicated in the shooting of 17-year-old Leo Norney in Ardmonagh Gardens on 13 September 1975. Despite attempts to justify the killing on the basis of a claim by the soldiers that Norney was a gunman, it was discovered in 2013 by the Historical Enquiries Team that evidence of firearms residue said by the British Army's Special Investigation Branch to have been discovered on his clothing was allegedly fabricated; he was not involved with any terrorist organization and was simply in the wrong place at the wrong time, getting out of a taxi with his 17-year-old fiancée on their way to do some babysitting. At the time of writing it is understood a fresh inquest into his death will be held in Banbridge Court House on 25 April 2022.

Upon sentencing the soldiers, Ambrose is reported to have 'denounced' them as being 'no better than terrorists … they had descended to the level of the terrorists and criminals they were supposed to be policing in Northern Ireland.'

While Ambrose would naturally have had some insight into and understanding of the soldiers' position, it is worth noting, in a curious parallel, that some thirty odd years earlier, Eoin's stick on Operation Squatter included Billy Morris, a member of the Black Watch – it is an honourable regiment with a formidable history and reputation, its kilted soldiers called the 'Ladies from Hell' by the Germans in the Great War.

In short, as some of these cases show, it was a time when conflicting loyalties and sympathies were especially tested, and Ambrose was popular neither with the Provisionals nor the Unionist paramilitaries, nor indeed even sometimes with the State.

Chapter 38

'A Torturer's Charter'

Ambrose was also involved in a number of controversial cases which considered the admissibility of statements taken under the so-called Diplock rules and which permitted a degree of maltreatment of the accused.

The Diplock courts were criminal courts in Northern Ireland for non-jury trials of specified serious crimes ('scheduled offences'). They were introduced by the Northern Ireland (Emergency Provisions) Act 1973 ('the Act'), to be used for political and terrorism-related cases during the Troubles, and remained in place for over thirty years, only being abolished in 2007. Section 6(2) of the Act essentially introduced grounds on which a certain degree of maltreatment of an accused would be acceptable but stated: 'If … prima facie evidence is adduced that the accused was subjected to torture or to inhuman or degrading treatment in order to induce him to make [a] statement, the court shall, unless the prosecution satisfies them that the statement was not so obtained, exclude the statement.' 'Prima facie' implies a theoretically low standard of proof under which only such evidence as is necessary to create a rebuttable presumption that the matter asserted is true need be presented. In contrast, under the old common law rule (and for non-scheduled offences), the burden of proof is reversed such that before a confession or self-incriminating statement is admitted into evidence, it is the Crown that must first prove beyond a reasonable doubt that the statement was given freely and voluntarily, and the accused was not induced to give it by any promise of favour or menace or threats.

In R v McCormick in 1977, Ambrose conducted a detailed review of section 6(2) of the Act, including the exercise of judicial discretion to exclude evidence, described as 'an extra-statutory control over the means by which statements are obtained'. Controversially, Ambrose held that, subject to the court's overriding discretion, 'treatment of a less severe degree of treatment which though otherwise within [section 6] was not used for the purpose of inducing the accused to make [a] statement will not exclude the statement under section 6(2).' It was a nuanced point, but the judgement was nevertheless later described by one commentator as a 'torturer's charter'.

Referring to the European Commission case of 'Republic of Ireland v United Kingdom' [1976] and an earlier matter referred to as 'the Greek Case' [1969], which dealt with a review by the European Commission of the meaning assigned to terms such as 'torture' and 'inhuman treatment' as well as 'permissible conduct' under Article 3 of the European Convention on Human Rights (ECHR) from which the wording of s.6(2) of the Act derived, Ambrose noted that the Commission 'distinguished in the Greek Case between acts prohibited by [the ECHR] and what it called 'a certain roughness of treatment'. The Commission considered that such roughness was tolerated by most detainees and even taken for granted. It 'may take the form of slaps or blows of the hand on the head or face. This underlines the fact that the point up to which prisoners and the public may accept physical violence as being neither cruel nor excessive varies between different societies and even between different sections of them.'

Ambrose concluded that taking into account the relevance of the ECHR to the genesis of s.6(2), this interpretation by the European Commission 'appears to accept a degree of physical violence which could never be tolerated by the courts under the common law test and, if the words in section 6 are to be construed in the same sense as the words used in [Article 3 of the ECHR], it leaves it open to an interviewer to use a moderate degree of physical maltreatment for the purpose of inducing a person to make a statement.'

Nevertheless, Ambrose went on to say:

> That does not mean, however, that these courts will tolerate or permit physical maltreatment of a lesser degree deliberately carried out for the purpose of, or which has the effect of, inducing a person interviewed to make a statement. Not only would such conduct amount to an assault and in itself an offence under the ordinary criminal law but it would be repugnant to all principles of Justice to allow such conduct to be used as a means towards an end, however desirable that end might be made to appear and pointed to the judges' discretionary powers, which provide an extra-statutory control over the means by which statements are induced and obtained.

The decision was later criticized on the grounds that the Court had not recognized any difference between tests applied in national and international law settings, in the sense that in order to generate international concern, a much greater infringement of a person's rights and freedom may be necessary than would warrant interference by a judge upholding the rule of law on a national level. Accordingly, later cases approached this issue on the basis that it would be 'difficult … to envisage any form of physical violence which is relevant to the interrogation of a suspect in custody and which, if it had occurred, could at the same time leave a court satisfied beyond a reasonable doubt [as to the confession's voluntariness]', concluding instead that it should not be permissible to use even a 'moderate' degree of physical mistreatment to induce a confession, the international standard notwithstanding.

Still, Ambrose took the view that this was a matter for parliament not the courts – concerned as to how a potentially unfettered use of a court's discretion could negate the intended effect of s.6. In his opinion, 'Judicial discretion should not be exercised so as to defeat the will of parliament.'

Interestingly, it has been contended that the establishment of the Diplock Courts can be seen as an early, and arguably successful, example of the IRA's long-term aim of making 'the Six Counties … ungovernable except by colonial military rule' – a central pillar of their so-called 'Long War' strategy. In practice, conviction rates in Diplock courts were not appreciably higher than in jury trials; between 1984 and 1986 the conviction rate was 51 per cent, compared to 49 per cent for jury trials in Northern Ireland and 50 per cent in England and Wales.

In any event, in exercising his judicial discretion, Ambrose excluded one out of four statements that were challenged in McCormick, holding that despite the express terms of s.6(2), the courts need not tolerate physical mistreatment 'purposely designed' to induce a person to make a statement.

Ambrose had an opportunity to develop the test and further demonstrate the importance of the court's discretion in a 1978 case (In Re Ian Milne) as a counterbalance to s.6(2) in appropriate instances, when he noted that 'although the accused has taken no point on the admissibility of the statement it is still for me to be satisfied that it is … admissible.' In short, Ambrose explained that if not satisfied that a statement was voluntary, or if not satisfied that the accused person had not been driven by the conditions and circumstances under which the statement was made to act against his will or conscience, then the court should exercise its discretion to exclude the accused's statement.

Accordingly, he went on to acquit an unrepresented defendant on six out of twenty serious counts, including a charge of murder. Ambrose concluded that the admissions had not been shown to be voluntary when the defendant was interviewed for thirty-nine hours out of a total of seventy-two hours' detention, and where there was evidence that he was confused before making a confession of murder. It was an approach which bore more resemblance to the old common law than to s.6(2).

Chapter 39

'A lawyer, a judge, a soldier and a gentleman'

Ambrose remained on the bench until his death in 1979 aged sixty-one soon after receiving a diagnosis from his doctor. Regrettably, the news had spread quickly – on the very same day that Ambrose learnt of his diagnosis, the Bar did too. As a result, his colleagues never saw him again – Lord Justice Deeny believes that Ambrose stayed away because he wasn't interested in people's sympathy. Six months later, he was gone, and his private funeral was attended, at his request, by immediate family only.

His obituary in the *Belfast Telegraph* described him as:

> A tall imposing figure he was looked upon as strong and fearless – a judge who could and did impose the full rigours of the law on Protestant and Roman Catholics alike who appeared before him on charges arising out of the Troubles of recent years. While those convicted of terrorist type offences could expect little or no leniency the firm and meticulous Sir Ambrose was not averse to tempering justice with mercy when the occasion arose.

Whether it was mercy or simply recognition of the situations that people sometimes find themselves in, a few years before he died, Ambrose reversed a decision of the Belfast Recorder's Court to deny an award of compensation to the wife of a man shot in the neck on a night of clashes between rival community crowds. Following a march, an Orange band had started playing near a Catholic enclave and church off the Newtownards Road. Ambrose described the evidence of an RUC officer as 'unreliable and unconvincing' in attempting to implicate the woman's husband in the shootings and awarded her substantial compensation, noting that 'Many things happened that night which people on both sides of the community must be deeply and thoroughly ashamed of.' Similarly, in a separate case, two men were caught in possession of firearms but defended on the basis that they had no intent to cause harm; 'they had simply been caught up in the present situation' and were armed in case they needed to defend themselves. Ambrose sentenced them to two years but demonstrated some understanding, perhaps born of personal experience and difficult decisions made during the war, commenting, 'When you found yourselves in a position to take life or cause injury, your better nature just revolted.'

He had a brief but noted career on the Appeal bench during difficult times and had been earmarked as a future Chief Justice before his premature death. The then Lord Chief Justice Lowry noted in internal court records at the time of Ambrose's appointment to the Appeal Court that Ambrose was

> a good thinker and an independent brave man who served well in the war … [the L.C.J.] thought that McGonigal should replace Curren, L.J. in the Court of Appeal. He would be a better choice for L.C.J. than [X] if anything happened to Lowry himself or to Jones, L.J. There had once before been a Roman Catholic L.C.J.

After Ambrose's death, Professor Kevin Boyle (a Northern Irish-born human rights activist, barrister and educator), wrote to Ambrose's wife, offering condolences: 'I want you to know that I regarded your husband as one of the great judges in Ireland.'

Lord Lowry and Lord Hailsham also spoke of him, on the occasion of the swearing-in of his successor, with Lord Hailsham saying:

> As Lord Lowry had already informed the court on a previous occasion, it was the express wish of Ambrose McGonigal, whom he had the privilege of knowing personally, that there should be no formal tributes. I therefore simply say the late Lord Justice was the epitome of all that a lawyer, a judge, a soldier and a gentleman would wish to be.

Irish *Who's Who* noted:

> A handsome but stern appearance, coupled with natural authority, meant that at times on the bench McGonigal conveyed an intimidating demeanour to counsel and witnesses alike. He was a man of decisive judgment and unimpeachable integrity, and any hint that the court was being misled or not told the full truth, or that counsel was not fully prepared, would result in an uncomfortable experience for the person concerned as the error was exposed in icy terms. Nevertheless, any counsel who had been found wanting knew that on his next appearance before McGonigal he started with a clean slate.

To put these assessments into context, Sir Donnell Deeny recalled a number of anecdotes. One concerned a dilemma Ambrose faced when as counsel he recommended settlement in a case where legal costs were still in issue (and would fall outside the terms of the recommended settlement). Ambrose felt that from the client's perspective the proposed settlement was the right thing, even if from his solicitor's (and his own) perspective it was not. At the time, Ambrose's main source of work was from this particular solicitor – he handled a lot of the PI and trade union cases – and by recommending the settlement to his client, Ambrose would risk falling out with his instructing solicitor. Acknowledging that, he said, 'I will settle this matter but I will lose a large part of my practice when I do.' Ambrose always played things straight down the middle.

On a later occasion, at the time of Blair Mayne's funeral (attended by both Ambrose and his wife Paddy), several old lawyer and army colleagues were reminiscing over a few drinks and discussing the difficulties Blair

Ambrose at his son Eoin's wedding.

had faced adjusting to civilian life. Someone lamented the fact that the army had turned Blair into a killer and suggested that may have been the real reason why he had struggled so much to readjust. However, somebody else noted that in contrast, Ambrose seemed to have managed the adjustment very well. Lord Chief Justice MacDermott (aka 'the baron'), the winner of an MC in the Great War and a large, intimidating man with a deep voice, interrupted: 'While the army may have made a killer of Blair Mayne, Ambrose McGonigal had always been a killer.' By the same token, his son, Sir John MacDermott, later added that 'if he had ever wanted someone to have his back it would have been Ambrose.'

There certainly were a number of apparent contradictions that went to make up Ambrose. In a memoir that appeared in the SAS magazine *Mars & Minerva*, the writer notes that having joined the SBS and as

> a natural ally of Andy Lassen, with a talent for good-natured escapades, both on operations and in camp, I can only remember his being ruffled once, when he surprised us all by vehemently defending de Valera's action in mourning the death of Hitler in a speech he gave in Dublin. We had all been denouncing this as Free State treachery, but Ambrose regarded our comments as an insult to the Irish people as a whole.

Clearly, if anyone was entitled to defend de Valera's demonstration of extreme political protocol, then it was an Irish Catholic major in the British special forces who had lost a brother in the war.

For Ambrose, although it was not something he ever discussed, the time he spent in the British Army remained important to him throughout his life. The war had marked a turning point for some of the obvious reasons already mentioned, but it also resulted indirectly in his not completing his legal studies in Dublin and perhaps, like his brother Dick, going on to pursue a career based there. However, in November 1971 Ambrose made a return visit to Dublin to share the bench of the Supreme Court with the Irish Chief Justice, Mr Cearbhall O'Dalaigh, in presiding over a ceremony marking the call of his son Eoin to the Irish Bar. Ambrose would have been familiar to many there from his time at Clongowes and later King's Inns. No photos were taken, but speckled with daggers, he was noted to have been wearing his green Commando tie.

Chapter 40

Brothers and Brothers in Arms

One of Ambrose's constant companions in those early years after the war was Blair, who had always been close to the McGonigal family. Another lawyer and ex-serviceman tells of what happened in the Belfast Tramways Club, a less than exclusive watering hole of those days.

After an evening of whiskey, Ambrose declared, 'Mayne, you big ape, I'm not afraid of you.'

'Right,' replied Blair. 'Stand against the wall.'

So, like William Tell's son, Ambrose, with his back to the wall, stood unflinchingly while Blair smashed a succession of tumblers just above his head. Satisfied, Blair insisted that the entire company drink to Ambrose McGonigal's steadiness under fire. A County Court judge recalls the gentler side of the relationship and Blair's continuing sense of responsibility: 'Ambrose and he had some kind of row in the Grand Central Hotel in Belfast at a very late hour. Ambrose, well-wined, stalked out, determined to walk home. Blair kerb-crawled after him at a discreet distance, to make sure he got home safely.'

It is known that Blair struggled to adjust to the norms of civilian life. After an abortive involvement with the British Antarctic Survey in the Falkland Islands – cut short in part because of the back injury he had sustained during that fateful first operation with 'L' Detachment – he made use of his qualification as a solicitor, returning to Newtownards and accepting the role of Secretary of the Incorporated Law Society of Northern Ireland. However, he never really settled – he probably drank more than he ought, but his back caused him great pain. He did, however, take more easily to time spent tending his garden, and after his mother passed away he arranged a substantial redesign of the family land in Newtownards, introducing literally hundreds of new plants. He also started a new business there raising hens which became a profitable venture.

From time to time Ambrose would visit his old friend, and on one occasion, not long before Blair passed away, he took with him his first son, named 'Eoin' after his brother. Ambrose proposed a short drive out of the city, but young Eoin, about nine at the time and the spit of his uncle, was not hugely impressed. He was just back from boarding school on holiday and not thrilled by the thought of a drive over to Newtownards – it would only take about half an hour, but he could think of better things to do.

'Where are we going?' he asked.

'To see an old friend and his hens,' came the reply.

'What?!' mouthed Eoin in silent reply, preferring to pick his battles rather than question 'the father' at this point.

It was a bright sunny day when they arrived to find Blair tending his roses. Ambrose explained that Blair used to play rugby for Ireland and this changed things immediately.

Blair seemed a little quiet and just said, 'So this is Eoin. Do you play any rugby yourself?'

'Yes, and I box.' confirmed Eoin.

'Is that so – well have you had many fights?'

'One or two but mainly only at home,' Eoin replied wryly.

'I can well imagine that. Tell me, have you ever smoked?' asked Blair.

Eoin, after a quick glance over at his father, just replied, 'Oh, well we're not supposed to smoke at school.'

'I see – probably very wise, but I'll take that as a yes,' said Blair, before asking Ambrose and Eoin to wait a moment. 'I have something I have been meaning to give to you for some time.'

Blair went into the house, came back with a small rectangular package wrapped in material and gave it to Eoin. Glancing briefly at Ambrose and then fixing Eoin with a serious look, Blair said, 'This used to belong to your uncle – he was a great friend of mine. You're very like him and I know he would've liked you to have it … But perhaps not use it for a few more years yet.'

Eoin waited until they were back in the car and then quickly started to unwrap the package. The material seemed to be some sort of scarf – Ambrose staring intently in his rear view mirror quietly said the word 'keffiyeh' (traditional Arab headdress) – and as the scarf fell away, Eoin spotted the initials 'E.McG' in the corner of a flat shiny, metal box. They were his initials! Where had this come from? It was his Uncle Eoin's lucky silver cigarette case, all that remained of Margaret's unknown soldier. It was a quiet drive home.

KILLED IN ACTION

McGONIGAL – Killed in action in November, 1941, Eoin Christopher McGonigal. The Royal Ulster Rifles (Commandos), aged 20 years, dearly-loved youngest son of Judge and Mrs. McGonigal, 6 Windsor Gardens. No mourning, by his special wish. – R.I.P.

ULSTER OFFICER MISSING.
JUDGE M'GONIGAL'S SON.

Judge M'Gonigal and Mrs. M'Gonigal, 6 Windsor Gardens, Belfast, have been notified that their third and youngest son, Lieut. Eoin Christopher M'Gonigal, R.U.R., is missing in the Middle East.

Mr. M'Gonigal had volunteered for the Commandos and was acting with this crack force during the Libyan battle. He was educated at St. Dominick's Prep. School, Cabra, and Clongoweswood College, Kildare, and received his commission in August, 1939.

His elder brother, Lieut. Ambrose Joseph M'Gonigal, is also in the Rifles and was married on the 19th inst.

His Honour's eldest son is a K.C. in Dublin.

Lieut. M'Gonigal

An article reporting on Eoin McGonigal MIA; his cigarette case; Ambrose's son, Eoin, at Clongowes.

Chapter 41

The Brothers – final notes

Encouraged by a patriotic belief in the nobility of battle, they remain noble, even if the cause for which they died was not. It is a story of its time, speaking to the idealism of the young. Many go through a voyage of youthful hope and ambition, imagining the world to be one way, only to experience another as they encounter a more challenging and uncertain reality. For some this may happen quickly; for others it involves a lifetime's journey.

The Ireland in which the brothers grew up was witness to a period of truly revolutionary change and, regardless of political or religious leanings, few could have avoided its impact. Against a backdrop of global economic upheaval and the Anglo-Irish trade war of the 1930s, any sense of youthful hope and ambition would have struggled when set against the turmoil of the fight for Home Rule, the 1916 Rising, a War of Independence and a Civil War – all bookended by two World Wars, Revolution in Russia and the Spanish flu: events which famously inspired Yeats to write of things falling apart as 'mere anarchy is loosed upon the world'. Allegiances became entangled with, at different times, Irishmen fighting for each other, against each other, against the British and with the British. And then, returning from war and throughout the latter part of his career as a lawyer and judge in the Six Counties, Ambrose encountered further conflict between neighbouring communities and was a primary target for some of it, living life always on his guard. It was a life of adventure, clashing loyalties, sacrifice, killing, death and heroism. Rarely can it have been comfortable. And rarely can it have felt over.

Plato is said to have remarked that 'Only the dead have seen the end of war.' There are many stories about the towering figures of SAS and SBS legend, growing ever more fantastic with each retelling (for 'history prefers legends to men'). However, reality is never so neat, and there is a good case for saying that one of the reasons Ambrose was able to re-adjust to civilian life and a burgeoning career at the Bar is that he was unreservedly single-minded in moving on from the memories of war – but perhaps failing therefore to live up to the standards of today's apparently enlightened millennial, co-parenting family men. He was known for his sometimes short temper – no doubt in part because of the lingering pain of various war-related injuries to his back and shoulder in particular. As a junior barrister he also maintained his reputation for being a little boisterous – a well-known incident involved him being called up to the top table at a dinner by the Father of the Bar so that he could be publicly admonished for some rowdy behaviour. However, Ambrose was having none of it and, although a mere junior, he responded by launching a firecracker under the top table! Quite what his actual father would have made of this as a former Father of the Bar himself is probably not too hard to imagine. In any event, over time whiskey was put aside and Ambrose adopted a far more solemn approach to life, devoting himself to his career and his obligations on the bench – never half-heartedly, for it was always all or nothing with Ambrose. Still, the reality was that the war did not end for many of those who survived it, and these unacknowledged sacrifices continued. The so-called celebrated 'originals' were not unique in this sense, and not all adjusted well to civilian life. The internal battles raged on, but there was no post-war award of medals, or more importantly, support – and sacrifice without an informed choice is somebody else's sacrifice.

So, where does this leave things? As a young boy I was an avid reader of the (now non-PC) Commando comics – my reading of them enhanced by the vague stories I would sometimes hear about my grandfather's and his brother's exploits which all sounded thrilling and inspiring. Were they really Commandos?! Even the holiday visits from Ambrose, 'my grandfather in Belfast', were exciting – it was at the height of the Troubles and the daring of my grandfather, still doing his best on crossing the border to lose his police protection on high-speed drives down from the North, felt like a scene straight from one of my comics. Playing 'Crossfire', the ball-bearing shooting game, with him on Christmas morning, or the board game 'Escape from Colditz' – to say nothing of the treasured toy sub-machine gun I received when I visited the house in Downpatrick and would use to chase his bodyguard around the garden. *The Great Escape* with Steve McQueen was a favourite in those days, but the thought that my grandfather and his brother could have known some of the PoWs was unbelievable. On one occasion, when we were together getting ready for a family wedding, I sneaked a glance as his handgun came out while changing jackets – I think time stood still at that moment; I know my heart did. All the same, his was a pretty remote life as a judge in those days – the threats were real – and as for many former soldiers, I think he may have found it easier to lower his guard with grandchildren. There were too few meetings but they were always memorable, and even then I knew I wanted to remember. As a Dubliner, I always thought his name a bit ridiculous, plummy even, but had no hesitation in adopting it for my confirmation name, even if it took quite a while to find a saint with the same name (one for the 'papists'!). However, now as a much older man and father, I see a slightly different picture of the brothers' wartime lives – there seems to have been a lot of luck involved, lots of waiting around for the next operation, much naivety, old fashioned resolve, amateurism, the exploitation of bold youth and ruthlessness, as well as unexpected disillusionment and trauma. This makes the events all the more inspiring when I think of the individuals involved. They had choices, but they did what they believed was right. In many cases there was quite literally no going back – they left everything familiar and comfortable behind and just got on with what was in front of them. But how do you remember people who, as in Eoin's case, you never actually knew but sometimes end up tricking yourself into feeling that you somehow did? Piecing together the fragments of a family's saved mementos, the few remaining blurred images, fragile letters from the front, anecdotes, records – it's not enough. No matter how many times you might stare at a photo, hold something that was theirs, walk the same ground, breath the same air in Arran or Ireland (Libya will have to wait), an unknowable space remains. There is a feeling that so long as people are remembered they are never truly gone. But of course they are, it's just sand and flies. It's all imagination and unreal. And although Joyce was of the view that imagination is memory, it is often hard to know where one begins and the other ends. So, you remember what they did, the examples they set and wonder 'what if'; the different lives dealt them by fate and the extraordinary qualities it brought out in both brothers; how you would have liked to have known them, to have been a little older when they were around. It is a pretty common wish amongst descendants of that generation. My own children are now close to the age that Eoin was when he disappeared, and this is partly why I wanted to find out more about the brothers; to remember them so that in time others in our family might also.

'Once you hear the details of victory, it is hard to distinguish it from a defeat.' The war was won but Sartre's words must be true in many cases and particularly apt in the context of battles small and large, such as for Ambrose on Sark and at Villa Punta, or for Eoin at the River Litani, when so many of 11 Commando from Arran were killed, wounded or taken prisoner, and again, with Operation Squatter, from which so few returned. However, for me, in fighting for what they believed in and delivering a statement of intent, Eoin and his brothers were victorious. And I'm with Stirling: *I know Eoin made it to Tmimi.*

* * *

Chapter 42

Heroes

The brothers are heroes of mine. But not all heroes are heroes to all – clear meaning is as elusive as a dry fuse in a sodden desert under a setting November sun – the meaning *can* change with time. Heroes may be fantastic killers, survivors, martyrs, conscientious objectors, participants in historic events or unheralded team members – 'average Joes' (or Janes) who never give up, who endure. They can inspire, give hope and lead. There are many brave, stoic and inspirational people who have not been recognized as heroic. Queen Victoria insisted that the Victoria Cross should be inscribed with the phrase 'for valour', not 'for the brave', since otherwise it might suggest that only recipients of the VC were brave. However, pinning down what distinguishes the two is as likely as having a VC pinned to your breast. Heroic status seems quite often to be a creature of propaganda if not otherwise driven by public opinion and the media – not always the most consistent of barometers as in the debate over Blair Mayne's VC, withdrawn when Britain no longer had need of heroes ('they had no bard to sing their praises').

In classical mythology, heroes were often, although not exclusively, the descendants of gods and quite literally 'protectors'. These heroic figures usually fulfilled a great task, elevating them from the realm of mere mortals. They were generally warriors who lived and died in the pursuit of honour alone (not adulation or reward), proving their greatness by their courage in the face of a mortal danger as well as the brilliance and efficiency with which they killed.

However, heroic status does not guarantee popularity or even likeability. Whether real or mythological, heroes are not always forever heroic – an act of valour may represent just a brief but extraordinary moment in time, as opposed to a lifetime of steadfast fortitude. Many fall from grace, their heroic status expiring and their worshippers vanishing. Others rise to heroism from a great depth. The appropriately named Steve Gallant, a convicted murderer who tackled a knife-wielding terrorist with a narwhal tusk in London in 2019, is now considered a hero by many and was granted clemency by the Queen.

King George V insisted that the recipient of a VC must never be relieved of that honour, no matter his subsequent crimes. A VC is bestowed for life and cannot be forfeited. Even if its holder is hanging from a scaffold, the VC should hang from his lapel, as a reminder that he did once act with valour in the presence of the enemy.

This may have come in the form of an instinctive reaction or as an example of 'cold courage', where there is a clear choice between self-preservation and self-sacrifice for a greater good. But is selflessness in circumstances of almost certain jeopardy not simply an acceptance of reality, the futility of hope – the very opposite of what a hero can inspire? Are kamikaze pilots brainwashed zealots or heroes giving their lives in the service of their emperor? What about the pilot who is brave enough to refuse his emperor? Is this any different to a soldier who throws himself on a grenade to protect his comrades? How about suicide bombers? Where does it end?

From a time when the designation of hero status generally went hand-in-hand with armed conflict, our concept of heroism has developed. The classic bravery of an Achilles can be set against the more contemplative but no less heroic course taken by a Socrates; somebody willing to risk everything for their values, livelihood, reputation, the lives of family members, imprisonment, even death. Chiune Sugihara, the 'Japanese Schindler', was a classic hero of this kind – a diplomat spurned by his country for his heroic wartime resistance, only to be feted in later years. He knew he would lose his job and status in Japan but did what he thought was right for the thousands of Jewish refugees in Lithuania to whom he granted transit visas.

Has there perhaps been a subtle diminution of our concept of heroism? With the development of a more technological form of warfare, the original ideals of military heroism have become more remote and harder to attain – fewer VCs will be awarded for acts of valour in the presence of the enemy. What need of an 'L' Detachment today, when an unmanned drone can swoop in and inflict risk-free death and destruction? At the same time, our concept of heroism has expanded to include society's leaders – politicians, bankers, lawyers, accountants, priests, CEOs and so on – some of whom are routinely embroiled in scandal and, save for the failure of expectation, often held in contempt. Idols are torn down as quickly as they are built up. Soldiers of today may find themselves fighting wars with which the general population disagrees, or doing so remotely against less sophisticated opponents and sometimes causing collateral damage – armchair warriors watching a screen and pulling triggers, or watching CNN and periodically feeling ill at ease (but absolved through distance). Now we idolize our sports men and women and other entertainers – who also sometimes fall from grace, whether it is a tax dodge, sex scandal, drugs or even worse. And is sport not the antithesis of a selfless pursuit, inspiring though it sometimes may be? Altruism is irrelevant – possession of an ego is now considered indispensable to success and the flawed hero, who achieves redemption is best of all in the eyes of the public.

Success in any field of endeavour today is often just a brief precursor to the development of a brand and the monetizing of that success. Perhaps, if Eoin and Ambrose were in action today as members of an elite military squad, they could be captured digitally, commentated on in real time, emblazoned with a swoosh and followed by a media tour. The sponsorship opportunities would be significant and the naïve romanticism of dying an unknown soldier would appear ridiculous.

In Brecht's play, in response to his pupil's contention that, 'Unhappy is the land that has no heroes!', (the heroic) Galileo answers, 'No. Unhappy is the land that needs heroes.' They may not have needed a protector but was this a land where people still believed in heroes?

Our heroes may not be perfect but any shifting of the sands, the adoption of an arguably diminished ideal, risks lowering the bar of what we expect of ourselves individually and as a society – our heroic imagination. It also risks devaluing the contribution of so-called 'true' heroes, whether they are imperfect figures of legend like Blair Mayne or the hero next door. This may not matter. Some consider it a juvenile concept, a false narrative based on stories told to children – a hero is someone out of this world, not human, or superhuman – whereas we should be looking to real people who do extraordinary things. The rest is an exercise in myth-making, comic book material and putting people on pedestals will not solve anything – as Banksy has sprayed, 'We don't need any more heroes, we just need somebody to take out the recycling.'

Ultimately, just as with our choice of moral or spiritual codes, we will each draw our heroic imagination from whatever source that inspires – whether it is a story or idea from the Bible, Homer, Marvel, Instagram, or *Rogue Warrior of the SAS*. We cling to memories but it is not the past which defines us, it is what we do now. But, as individuals we *are* our memories – both imagined and real. This is a story about two of my heroes growing up in Dublin: Eoin McGonigal about whom I knew so little other than that he was lost at the age of just 20, fighting with the original SAS in the Libyan desert – with no identity tags, the archetypal 'unknown soldier'; and his elder brother, Ambrose McGonigal, my grandfather – a soldier, judge and gentleman. Neither wished to be mourned but they are remembered.

Chapter 43

Commando

In an extract taken from 'Combined Operations, 1940–1942' (the pamphlet referred to by Margaret in her letter to Blair), Hilary St George Saunders MC (although not credited) describes the qualities sought of a Commando in a chapter entitled 'To Be Known as Commandos':

> To get in and out of a small boat in all kinds of weather, to swim – if necessary in full equipment with firearms held above the water, to be familiar with all the portable weapons of the soldier from the rifle and the tommy gun to the three-inch mortar and the anti-tank rifle, to be able to carry and use high explosives, to hunt tanks and their crews – here are some of the things that the Commando soldier must learn. To do so, however, is only to become proficient in the use of the tools of his trade of war. He must do more than this; he must master his mind as well as his body and become not only a specially trained soldier but a trained individual soldier. In other words, self-reliance and self-confidence form an integral, a vital part of his mental and moral make-up. To achieve these mutually dependent qualities the men, on entering the depot, are treated as far as possible as individuals. They are required to do everything for themselves. It is not for them to await orders from their officer or their N.C.O. They must do the sensible, obvious thing just because it is the sensible, obvious thing … Self-confidence springs from the possession of confidence in those appointed to lead. At the depot the embryo Commando soldier soon discovers that his instructors do exactly what he does, only always a little better, however hard he may strive.
>
> The physical conditions of Commando training are strenuous, but well within the endurance of young men all of whom have passed a severe medical test. They march many miles over all kinds of country; they swim rivers or cross them on bridges made of toggle ropes … They go over specially-prepared assault courses where only live ammunition and live bombs are used. They climb cliffs; they do physical exercises in parties of eight together bearing a log eight inches thick on their

shoulders … when they reach their Commando Units they are already hard men, physically and morally, able to perform considerable feats of endurance. They have need to be so, for the men they join are harder …

Finally, the young Commando soldier is taught to appreciate to the full the meaning and value of friendship in war. He is encouraged to do everything and to regard himself as being one of a team of two … Their team work is vital to the safety and success of the troop moving through enemy country … Friendship between two men engaged in the business of war is as old as war itself. Achilles and Patroclus, David and Jonathan, Roland and Oliver, the names change; the spirit remains … the officers who take [the Commandos] into action … know that their men will fight, not with steel only, but with strong united hearts.

And so went Eoin, Blair and Ambrose – brothers in arms and brothers, perhaps not always together in time but forever united in spirit. They were unconventional men recruited as much for their independent ways as their athleticism, resilience, aggression, intelligence and leadership. Unimpressed by status and authority, they were brothers in all senses of the word, untraditional and prone to acting impetuously in their down time but deadly serious in action. A final image to leave in the memory is the now infamous tale of Eoin and Blair riding bareback across the sands in Cyprus. Recalling the spirit of the ancient warrior Celts who would go into battle bearing only their shield and a sword (or perhaps they were just 'three sheets to the wind'), they had been swimming with other Commandos from Layforce, spotted the horses, challenged each other to a race and each hopped on and tore off across the beach. What a scene! No doubt, the ORs in whose minds the image was firmly fixed (Bob Bennett, Chalky White and others) were left with a pretty strong impression of the madmen from Ulster. However, three years later – not to be outdone – it is said that Ambrose and Ian Smith, his old mucker from 12 Commando, took off naked on their motorbikes in Crete, in memory of Eoin.

They lived life not timorous but bold.

Siegfried Sassoon, *To Any Dead Officer* (14.7.1917)

So when they told me you'd been left for dead I wouldn't believe them, feeling it must be true.

Next week the bloody Roll of Honour said 'Wounded and missing' – (That's the thing to do When the lads are left in shell-holes dying slow, With nothing but blank sky and wounds that ache, Moaning for water till they know It's night, and then it's not worth while to wake!)

Good-bye, old lad! Remember me to God,

And tell Him that our Politicians swear

They won't give in till Prussian Rule's been trod Under the Heel of England ... Are you there? ...

Yes ... and the War won't end for at least two years; But we've got stacks of men ... I'm blind with tears, Staring into the dark. Cheero!

I wish they'd killed you in a decent show.

> He will not grow old, as we who are
> left will grow old.
> Age can not wither him or the
> Weary years condemn.
> At the going down of the sun &
> In the morning
> We will remember him.

> When you go home,
> Tell them of us & Say
> For your tomorrow, we gave our Today.

Pages from Margaret McGonigal's prayer card for Eoin.

Appendix A

The record of Eoin's transfer from the RUR (when attached to C Battalion Layforce [11 (Scottish) Commando]) 'posted to parachute unit with Capt Stirling' (formerly of 8 [Guards] Commando) on 15 August 1941.

A handwritten War Diary / Intelligence Summary sheet for C Bn Layforce, August 1941, recording events dated 6–31 August at Alexandria and Training camp, including the entry noting Lt. E.C. McGonigal R.U.R. posted to parachute unit under Capt. Stirling.

Appendix B

Early 'L' Detachment roll call dated Kabrit 27 August 1941 but with much later (1945) typewritten/manuscript notations recording the fate of original members, whether prisoners (P.O.W.), 'returned' to parent unit (R.T.U.), non-operative (Non Op), or lost in action (Killed) [NOT in SAS War Diary].

```
                    L. Det. 1st. S.A.S. Bde.  O.C. Capt. Stirling.  (P/O/W/)

                              C.S.M. Yates.
No. 1 Troop.              Lieut. Lewes. (Killed)    Sgt. Riley.
   No. 1. Section.                                     No. 2. Section.
   A. Group.                                           D. Group.                    (Killed
   Lieut. Fraser. .        now master                  Lieut. Mc Gonical.           (Killed)
   Sgt. Cheyne.            (Killed)                    Sgt. Lazenby.                (P.O.W.
   L/C. Byrne.             (P.O.W.) escaped            L/C. Leitch.                 (Non E
   Pet. Cattell.                                       Pct. Davies. RETURNED (P.O.W.
     "  Cooper.                                          "  Mc Kay.                 (P.O.W.

   B. Group.                                           E. Group.
   Cpl. Bait.              (2nd. S.A.S.)               Cpl. Badger.                 (Wounded
   L/C. Orton.             (P.O.W.)                    L/C. Hildreth. (             (P.O.W.
   Pct. Cockbill.          (P.O.W.)                    Pct. Westwater.   (P.O.W. Re
     "  Keith.             (Killed)                      "  White.                  P.Q.W.)

   C. Group.                                           F. Group.
   Cpl. Du Vivier..                                    Cpl. Corps.                  (Non O
   L/C. Storrie.           (P.O.W.)                    Pct. Harvie.                 (R.T.U.
   Pct. Warburton.         (P/O.W.)-SHOT IN PRISON       "  Trenfield.             (P.O.W.
     "  Phillips.          (R.T.U.)  CAMP FOR SABOTAGE   "  Morris.                 (P.O.W
                                                                                    RETURN

No. 2. Troop.             Lieut. Mayne.              Sgt. Stone.    (Killed
   No. 1. Section.                                     No. 4. Section.
   G. Group.                                           J. Group.
   Sgt. Almonds.           (P.O.W.) RETURNED           Cpl. Kershaw.               (2nd S
   L/C. Walker.            (P.O.W.)                    L/C. Bose.
   Pct. Hill.              (P.O.W.)                    Pct. Baker.
     "  Sadler.            (P.O.W.)                      "  Bennett.
                                                           WHITE H.

   H. Group.                                           K. Group.
   L/Sgt. Colquhoun.       (P.O.W.)                    Cpl. White.                 (P.O.W.
   L/C. Evans.             (P.O.W.)                    L/C? Kendall.               ((P.O.
   Pct. Carrington.        (Non Op.)                   Pct. Seekings.
     "  Bolland.           (Killed)                      "  Chesworth.             (R.T.U

   I. Group.                                           L. Group.
   Cpl. Monachen.          (P.O.W.)                    L/C. Brough.
   L/C. Smith.             (P.O.W.)                    L/C. Kaufman.               (R.T.U.
   Pct. Keenan.            (P.O.W.) RETURNED           Pct. Leadbetter.            (R.T.U.
     "  Bridger.           (P.O.W.)                      "  Rhodes.

   ALSO.  ALSO
   Cpl. Mc Ginn.      L/Sgt. Mc Donald. (2nd. S.A.S.)  Pct. Austin.    (R.T.U
   Pct. Arnold.  (P.O.W.)     Pct. Hawkins.  (R.T.U.)    "  Lilley.
   ------------------------------------------------------

   (Unaccounted For)              P.o.w. Returned 11-7-45
   Capt. Thomson.  Adjutant?    2/Lt. Bonnington.  Pct Arnold.  R.H.F. (Killed
   Pct. Robertson.   F/Sgt. West. (YABSI.)(?) Sgt. Toms.
                                  R.A.F.
                         KABRIT......27/8/41.      P. O.
```

Appendix C

'L' Detachment nominal roll dated 1 September 1941 but with subsequent typewritten and manuscript notations recording the fate of original members (whether taken prisoner [P.O.W.] or lost in action [Killed]). *SAS War Diary 1941–1945*, p.33

A NOMINAL ROLL, 1, 9, 1941.

"L" DETACHMENT, 1ST S.A.S. BRIGADE, COMDR.,

Capt. DAVID STIRLING, (P.O.W.)

No. 1 Troop:	Lt. Lewes (Killed)	No. 2 Troop:	Lt. R.B. Mayne
	CSM Yates (P.O.W.)		Sgt Stone (Killed)
	Sgt Riley		Sgt. F.Bond (Pow)

No. 1 Section		No. 3 Section.	
A.Group	Lt. W. Fraser	C Group	Sgt Almonds
	Sgt Cheyne (Killed)		L/C Walker
	L/C Byrne (P.O.W.)		Pot Hill (P.O.W.)
	Pot Cattell		Pot Sadler (P.O.W.)
	Pot Cooper		

B.Group	Cpl Tait	H.Group	L/S Colquhoun (P.O.W.)
	L/C Orton (P.O.W.)		L/C Evans (P.O.W.)
	Pot Cockbill (P.O.W.)		Pot Carrington
	Pot Keith (Killed)		Pot Bolland (Killed)

C.Group	Cpl DuVivier	I Group	Cpl Monaghan (P.O.W.)
	L/C Storrie (P.O.W.)		L/C Smith (P.O.W.)
	Pot Warburton (P.O.W.)		Pot Keenan (P.O.W.)
	Pot Phillips		Pot Bridger (P.O.W.)

No. 2 Section		No. 4 Section.	
D.Group	Lt. McGonigal (Killed)	J Group	Cpl Kershaw
	Sgt Lazenby (P.O.W.)		L/C Rose
	L/C Leitch		Pot Baker
	Pot Davies		Pot Bennett
	Pot McKay		L/C Arnold

E.Group	Cpl Badger	K Group	Cpl White (P.O.W.)
	L/C Hildreth (P.O.W.)		L/C Kendall (P.O.W.)
	Pot Westwater (P.O.W.)		Pot Seekings
	Pot White (P.O.W.)		Pot Chesworth

F.Group	Cpl Corps	L Group	L/C Brough
	Pot Harvie		L/C Kaufman
	Pot Trenfield (P.O.W.)		Pot Leadbetter
	Pot Morris (P.O.W.)		Pot Rhodes

Also:- Capt. Thomson (P.O.W.), Capt. Bennington (P.O.W.), Cpl. McGinn, L/S. McDonald, Pot Austin, Pot. Hawkins, Pot. Blakeney, Pot. Lilley, Pot. Robertson, F/S. West (Killed)

Appendix D

Preparation order for Operation SQUATTER, 9 November 1941

MOST SECRET

S.A.S.O.
Ops. 1
S.I.O.

1. The 'Squatter' operation has now been fixed for the night of D-2.
2. Five Bombays will arrive at Bagush at about 1200 hours on that day and will take off again at 1730. The first one will be over the objective at 2015 hours and will be followed by the other four at 15 minute intervals between each.
3. The Albacores will, therefore, be required to drop flares over Gazala No. 1 Landing Ground from 2000 to 2130 hours, and the Blenheims to bomb this Landing Ground between these times. The Bombays during this period will be carrying out their operation some 15 miles to the south west and it is desirable that when approaching or leaving the target, Blenheims should fly at not less than 3000 feet over the same area. Continued desultory bombing throughout the night (of GAZALA and TMIMI L.Gs) would help as a distraction to the enemy.
4. In order to ensure success and to synchronise times, a Conference between O.C. 'Squatter' O.C. Bombays, and the O.Cs. Albacores and Blenheims who are taking part should be held here at 1300 hours on D-2.
5. It is essential that O.C. 'Squatter' should be provided with one mosaic and two sets of (a) Tmimi Landing Ground with an area ten miles to the south and west of it and (b) two strips in the Got Taray – Bir Temrad area west of Gazala and south of Tmimi.
6. Will the S.A.S.O. please issue the necessary instructions regarding (a) proposed conference on D-2, and (b) the operations of the Bombays and Albacores, and will the S.I.O. please check that the necessary action has been taken by the Army Survey Flight or the Photo Interpretation

Section, to ensure that the photographs required are produced and issued to Captain Stirling immediately.

PLANS
A.H.Q.W.D.
9.11.41
Signed: [illegible], Group Captain
Copy for information to the A.O.C.

Appendix E

Eighth Army Operation Instruction No. 16 dated 10 November 1941, taken from: *SAS War Diary 1941–1945*

Copy No. 3
10 Nov 41.
HQ/8A/12/G(0)

EIGHTH ARMY OPERATION INSTRUCTION NO. 16

Capt. D. Stirling
    Comdg. 'L' Sec 1 S.A.S Bde.

Ref Maps – LIBYA 1/500,000 – DERNA sheets 5 & 13 – BARDIA sheet 14 1/100,000 BOMBA, GAZALA.
----

1. Your force will consist of 54 men from 'L' Sec 1 S.A.S. Bde.
2. Your primary task is to raid both aerodromes at TMIMI in sq (S) P 70, GAZALA No. 1 355446 and GAZALA No. 2 362443, the latter including the new ground cleared to the East, destroying as many aircraft as possible.

   Other objectives such as H.Qs. and communications should only be attacked if they will in no way prejudice the success of your primary task.
3. You will plan your raid so that it takes place on the night D-1/D1 at an hour to be decided upon by you.

   It is important that your plan should co-ordinate the efforts of all parties on the various aerodromes in order that the first explosions will take place at the same time, and it is most important that the enemy should be unaware of your having landed or of your presence during the whole of D-1 day.

4. The types of aircraft likely to be found are given below in order of priority for destruction:-

    (a) <u>GERMAN</u> – ME 109 E & F
                     ME 110
                     HE 111
                     STUKA JU 87
                     JU 88

    (b) ITALIAN – G 50
                    MACCHI 200
                    CR 42
                    BR 20
                    S 79

The destruction of fighter aircraft is of greater importance than bombers and GERMAN aircraft of more importance than ITALIAN.

5. HQ. RAF, Western Desert have arranged to bomb all aerodromes in para. 2 at dusk on D-1 and after moonrise night D-1/D1, you must therefore be clear of the aerodromes at these times.
    During the whole night D-2/D-1 all aerodromes will be bombed.

6. You will land at a place, which you will select from previous reconnaissance and air photos, in the area BIR TEMRAD (S) U 7982 between the hours of 2030 hrs and 2130 hrs on night D-2/D-1.
    During 2000 hrs to 2130 hrs the RAF have arranged to drop flares over both aerodromes at TMIMI and GAZALA to assist you in locating your position.

7. HQ. RAF. Western Desert are arranging with 216 Sqn. RAF for the five aircraft which will carry your force to land at BAGUSH before 1200 hrs D-2 which will allow them time to refuel and for your force to have a meal before taking off for operations.
    The meal is being arranged by RAF. The exact time you will take off from Bagush will be notified to you by the Senior RAF Officer of the transport aircraft after a conference arranged by RAF Plans for 1300 hrs D-2 at HQ. RAF. WD.
    You will attend this conference.

8. Arms, ammunition and explosives to carry out the operation will be as selected by you.

9. For this operation you will carry 6 water bottles per man and sufficient food for 5 days. The type and quantity of food to be selected by you.

10. Having completed your task you will march, preferably in small parties, to the RV selected by you and Capt. EASON-SMITH, LRDG and, having met your vehicles, you will return to GIARABUB by the quickest route reporting your arrival through the HQ there to Battle HQ EIGHT ARMY, and await further instructions.

11. You should reach the above RV in time to be picked up by the LRDG patrol between the hours of 0600 – 0700 hrs G.M.T. (i.e. 0800 – 0900 hrs EGYPTIAN STANDARD TIME) on D3.

    For reasons of security the LRDG patrol has been instructed not to wait later than 0700 hrs G.M.T. on D3.

12. If you are unable to reach the RV by the appointed time the LRDG patrol will leave 12 galls of water and two 4 gallon tins of dates at the R.V. if possible near one of the Sheik's tombs marked on the map.

13. The two lorries belonging to your unit, with 1 officer and 3 O.R's, which are now being sent to SIWA will be taken by the LRDG patrol to a second R.V. already arranged between you and Capt. EASON-SMITH. This R.V. will be in the area of WADI EL MRA sq (S) U 42 and will be within walking distance of the first R.V.

    It is to this second RV that the LRDG will take your force having picked it up at the first RV or in the event of you failing to contact each other, to which you will march.

14. Your lorries before leaving SIWA will carry sufficient POL for the journey from SIWA to the second R.V. and return. The LRDG will give instructions as to exact quantities to be carried.

    They will also carry sufficient water and rations for 55 men for 6 days plus sufficient for their own party of 4 from the time they leave SIWA until D 10

15. The party at the second R.V. will wait until all your party have come in but not later than D.8.

16. Recognition signals between your force and the LRDG patrol will be arranged between you and Capt. EASON-SMITH.

17. The date of D.1 will be notified to you separately.

by hand
Method of issue……………..   <u>A. Galloway</u>

1810 hrs
Time of Signature…………..   Brigadier,
                                    General Staff.

Distribution:-	Copy No.
Capt. D. Stirling, Comdg. 'L' Sec S.A.S. Bde.	1
A.O.C. RAF. Western Desert	2
Lt-Col. G.T. Prendergast, Comdg. LRDG.	3
B.G.S. EIGHTH ARMY	4
C.G.S. G.H.Q.	5
File	6
War Diary	7 & 8

Appendix F

Reported bombings and other activities at airfields in Libya, extracts covering Tmimi and Gazala.

Henry L. deZeng IV, *Luftwaffe Airfields 1935–45 Libya (Tripolitania & Cyrenaica) & Egypt*

[Sources: AFHRA A5263 pp. 004-175 (31 Dec 42); chronologies; BA-MA; NARA; PRO/NA; website ww2.dk]

pp.1–2

Preface

The Italian colonization of Libya began with an attack on the Ottoman Turks at Tripoli and the ceding of Libya to Italy a few months later in 1912. From 1934 it was officially known at Italian Libya and its status on June 1940 was that of an Italian colony with an Italian administration. Egypt on the other hand, was an independent monarchy with a strong British civil and military influence. The British Royal Air Force already had significant assets in Egypt by June 1940, mainly to protect the Suez Canal.

In Libya, the Italians had developed a modest number of airfields, landing grounds and emergency landing grounds (ELGs) throughout the country but the exact numbers are not known. What is known is that by the end of December 1942 there were in Tripolitania 7 airfields (airdromes), 25 landing grounds, 52 emergency landing grounds, 1 seaplane station, 1 seaplane anchorage and 1 emergency seaplane anchorage. At the same time in Cyrenaica there were 5 airfields (airdromes), 73 landing grounds, 50 emergency landing grounds, 3 seaplane stations and 2 seaplane anchorages. Some of these were built or established by the Italians and Germans while the remainder were constructed by the Allies, mainly the British and South Africans. The vast majority were simply patches of open desert with markers, no buildings and no facilities. Tents were used for accommodations, operations and supply shelters. These landing grounds were typically used for a few days or weeks and then the war moved on leaving them vacated and abandoned. Nearly all of them flooded out during the fall and winter rains which made them unserviceable for days at a time.

In Egypt, the airfields were much more developed and were mainly centered in the Alexandria – Cairo – Port Said area. Those in the northern coastal area west to Sidi Barrani were less developed and even primitive in some cases, not unlike their counterparts in Libya. By the end of December 1942 there were in Egypt 26 airfields (airdromes), 77 landing grounds and emergency landing grounds (ELGs), 2 seaplane stations, 6 seaplane anchorages and 9 emergency seaplane anchorages.

Axis airfield construction efforts were minimal aside from laying out an airstrip of sorts, and this was largely due to the lack of building materials caused by the shortage of shipping space for lower priority war material such as prefabricated huts, concrete, etc. Few details regarding this subject have been found, but here are two exceptions: (1) on 8 November 1941 the senior Luftwaffe territorial command (ITALUFT) ordered Luftgaustab Afrika to increase the light Flak defenses around the existing airfields and, presumably, build Flak positions for these defenses; and (2) on 29 March 1942 OBS (Luftflotte 2) in Italy ordered the construction of blast bays and aircraft shelters to proceed as quickly as possible despite the shortage of matériel. The one airfield that probably received the greatest amount of attention and improvements from the Germans was Benina. On the other hand, the Allies had far more resources and were much better organized for this construction work and, accordingly, were able to build new airfields and landing grounds and improve existing ones at a comparatively rapid rate.

Airfields Listed

A total of 14 airfields, 147 landing grounds, 27 satellites and 101 emergency landing grounds are listed below along with 4 seaplane stations and 3 seaplane anchorages. Additionally, 90 landing grounds used by the Allies but not by the Axis are listed without details aside from the coordinates. It should also be pointed out that quite a few of the airfields and landing grounds had multiple airstrips. Some named airfields deep in Egypt along the Suez Canal and in the Sinai Peninsula that were well behind Allied lines are not listed. The grand total of all listings in this monograph is 386.

While the primary source documents and a few secondary works cited after each listing provided 90 per cent or more of the data used in this monograph, it was necessary to rely on four excellent reference books for some of the details concerning the order of battle and losses of the *Regia Aeronautica* (Italian Air Force), and these are:

Dunning, Chris. *Courage Alone: The Italian Air Force 1940–1943*. Manchester: Crécy Publishing Limited, 2009. ISBN: 9 781902 109091.   360p.

Shores, Christopher and Hans Ring. *Fighters Over the Desert: The Air Battles in the Western Desert June 1940 to December 1942*. London: Neville Spearman Ltd, 1969.   256p

Shores, Christopher and Giovanni Massimello with Russell Guest, Frank Olynyk and Winfried Bock. *A History of the Mediterranean Air War 1940–1945. Volume One: North Africa June 1940 – January 1942*. London: Grub Street, 2012. ISBN-13: 9781908117076.   560p

Shores, Christopher and Giovanni Massimello with Russell Guest, Frank Olynyk and Winfried Bock. *A History of the Mediterranean Air War 1940–1945. Volume Two: North African Desert February 1942 –* March 1943. London: Grub Street, 2012. ISBN-13: 9781909166127.   736p

Copyright © by Henry L. deZeng IV (Work in Progress). (1st Draft 2016), pp. 9–10

Ain el Gazala (LIB) (a.k.a. Ayn al Ghazālah, Ayn al Ulaymah?, Al Qardabah?) General: landing grounds in N Cyrenaica 62 km WNW of Tobruk. There were 3 landing grounds – Gazala/North, Gazala/South, Gazala No. 3, plus 1 seaplane anchorage – Mersa Ain el Gazala.

Remarks:

Jun 40: in Italian hands.

16 Dec 40: attacked by Blenheims – 1 x Ca.133 bomber-transport destroyed on the ground.

1 Jan 41: bombed by RAF Wellingtons – 1 x S.M.79 destroyed and 2 more damaged on the ground.

5(8?) Jan 41: low-level attack by 2 RAF Hurricanes – *claimed* 2 x S.M.79s destroyed. Evacuated by the Italians and taken over by the British the last week of January.

10 Apr 41: landing ground captured by German forces.

16 Apr 41: landing ground being subjected to nightly naval gunfire.

19 Apr 41: low-level attack by RAF Blenheims – 3 x Hs 126s and 1 x Ju 52 from 2.(H)/Aufkl.Gr. 14 destroyed on the ground, plus 5 KIA and 10 WIA.

9 Jun 41: low-level attack by RAF Hurricanes – *claimed* 6 x Bf 109s and Fiat G.50s set on fire.

12 Jun 41: bombed – 2 x Bf 109 E-7s from I./JG 27 damaged on the ground.

26 Jun 41: bombed by 15 Blenheims – 2 x Bf 109s destroyed and 3 more damaged. (German report)

28 Jun 41: bombed by SAAF Marylands – 2 x Bf 109 E-7s from I./JG 27 damaged on the ground.

3 Aug 41: bombed – 1xBf109E-7 from I./JG27 destroyed and 1xBf109 E-7/N from 7./JG 26 destroyed.

1 Sep 41: bombed – 1 x Bf 109 E-7 from 2./JG 27 destroyed on the ground.

21 Oct 41: 1 x Bf 109 F-4 (trop) from 5./JG 27 blown up to prevent capture.

9 Nov 41: bombed – 1 x Bf 109 F-4 (trop) from II./JG 27 damaged.

10 Nov 41: bombed – 1 x Bf 109 F-4 (trop) from II./JG 27 badly damaged.

21 Nov 41: night bombing – 1 x C.200 fighter destroyed and at least 3 x G 50 fighters damaged.

23 Nov 41: bombed – searchlight and tents damaged.

24 Nov 41: bombed – 1 x Junkers W 34 hi from II./JG 27 destroyed.

25 Nov 41: bombed – 2 x Bf 109s damaged on the ground.

27 Nov 41: bombed – 3 Messerschmitt Bf 109s damaged on the ground.

1 Dec 41: bombed – damage to rations stores and Flak positions.

7 Dec 41: 1 x Bf 109 F-4 (trop) from II./JG 27 blown up to prevent capture.

9 Dec 41: bombed – 3 x Fi 156s from Wüstennotstaffel destroyed or damaged on the ground.

Dec 41: 71 abandoned Axis aircraft, about half German, were found on the 3 Gazala landing grounds when they were overrun by British forces.

c. 13–14 Jun 42: Gazala landing grounds taken by advancing Axis forces. 17 Jun 42: low-level attack by RAF and RAAF Curtiss Kittyhawks – 3 x Bf 109 F-4 (trop) from 1./JG 27 damaged on the ground, while the Kittyhawk pilots *claimed* a total of 10 x Bf 109s destroyed or damaged plus 2 x Fi 156s damaged during repeated strafing runs.

21 Jun 42: bombed – 6 x Bf 109 F-4 (trop) from III./JG 53 destroyed (5) or damaged (1) on the ground.

14-15 Nov 42: re-occupied by British forces.

[pp. 123–5]

Tmimi No. 1 (LIB) (a.k.a. El Tmimi, Tmimi/South, At Tamïmï) (32 18 00 N – 23 01 30 E)

General: landing ground in Cyrenaica 88 km WNW of Tobruk, 63 km SE of Derna and 4.5 km SSW of the village of At Tamimi.

History: an important Axis landing ground that changed hands several times during 1941–42.

Surface and Dimensions: firm natural sand surface with sparse camel scrub measuring approx. 1510 x 1005 meters (1650 x 1100 yards).

Fuel and Ammunition: no details found. Infrastructure: none.

Dispersal: had 10 to 12 aircraft blast bays on the SE side in Dec 41 and Jun 42.

Defenses: Tmimi No. 1 and No. 2 were surrounded by 8 Flak positions in Jan 42.

Remarks:

21 Aug 40: landing ground raided – 2 x S.M.79 bombers destroyed on the ground.

6 Sep 41: bombed by RAF Wellingtons – 25 H.E. bombs dropped, 1 x Ju 87 R-2 destroyed on the ground.

15 Nov 41: RAF dropped 40 to 50 bombs – 1 x Ju 87 destroyed on the ground.

18 Nov 41: Tmimi unserviceable and tents washed away due to heavy flooding along the road to Gazala.

18 Nov 41: low-level attack by 6 RAF Beaufighters– claimed 5 x Ju 52s, 4 x S.M.79s and 1 x Hs 126 destroyed. Italian records only show 2 x S.M.79s damaged.

19 Nov 41: low-level attack by 6 RAF Beaufighters – claimed 5 x Ju 87s and 2 c Bf 109s destroyed.

20 Nov 41: low-level attack by 4 RAF Beaufighters – 1 x Ju 87 R-2 from II./St.G. 2 shot up and badly damaged on the ground and 3 others slightly damaged, while the Beaufighters *claimed* a total of 14 x Ju 87s and 1 x Bf 109 destroyed. A stock of 5,400 litres of B4 fuel was also ignited.

5 Dec 41: bombed – 2 x Bf 109 F-4s from III./JG 53 severely damaged on the ground.

6 Dec 41: low-level attack by 4 RAF Beaufighters – 1 x Ju 87 R-2 (Trop) from II./St.G. 2 shot up and badly damaged on the ground, while the Beaufighters claimed 5 x Ju 87s.

11 Dec 41: low-level attack – 1 x Ju 88 A-5 from I./LG 1 shot up and destroyed on the ground and 4x Bf 109 F-4s from III./JG 53 demolished to prevent capture by the advancing enemy.

12 Dec 41: Tmimi evacuated by the Axis.

3 Jan 42: 23 wrecked and abandoned aircraft found here by the advancing Allied troops, 14 German and 9 Italian.

Dec 41 – late May 42: occupied by the Allies.

25 May 42: bombed – 2 x Bf 109 F-4 (trop) from 4./JG 27 destroyed (1) or damaged(1).

22 Jun 42: air attack – 1 x Ju 87 D-1 from I./St.G. 3 destroyed on the ground.

Nov 42: reoccupied by the Allies.

Appendix G

Extracts of statements on Operation Squatter, SAS operation number one taken from PoWs who escaped through Switzerland in September/October 1943, from Corporal Bob Tait of Stirling's stick, 1945 and an undated statement from Pct Bennett. Also, included are contemporaneous reports from Captain Easonsmith and Blair Mayne.

Statement by No. 2660354, Tpr. Blakeney

The above-mentioned soldier proceeded on operations in the Western Desert on 16th November, 1941, and was dropped in a gale. After landing he lay up until dawn and found himself along with other members of his party, including Lt. MacGoneagle, who was badly injured and died later. Other members of his party were as stated in the following report by Tpr. Davies.

This party, which endeavoured to make for L.R.D.G. RV got lost, and so made their way to the coast and were picked up by an Italian Guard at TMIMI airfield, as per report of Tpr. Davies, prior to arriving on the Italian Mainland.

Statement by No. 2734997, Tpr. Davies

This soldier proceeded on operations in the Western Desert on 16th November, 1941, and was dropped in a gale over the DZ. After a rough landing he lay up until daylight when he met some other members of the operational party, which included Lt. MacGoneagle, Sgt. Lazenby, Cpl. Westwater, Cpl. Evans, Pcts. McKay, MacCormick, Malone, Morris, Robertson, and Haldreth. The last-named member died later. Lt. MacGoneagle, who was badly injured, died the same day. Members of the party commenced to make their way to the L.R.D.G. RV, but got lost in the desert.

They had no supplies, as all their containers were lost. On making their way to the coastal sector, they were picked up by Italian Guards on the edge of TMIMI airfield.

PoW Statement by No. 811911, GDSM Robertson

Date and Place of Capture: 21.11.41 Tmimi
Date of Arrival in Switzerland: 30.9.43

Dropped by parachute 16.11.41, 20 miles south of Tmimi Aerodrome without Arms (except revolver) ammunition ar [*sic*] food or water. Officer i/c party killed on landing. Forced to go to Tmimi after five days without water. 19.7.44

PoW Statement by No. 2734997, Tpr Davies

Date and Place of Capture: 23.11.41 South West of Tobruk
Date of Arrival in Switzerland: 26.10.43

Dropped from the air, by plane, wrong place, no supplies, marched six days, and picked up by the Germans, South West of Tobruk. 4.8.44

Operation Squatter Report: Cpl. R.D. Tait

We were scheduled to arrive over the dropping area about 2230 hours but owing to the weather which I think was of gale force, and the heavy A.A. barrage we were much later.

The pilot had to make several circles over the area, gliding in from the sea, coming down through the clouds right over Gazala, which was well lit up by flares dropped by the bombing force, covering out [*sic*] arrival.

During this glide, we came in for an uncomfortable amount of A.A.

We finally were dropped about 2330 hours, and owing to high wind – I estimated this at about 30 miles per hour – we all made very bad landings.

I myself being the only one uninjured. Captain Stirling himself sustained injuries about both arms and legs.

Sergeant Cheyne, we never saw again.

We had considerable difficulties in assembling, the wind having scattered us over a wide area but finally set out about 0100 hours.

Complete report on Operation Squatter by Cpl. R.D. Tait

Report on the operation against Gazala
By 2888693. S.S.M. R. Tait

The object of this operation was the destruction of the aircraft on the aerodromes at Gazala and Tinime principally the 109 F fighters. The attack was prepared to be made the night before the offensive launched by the Eighth Army, and if successful would help us toward air supremacy during the offensive. Our force consisted of five plane loads of approximately ten men in each, in our plane were Lieutenant-Colonel Stirling, C.S.M. Yates, Sergeant Chain, and myself with six other ranks. On the morning of 17th November, 1941 the Force moved up to the forward drome of Bagoush where we rested throughout the day and at about 1930 hours that evening took off for our objectives. From here on I can only report with any accuracy of our own flight, plane loads and own movements.

We were scheduled to arrive over the dropping area about 2230 hours but owing to the weather which I think was of gale force and the heavy A.A. barrage we were much later. The pilot had to make several circles over the area, gliding in from the sea coming down through the clouds right over Gazala, which was well lit up by flares dropped by the bombing force, covering our arrival. During this glide we came in for an uncomfortable amount of A.A. We finally were dropped at about 2130 hours, and owing to the high wind (I estimated this at about thirty miles per hour) we all made very bad landings. I myself being the only one uninjured. Lieutenant-Colonel (then Captain) Stirling himself sustained injuries about the arms and legs, Sergeant Cheyne was never saw again. We had considerable difficulty in assembling, the wind having scattered us over a wide area, but finally set off at about 0100 hours on the 18th November, 1941.

Our march towards the rendezvous to contact with the other parties, overlooking the two aerodromes (Gazala). From there we would have been able to observe during the daylight and make our attack after dark, zero hour was 0300 hours. We should have reached this Wadi before daylight, but the delay in dropping and assembling and the fact that we were dropped out of position, threw the time schedule, and by daylight we were still in the open and had to lie up. Very little enemy activity was observed during the day. By nightfall, Colonel Stirling had decided to send all of the party except myself back to first withdrawal R.V. which lay about seventy miles to the South-West, where we were to pick up the L.R.D.G. Patrol. He and I were to continue to the attack by ourselves. The injuries of most of the party had made marching very difficult, also we lacked supplies, not all of the containers dropped, having been recovered. The return party then left under C.S.M. Yates, and Colonel Stirling and myself marched towards the escarpment.

We had reached the high ground behind the escarpment about 2000 hours, when a terrific electric storm broke with hail and rain. We were unable to see more than a few yards in front and within fifteen minutes the whole area was under water. Eventually reaching the fork Wadi we endeavoured to make our way down it on the flat coastal strip, but found this impossible owing to the water which rushed down with great force. From then until long after midnight we moved along the escarpment, attempting to go down the various Wadis but with no success, so accordingly about 0100 hours, Colonel Stirling abandoned the attempt and we turned away and marched South.

The fact that the desert, except for the top of the ground folds, was flooded, made our march very difficult, also the cold and lack of food slowed us considerably. We were to R.V. with the L.R.D.G. on the night of the fourth at the junction Rotondo Segnaly formed by the Trigh Enver Bu and the track leading to a Southern Wadi at a point about two miles South-East of the junction on high ground where the patrol would burn two blue lights throughout the night, and before withdrawing a smoke flare at dawn. If it proved impossible to contact the patrol at this R.V. we had another R.V. about seventy miles to the South where Mr. Fraser, one of our officers, would wait for a fortnight with transport. Lieutenant-Colonel Stirling's plan was to march South until we struck the Trigh Enver Bu track, then turn West along it until we came into sight of the lights. We had timed our journey to arrive at this point after dark.

This we did and arrived at the R.V. at 0430 hours, 22nd November, 1941. We found that none of the party under C.S.M. Yates had reported in. After spending some days in the area searching for missing personnel we withdrew with the L.R.D.G. to Giarabub, arriving there on the [25th]. C.S.M. Yates and some of his party were later reported prisoners of war.

*   *   *

LRDG Report (extract): Capt. Easonsmith

Date: 26/11/41
Period: 17–26 November 1941

<u>Nov 17</u> Left SIWA 05.30 hours GMT with six patrol trucks, two 15-cwt Bedfords supplied by Captain Stirling with Lieut. Fraeser and four of his men

as crews and one 3-ton Bedford supplied by the LRDG as it was considered that the transport supplied by Captain Stirling might not prove adequate.

Having crossed the wire at UWANYA reached a point some 15 miles to the west for the night. No incident save that the 3-tonner blew a gasket after 80 miles and had to be left.

Nov 18 Ran on a general bearing of 255°, made a poor days run over 110 miles due to the many minor breakdowns. Saw a lot of aircraft, largely British but were not seen.

Nov 19 Reached R.V.2 (map ref. XX. 3584 in Wadi Mra) at 08.00 hours and harboured up Lt Fraeser and his two Bedfords which were carrying rations and water for Capt. Stirlings party. Pushed on at an average bearing of 25° towards R.V.1. As we approached it crossed many fresh tracks, hid my vehicles and waited until the late afternoon before finally locating it. Examination of the debris in the area proved that various units of the Trieste Divisions had been using it, probably for manoeuvres up to a fortnight before. There are many scarps and pimple-like hills with sides some 20 to 60 feet in height and at the base of the slit trenches, machine guns pits and vehicle pits had been dug. The two former of no great depth than a couple of feet and the latter done quite elaborately making good camouflage. Many of the trenches were on the western slopes of the hills. On approaching our R.V. we contacted LRDG Patrol Y 2 who were on another job in the area and who also reported seeing no ground movement. Drove along TRIG CAPUZZO (ENVER BEI) to the GADD EL AHMAR track junction which incidentally is marked with a sign post, and then picked up our agreed position three miles S.E. of it. At 05.20 hours two hurricane lamps were placed on a very high point some 3/4 mile from our camp. At 09.00 hours one was seen to be lifted and swung from side to side, the pre-arranged signal, this was answered by us and contact was made with the first party, Lt. Lewis and 9 O.R's.

Nov 20 At 01.00 hours there was a similar signal and Capt. Stirling and one Sgt came in. At dawn we moved our camp to good cover but left a small party who built a smoke fire on the high point previously mentioned. This brought in Lt Mayne and 8 men. I decided to remain at R.V.1 until the afternoon as a further party of 6 men had been sighted by Capt. Stirling on the previous evening heading in the right direction. The Italian vehicle pits afforded good shelter. However, no one else came in or were sighted by men placed at vantage points. I contacted our Y 2 patrol again and asked them to keep on lookout also, withdrew in the late afternoon to Fraesers party at WADI MRA having stayed 8 hours over the contracted time at R.V.1.

Nov 21 Kept a lookout all day with trucks displayed over a front of approx 8 miles. No incidents, no results.

Nov 22 Repeated the process with similar results until mid-day. Received a wireless signal telling me to take Capt. Stirlings' party to the BIR TENGEDER area to contact R.2 Patrol who would bring them to SIWA. On the way there we were seen and machine gunned by a Savaia 79, he scored no hits and the patrol replicd vigorously so he soon cleared off evidently to fetch aid as a Heinkel III arrived about 40 minutes later. This lost our trucks amongst some stones and failed to locate us, bombing and machine gunning (probably derelicts) some 3 miles from us. We camped 3 miles from BIR TENGEDER.

Nov 23 Failed to contact R.2 Patrol. Movement was rather restricted as planes were out looking for us for a high percentage of the day. On two occasions bombs were dropped and once machine gunning but we were not seen and the targets were all probably bushes or derelicts.

Nov 24 Received instructions to bring in Capt. Stirlings' party as R.2 were not to be found. Went back through Fraesers camp and ascertained that no one else had come in. No incident save the overturning of one of my trucks, fortunately without serious injury to men or machine.

Nov 25 Trouble free run, dropped Capt. Stirlings' party at Brigade H.Q. JERABUB at 12.30 hrs.

Nov 26 Arrived at SIWA 0700 hrs.

Lt. R.B. Mayne's Report (extract)

'To Commanding Officer, SAS Brigade'
'L' Detachment, Special Air Service Brigade.
Operational Report No.1

Personel: 'B' Troop, No.3 & No.4 Sections
Date: 27/11/41

Raid on TMIMI airfield
16th – 25th November 1941

Equipment:
No. 3 Section; Five containers of two packs each, one container with two TMSGs, one container of reserve dates and water.

No.4 Section; Six containers of two packs each, two containers of TMSGs. Personal equipment per man as per Squadron arrangements.

Plan:
No.3 Section under Lieut. Bonington was to take off from Bagoush with nine O/R's at 1920 hours on Flight No.4, No.4 Section on Flight No.5 would follow at 1940 hours on the 16/11/41.

After landing and regrouping both sections were to make contact and advance as a troop with No.4 Section leading and lie up for the day approximately five miles from the airfield.

At one minute to midnight on the 17/11/41 No.3 Section would attack planes on the east side of the airfield; No.4 Section were to attack those to be found on the south and west sides.

All contact with the enemy was to be avoided until fifteen minutes past midnight; thereafter TMSGs and instantaneous fuses could be used if necessary.

After completion both Sections would regroup and head for the RV.

Execution:
No.3 Section took off at 2000 hours some forty minutes late and I did not See them again.

No.4 section left at 2020 hours and reached the landing ground at 2330 hours. There were no incidents on the flight there and we were dropped as arranged.

As the section was descending there were flashes on the ground and reports which I then thought was small arms fire. But on reaching the ground no enemy was found so I concluded that the report had been caused by detonators exploding in packs whose parachutes had failed to open.

The landing was unpleasant. I estimated the wind speed at 20-25 miles per hour, and the ground was studded with thorny bushes.

Two men were injured here, Pct Arnold sprained both ankles and Pct Kendall bruised or damaged his leg.

An extensive search was made for the containers, lasting until 0130 hours 17/11/41, but only four packs amd two TSMGs were located.

I left the two injured men there, instructed them to remain there that night, and in the morning find and bury any containers in the area and then to make to the RV which I estimated at fifteen miles away.

It was too late to carry out my original plan of lying west of Tmimi as I had only five hours of darkness left, so I decided to lie up on the southern side.

I then had eight men, sixteen bombs, fourteen water bottles and food as originally laid for four men, and four blankets.

We marched for three and a half hours on a bearing of 360 degrees covering approximately six miles and laid up in a small wadi which i estimated was four to six miles from the aerodrome.

Daylight reconnaissance made on 17/11/41 showed the aerodrome to be some 6 miles due north. There were seventeen planes on the southerly side. Some AFVs and motorcycles were seen also. There was one tent between us and the aerodrome.

I decided to leave our lying-up position at 2050 hours, leaving the packs there, taking one water bottle and two bombs per man, two group leaders carrying the TSMGs and returning by groups to the position after the attack and then proceeding as a section to our RV.

It had rained occasionally during the day and at 1730 hours it commenced to rain heavily. After about half an hour the wadi became like a river, and as the men were lying concealed in the middle of bushes it took them some getting to higher ground. It kept on raining and we were unable to find shelter. An hour later I tried two of the time pencils and they did not work. Even had we been able to keep them dry it would not, in my opinion been practicable to have used them, as during the half hour delay on the plane would have rendered them useless.

I tried the instantaneous fuses and they did not work either.

I remained there that night hoping to dry the fuses, but the next day was cloudy and there was insufficient sun.

Also, I found that a deep wadi about twenty five yards wide, was running between us and the aerodrome, was full of water.

I withdrew that night, 18/11/41, some twenty miles on a bearing of 185 degrees. The next night I did a further five miles on that bearing and then turned due west for approximately three miles, where we contacted the LRDG.

There was nothing of importance seen on the withdrawal except two Italian tents… We moved up to them at dusk hoping to get rations but we found them empty.

The whole section have behaved extremely well and although lacerated and bruised in varying degrees by their landing, and wet and numb with cold, remained cheerful. Sgt MacDonald the Section Sergeant proved himself an extremely good and able NCO.

I am certain that given normal or even moderate weather our operation would have been entirely successful.

Nominal Roll:
Lieut, R.B. Mayne O/C., Sgts. MacDonald, Kershaw, Cpl. White, Pct's. Seekings, White, Hawkins, Arnold, Kendall, Chesworth and Bennett.

Signed: R.B. Mayne
Lieut. Royal Ulster Rifles

*   *   *

Account of Operation Squatter by Pct Bennett (undated)

November 17th 1941.
Left Kabrit for parachute operation with intention of dropping in two parties, one at GAZALA and the other at TMIMI, I being a member of the latter. Our party consisted of Lieut. Mayne, Sgt. MacDonald, Sgt. Kershaw, Cpl. White and Pcts. White, F., Seekings, Hawkins, Arnold, Kendall, Chesworth and myself.

We proceeded to BAGUSH where we went into the Officers' Mess; we were made very welcome and sat down to a dinner which was fit for a king, the kind of 'scoff' which the average soldier sees only when in the arms of Morpheus. An officer waited on us at the table, and he looked at us in such a way that we could imagine him saying, "I will them all that I can, as the poor chaps may not be coming back again!" It was just like having whatever you wished before going to the gallows.

At 22.30 hrs., we were all sitting in our planes as detailed. The pilot passed the remark that the wind was getting up, a fact with which we were not at all thrilled. We set off, and the next two and a half hours seemed to me a lifetime. It was cold – intensely cold. On arrival at our dropping area, we were greeted by slight flack. The time came to jump, and I have never seen a party leave a plane so quickly – incidentally, the planes we were using were the old troop – carrying Bombays.

On hitting the ground I immediately found myself dragged by the wind, I could not stop myself, but made desperate efforts to release my harness, this being a job for Houdini. I don't know just how far I was dragged but after being used as a human bulldozer for what seemed like an age, a lull in the fury of the gale allowed my 'chute to collapse. Purely by instinct and training I managed to get out of my harness and roll up the 'chute and bury it, a job which should have been done with the utmost quietness, but owing to the ground in the vicinity being very hard indeed, I made enough noise with my entrenching tool to awaken the whole of the Africa Corps. The burying process completed, I caught sight of a figure approaching me. I was naturally dubious of his identity, but found that the man was one of the party – Pct. Seekings. Our next job was to find the rest of the party, and after walking round in ever increasing circles, we located them, to find that two members had received injuries on landing. We were then sent out in different directions to find the containers in which were our arms and rations and the main thing of all – water. Our luck was out; all we found were two out of eleven containers, the total bag being two tommy – guns, eight bottles of water and six blankets. Three bottles of water were handed to the injured members of the party together with a few rations. We shook hands with them, wished them luck, and set out to find our objective.

It was 0245 hrs. when we set off; we walked through the night and came across a Wadi in which we decided to lie up until darkness came again. In the meantime Sgt. MacDonald made a recce of the area. He reported back and gave the position of the drome which was two miles away.

The time for leaving our hide–out and proceeding to 'fix' the drome was laid down as 1830 hrs., the elements intervened – it rained as I have never seen it before – clouds broke by the score, and our nice dry little Wadi was transformed in a matter of minutes into a lake. We clambered to higher ground, trying to salvage what kit we had, but lost a lot in the process. We had to try to keep out some of the rain, by deciding to use one blanket per three men, having only managed to save three blankets for the nine of us. This proved none too effective, but was better than nothing at all, so with constant wringing out of the blankets, and an occasional sip at the old 'rum stakes' we managed to survive.

When morning came it was apparent that we were not now in a position to carry out an attack on the drome, so we made off for the rendezvous, where, by arrangement the L.R.D.G. should be waiting for us. A thirty-six hours' march brought us to the approximate position, and as we were by this time in an exhausted condition, we lay down. Seekings said that he could see a light in the distance; no-one seemed to take much notice, and Sgt. Kershaw said that it was not a light but a star low on the horizon, so the matter dropped.

Daylight came, we aroused ourselves, and started walking, when suddenly a truck appear-ed, but turned out to be one of the L.R.D.G. Patrol appointed to meet us. The first things to greet us were cigarettes. It was the finest fag I have ever tasted, as all ours had been destroyed by the rains. Those chaps got down to making a real good 'Scoff' and did we enjoy it!

We were then conveyed back to our base, the only incident being an attack by an Italian Savoya.

Appendix H

The five 'sticks' for Operation Squatter, 16 Nov 1941

Flight No. 1 – dep @ 19:30

1) Capt A.D. Stirling (Scots Guards/No. 8 Commando)
2) CSM G.H.A. Yates (Grenadier Guards/No. 8 Commando) – PoW
3) L/Sgt L. Colquhown (Scots Guards/No. 8 Commando) – PoW
4) Cpl R.D. Tait (Gordon Highlanders/No. 11 Commando)
5) L/Cpl J. Orton (Seaforth Highlanders/No. 11 Commando) – PoW
6) Pct S. Bolland (Scots Guards/No. 8 Commando) – not found but death from injuries sustained reported by Italians on 20.11.41
7) Pct E.J. Cockbill (Worcestershire Reg/No. 8 Commando) – PoW
8) Pct F.C. Trenfield (Oxfordshire & Buckinghamshire Light Infantry/No. 7 Commando) – PoW
9) Pct R.P. Alexander (Seaforth Highlanders/No. 11 Commando) – PoW (Participation unconfirmed but Casualty Report 684 records Alexander missing as of 16.11.1941 – a time when the Seaforths were not in theatre. It is therefore likely he took part in Operation Squatter with Stirling's stick the most likely candidate.)

Flight No. 2 – dep @ 19:40

1) Lt E.C. McGonigal (RUR/No. 11 Commando) – presumed dead from injuries sustained, Nov 41
2) Sgt R. Lazenby (Scots Guards/No. 8 Commando) – PoW
3) A/Sgt C. McCormack (Royal Scots/No. 11 Commando) – PoW
4) L/Cpl R.D. Evans (Welsh Guards/No. 8 Commando) – PoW
5) L/Cpl J.W. Maloney (Somerset Light Infantry/No. 8 Commando) – PoW
6) L/Cpl S. Hildreth (Sth Lancashire Reg/No. 7 Commando) – died from injuries sustained, 19.11.41
7) Pct W. Morris (Black Watch/No. 11 Commando) – PoW
8) Pct R.J. McKay (Scots Guards/No. 8 Commando) – PoW
9) Pct J.P. Robertson (Scots Guards/No. 8 Commando) – PoW

10) Pct R.D. Davies (Welsh Guards/No. 8 Commando) – PoW
11) Pct J. Blakeney (Coldstream Guards/No. 8 Commando) – PoW
12) Pct A. Westwater (Royal Artillery/No. 7 Commando) – PoW

Flight No. 3 – dep @ 19:50
 1) Lt J.S. Lewes (Welsh Guards/No. 8 Commando)
 2) Sgt J. Cheyne (Gordon Highlanders/No. 11 Commando) – presumed dead from injuries sustained, Nov 41
 3) Sgt C.G.G. Riley (Coldstream Guards/No. 8 Commando)
 4) Cpl J. DuVivier (Gordon Highlanders)/No. 11 Commando)
 5) L/Cpl J. Storie (Seaforth Highlanders/No. 11 Commando)
 6) L/Cpl G. Rose (Grenadier Guards/No. 8 Commando)
 7) L/Cpl W.G. Brough (Scots Guards/No. 8 Commando)
 8) Pct J. Cooper (Scots Guards/No. 8 Commando)
 9) Pct E.T. Lilley (Coldstream/No. 8 Commando)
10) Pct F. Rhodes (Grenadier Guards/No. 8 Commando)
11) Pct C. Cattell (East Surrey Regiment/No. 7 Commando)

Flight No. 4 – dep @ 20:00
 1) Lt C.J.L. Bonington (General List/50/52 ME Commando) – PoW
 2) Sgt E.R. Bond (Scots Guards/No. 8 Commando) – PoW
 3) Sgt S.J. Stone (Scots Guards/No. 8 Commando) – PoW but died from injuries sustained, 5.12.41
 4) Cpl R.S. Quinton (Royal Horse Guards/No. 8 Commando) – PoW
 5) Cpl J. Monaghan (Highland Light Infantry/No. 7 Commando) – PoW
 6) L/Cpl A. Smith (Scots Guards/No. 8 Commando) – PoW
 7) Pct D. Keith (Gordon Highlanders/No. 11 Commando) – PoW
 8) Pct D.M. Hill (Scots Guards/No. 8 Commando) – PoW
 9) Pct J. Sadler (Scots Guards/No. 8 Commando) – PoW
10) Pct A. Bridger (Scots Guards/No. 8 Commando) – PoW
11) Pct J. Keenan (The Green Howards/No. 7 Commando) – PoW
12) Capt F.C. Thomson (Frontier Force Rifles, Indian Army) – observer capacity – PoW

Flight No. 5 – dep @ 20:20
 1) Lt R.B. Mayne (RUR/No. 11 Commando)
 2) L/Sgt E. McDonald (Cameron Highlanders/No. 11 Commando)
 3) Cpl G. White (Royal Scots/No.11)
 4) Cpl D. Kershaw (Grenadier Guards/No. 8 Commando)
 5) L/Cpl D. Arnold (Liverpool Scottish/No.7 Commando) – PoW

6) L/Cpl J.W.E. Kendall (Royal East Kent Regiment/No.7 Commando) – PoW
7) Pct T.R. Chesworth (Coldstream Guards/No. 8 Commando)
8) Pct R. Bennett (Grenadier Guards/No. 8 Commando)
9) Pct A.R. Seekings (Cambridgeshire Regiment/No. 7 Commando)
10) Pct H. White (Royal Army Service Corps/No. 7 Commando)
11) Pct A. Hawkins (Royal West Kent Regiment/No. 7 Commando)

Second RV party (apart from Fraser, composition unconfirmed)
1) Lt W. Fraser (Gordon Highlanders/No. 11 Commando)
2) L/C J.V. Byrne (Gordon Highlanders/No. 11 Commando)
3) Pct J.H.M. Baker (Grenadier Guards/No. 8 Commando)
4) Pct A. Warburton (Welsh Guards/No. 8 Commando)
5) Pct A. Phillips (Royal Warwickshire Regiment/No. 7 Commando)

Active force: 54 plus 1 observer
Survivors: 21
PoWs: 29
Dead: 5

The number of survivors has often been stated as twenty-two as a result of the mistaken inclusion of Bill Fraser in the surviving officer count. However, Fraser was injured and his place in the operation was filled by Stirling. Fraser was instead put in charge of the second RV party.

Appendix I

Casualty Lists and Trenfield MID Award

SECRET
Casualty List No. 697 (Officers)
[As of 9am **17 Dec 1941**]
  1. Expeditionary Forces
     (a) Middle East
        Western Desert
        Missing
Royal Ulster Rifles
McGONIGAL W.S./Lieut. E.C. 97290 16.11.41

SECRET
Casualty List No. 892 (Officers)
[As of 9am **3 Aug 1942**]
  2. Expeditionary Forces
     (b) Middle East
        Western Desert
        Died of Wounds
Royal Ulster Rifles
McGONIGAL W.S./Lieut. E.C. 97290 17/18.11.41
(Previously shown on Casualty List No. 697 as Missing, 16.11.41)

714

  1. Expeditionary Forces (Contin.)   Date of Casualty
     (b) Middle East (Contin.)
        Cyrenaica
        Prisoner of War (Previously reported as Missing) Date of Missing
        Casualty

Seaforth Highlanders
The following was previously shown on Casualty List No.684 as Missing, 16/17.11.41
2819724 ALEXANDER   318.   Pte.   R.P.

RECOMMENDATION FOR AWARD

Brief account of activities whilst a prisoner of war

Pte. TRENFIELD, Frederick Charles
S.A.S. L Det.
D.D.P.W.

I propose to recommend TRENFIELD for the award of MENTIONED-IN-DESPATCHES for his Escaping Activities whilst a prisoner of war.

24 July 1946

The above Other Rank was a member of an Airborne Unit prior to his capture by the enemy.

I consider that, from the escape angle, he merits the award of MENTIONED-IN-DESPATCHES.

Pte. TRENFIELD, Frederick Charles.
S.A.S. "L" Det.

TRENFIELD was taken prisoner on the 30th November 1941 in LIBYA.

During his subsequent imprisonment in various camps in ITALY and GERMANY. He made six attempts to escape, all of which were unsuccessful. Methods of escape included tunnelling, disguise and wire cutting. TRENFIELD was finally liberated by the Americans on the 9th April 1945.

Appendix J

Extracts from a letter from the brothers' uncle David McGonigal in Cape Town to his sister, Dorothy McGonigal in Belfast

The *Cape Times*
Editorial Offices,
Burg Street, Cape Town
24/9/38

My dear Dorothy,

I have delayed writing to you until we had seen the boys off on their homeward journey once again, and now I can give you as much news as possible.

First of all, let me tell you about my evening with the Lord Justice, if you have not already heard of it …

The Rugby boys got back on Monday, September 5 after having lost the second Test match in Port Elizabeth on the Saturday. No one can blame them for they had to play in a temperature of 93 degrees in the shade. Such weather has never before been experienced at Port Elizabeth at this time of the year. It was too much for them, and almost too much for the South Africans.

It is said that in the dressing-room after the match, Sam Walker was sitting prostrate and asked for George Cromey – who, as you may know, was licensed as a Presbyterian minister the night before he sailed for South Africa. When George arrived he asked Sam what he wanted and got this reply: "Stand over there and talk to us about Heaven. We have had enough of the other place all afternoon."

Their journey back to Cape Town was by boat and they ran into a terrific storm just off Cape Agulhas. The bow rails of the ship were stove in and the baggage room got flooded, and altogether they had a nasty time.

During the week they took things very quietly to prepare for the final Test at Newlands on September 10. You will know by this time that all eight Irish boys were selected to play and that Britain won the match by 21 points to 16. It was the most wonderful Rugby international that I ever saw, and certainly was the most marvellous to be played in this country. Everyone was so thoroughly satisfied with the play that they are still talking about it and will go on talking about it for years to come.

There was one great feature of the game, and that was the crowd. As was natural over 90 per cent were yelling for South Africa and yell they did. But the display given by the British boys was so grand that the crowd simply forgot all about their favourites and ended by cheering the victors with full-throated roars. Sam Walker told me after the match that the greatest thrill of his Rugby career was when the final whistle blew and five of the Springboks hoisted him on their shoulders and chaired him off the field.

I was broadcasting the game for the Broadcasting Corporation, and my excitement got higher and higher until, in the end, it was only a hoarse voice that went over the air. However, everyone said it was a splendid running commentary and that was the main thing.

I was at the official dinner in the evening, which, under the circumstances, would have been better if it had been held at a later date. The boys were in no mood to listen to long-winded speeches, and the breaking of glass and the singing of songs and the shouting of happy hearts made a terrific din, above which the speakers' voices could hardly be heard.

I was impressed by the fact that the Cambrian Society had put up two evenings for the Welsh members of the party, and the Scots were entertained by the Caledonian Society, while the English lads had a night with the St. George's Association, but there was nothing for the eight Irish boys.

After a bit of thinking I got hold of my namesake, who is a male nurse in the Valkenberg Mental Hospital … one of the Donegal McGonigals had come out here years ago.

This member of the clan, whose name is Desmond … got married to a girl from Kerry. Of course, he belongs to the "True Church" and I have had many an evening with various Irish priests as a result.

This Kerry girl, Kathleen Leary, has given me potato cake, soda bread and wheaten bread, bacon and eggs on several occasions. So I had a brain-wave. I borrowed their flat at Green Point and we put up a real Irish tea for the boys. The whole eight of them came along and down they sat and bacon and eggs and soda bread and potato cake and wheaten bread disappeared like magic. Everyone of them, including wee George Cromey had five eggs each, and as for the rashers of bacon, no chartered accountant could have kept a tally of them.

After the meal some girls arrived and there was a sing song and a dance. The boys obliged with several of their team choruses and a pleasant time was had by all. They really did enjoy it all, for it was a complete break from their usual round of official functions, and I felt rather like father as I was by miles the oldest in the party.

On the Saturday I was again broadcasting the match they played against Combined Universities, when they won another wonderful game in the very last minute. On the Sunday I went and heard George Cromey preach, and was astonished. He is really good and should have a very successful career. He has a very natural style, without any arm flinging additions. He chose the parable of the Good Samaritan as his subject to talk on Neighbourliness, and there was no doubt that he got his message home to the congregation that overflowed the Church.

On Wednesday there was an unofficial match against the Combined Country, and in it the British selectors gave places to those who had not had a game for some time.

The result was a defeat, but then a defeat never upset our boys throughout the whole of the tour, which has been the most successful ever held in South Africa. Both on and off the field these lads have been tremendously popular and have made countless friends. This was proved in no uncertain way when they departed for home on Friday. Such a large crowd has never been seen at the Docks to bid farewell to a visiting team before.

Well, now they have gone and we are back to war and rumours of war. The situation appears to be critical at the moment, and everyone is wondering what will be the eventual outcome. The consensus of opinion here is that if only England and Germany can come to agreement, that fact, of itself, will bring France into the fold and then the peace of the world will be secure. On the other hand there is a doubtful feeling that the word of Hitler is not to be trusted, and that this move against the Czechs is but the prelude to further efforts to gain Rumania and Jugoslavia.

It is all very upsetting, for there can be no doubt whatsoever that Hitler has never given the world any idea that he is really the man of peace that he proclaims himself to be. The fact that he considered he is Divinely appointed to govern Germany and Germans everywhere, and that Germany, as a direct result, is appointed to rule the world, does not seem to me to spell the word Peace.

This week will see how it is all to end, but, at the moment, I fear that he will march into Chechoslovakia and will not be just satisfied with getting the Sudetens under his sway. He wants for more than that. He wants a port on the Mediterranean. Of course, he is in rather a difficult position. If he attacks the Czechs without reason, France and Russia will go to the assistance of the Czechs and where that move will end it is hard to foresee. To me it seems that the world will again be involved in a war of aggression. Another fear the Führer has is his inability to be sure if he can depend upon old Mussolini. Personally, I don't think he can for the Italian seems to me to be the kind of individual who will attack the untrained, unskilled and, to a large extent, the unarmed natives of a place like Abyssinia, but he will think twice and three times before he attempts to do the same with trained nations. Indeed, it will not be surprising if, in the end, he decides on benevolent neutrality until he sees which way the issue is likely to be decided, and then he will come in on the side of the victors and claim his share of the spoil.

The cruel thing about the whole business is, that while alleged Statesmen and mere politicians plot and plan the poor old world is steadily moving towards another period of slaughter, in which countless lives are to be sacrificed simply to satisfy the ill-judged vanity of two dictatorial puppets who have allowed things to get beyond their control. It is all too tragic for words, and it looks as if it will be far more tragic before it is all over. If ever a couple of bullets would help towards the settling of the world it is now – one in berlin and the other in Rome…

…It is interesting to contemplate what will occur in the courts now that Horner has died. It will not be at all surprising if some other outsider gets a job for a pal. How did they again pass over Uncle John when the Recordership of Derry was vacant. Has it now got to the stage that he is too old for an appointment. If so, they have jockeyed him about to their satisfaction. Sometimes I think he would have been a judge many years ago had he remained on in Dublin, where, at least, the law appointments have been made on merit and not because you beat a drum of a certain kind…

…I shall try to make it a weekly letter to you in the future. In the meantime alles van die beste, as they say out here.

Yours, David

Appendix K

Villa Punta operation instruction; Cherso operation instructions; 'L' Squadron nominal role; and Intelligence Report on Eastern Istria

"S" Squadron, Special Boat Service
Northern Adriatic Operation Instruction No. 5 – LUSSINO (VILLA PUNTA)

Ref Maps;- Italy 1/50,000. Sheets 89B – 3 & 4.
To;- Lieut Thomason.

1. COMPOSITION OF FORCE.

Lieut Thomason.	
Lieut Jones-Parry.	Rfn Lynch.
Sgt Geary.	Mne Bridger
Sgt McDougall.	Gnr Barlow.
Sgt Cameron.	~~Mne May~~
Cpl Morgan.	Mne Iggleden.
Cpl Bentley.	Rfn Stagg
Cpl Smith, K.	Rfn Lenney
L/C O'Lone	Pte Smith, A.
Cpl Mayall	Pte Madden
	Pte Potter
	Pte Allinson
	Mne Kitchingman
	1 Guide.

2. <u>TASK</u>.

You will attack and destroy the occupants of VILLA PUNTA 394485 and bring away any prisoners and equipment captured.

3. <u>METHOD</u>.

You will be landed at 413466 p.m. 6th March. You will proceed on foot to your objective. On completion of task you will return to point 413466 and be taken aboard the M.Ls.

In case of your party being disorganised and pick up point endangered you will go, after leaving one man to signal craft, to the alternative beach at point 400444 for two nights after the original pick up night.

4. <u>EQUIPMENT & STORES</u>.

Normal patrol weapons plus 1 PIAT & supply of bombs.

1 x 5 gallon can of petrol.

1 Everest carrier.

Supply of Lewis bombs.

4 rubber boats.

1 escape ration will be carried by each man.

5. <u>INTER COMMUNICATION</u>.

<u>LAMP.</u>   Shore to Ship – "A" – Come in and take off.

"K" – Go to alternative point.

"O" – th a WHITE light.

Major.

Field.   O.C. "S" Squadron, S.B.S.

6 March, 45

Distribution;-

Copy No. 1. Lt. Thomason.   Copy No. 2. Lt.Jones-Parry.

3. C.O.   4. O.C. "S" Sqn.

5. S.N.O.N.A.   6. HQ. LFA.

Capt McGonigal

"S" Squadron, Special Boat Service, Northern Adriatic Operation Instruction No. 11 – CHERSO (OSSERO 3167).

Ref Maps;- Italy 1/50,000. Sheets 77B II.
To;- Capt. A.J.McGonigal, MC.

1. COMPOSITION OF FORCE.

Capt. A.J.McGonigal. M.C.	Capt. J.C. Henshaw.
CAPT. ANDERSON ~~Capt K.H.J.L. Fox.~~	Lieut I.C.D.Smith.
Lieut B.J.S.S.Gallagher.	SSM Nicholson, J.
Sgt Henderson, P.	Sgt Holmes, R.
Sgt McDougall, W.	L/S Sibbett, J.
Cpl Jarrell, P.	Cpl Hawes, A.
Cpl Wright, D.	Cpl D'Arcy, M.
L/C Watler, R.	L/C Williams, D.
Pte Allen, W.	Pte Allinson, E.
~~Gnr Clark,~~ H.	Tpr Cree, J.
Pte Creevy, S.	Gnr Hendy, G.
Pte Laverick, G.	Rfn Lynch, J.
Rfn Lecomber, A.	Pte Madden, P.
Pte Millard, P.	Gnr Pirie, P.
Rfn Probin, L.	Gnr Ross, D.
Gnr Roberts, B.	Tpr Sanders, A.
Pte Smith, A.	L/C Millar, J. RAMC
L/C Bell, W. RE	*Gnr McKever.*
Tpr Harrison, C.)	
Tpr Shohot, V.)	Signallers.
Spr Howard, P.)	

2. INFORMATION.
Verbally from I.O., and photographs.

3. INTENTION.
   1. To attack and destroy the German Garrison at OSERO 3167.
   2. Render the Bridge unusable by the enemy.

4. <u>METHOD.</u>
    There will be two parties,
    (a) Folboat party.
    (b) Main Party.
        Folboat party will be landed at POINT OSSERO 2669 p.m. 16th.
        The Main Party will be landed by ML at 313687 p.m. 16th .
        Both parties will proceed to the target areas under party Commanders.
        The operation will be carried out in two phases.
    1. Destruction of the Garrison in the Town.
    2. The blowing of the Bridge at OSSERO.
        The Main Party will be picked up from the quayside at OSSERO, or
        in the event of the attack being unsuccessful at 313687. If this beach
        in endangered they will be taken off from BORA COVE 316678 on
        the night of 17/18.

5. <u>EQUIPMENT & STORES.</u>
    Patrol Weapons.
    3 PIATs & Bombs.
    Supplies of Lewis Bombs & Grenades.
    2 Depth charges & supply of plastic.
    Explosives & accessories.
    1 Goatley.
    3 Rubber dingys.
    3 B.C.611. Sets.

6. <u>INTER COMMUNICATION.</u>
    a. B.C. 611 Set.
    b. Lamp.

    <u>Shore to Ship.</u>
    "K" – OK Come into Jetty.
    "V" – Go to pick up point.
    "B" – Go to alternative pick up point tomorrow night between 2000 –
        2359 hrs

    <u>Ship to Shore.</u>
    White to flash.

Field.   Major.
16 March, 45 .   O.C. "S" Squadron, S.B.S.
                        Distribution;- Normal.

                                                    Copy No.…1.

"S" Squadron, Special Boat Service
Northern Adriatic Operation Instruction No. 11 – CHERSO (OSSERO 3167).

To;- O.C. "S". Squadron, Special Boat Service.
Ref Maps;- Italy 1/50,000. Sheets 77B II.

1. <u>COMPOSITION OF FORCE.</u>
    Capt. A.J.McGonigal. M.C. Capt. J.C. Henshaw.
    Capt. M.E. Anderson   Lieut I.C.D.Smith.
    Lieut B.J.S.S.Gallagher. SSM Nicholson, J.
    Sgt Henderson, P.   Sgt Holmes, R.
    Sgt McDougall, W.   L/S Sibbett, J.
    Cpl Jarrell, P.   Cpl Hawes, A.
    Cpl Wright, D.   Cpl D'Arcy, M.
    L/C Watler, R.   L/C Williams, D.
    Pte Allen, W.   Pte Allinson, E.
    Pte Creevy, S.   Tpr Cree, J.
    Pte Laverick, G.   Gnr Hendy, G.
    Rfn Lecomber, A.   Rfn Lynch, J.
    Pte Millard, P.   Pte Madden, P.
    Rfn Probin, L.   Gnr Pirie, P.
    Gnr Roberts, B.   Gnr Ross, D.
    Pte Smith, A.   Tpr Sanders, A.
    L/C Bell, W. RE   L/C Millar, J. RAMC
    Tpr Harrison, C.   )   Gnr McKeever, J.
    Tpr Shohot, V.   ) Sigs
    Spr Howard, P.   )

2. <u>INTENTION.</u>
    To attack and destroy the German Garrison at OSERO 3167.
    Render the Bridge unusable by the enemy.

3. <u>NARRATIVE.</u>

1532 hrs   18 March. Ship ZARA. aboard M.Ls 238 & 577.

2050 hrs   Off OSSERO Pt. Folboat party, Sgt Holmes & Rfn Lecomber, dropped off to land in Bay 304673.

2226 hrs   Off TANKA Pt. Launch assault boat.

2250 hrs   All boats away from M.Ls.

2310 hrs   Party landed and ready to move off from Pt 311685.

0245 hrs   19 March. Target was reached.
Lieut Smith and "K" Patrol investigate Church 313675 for reported M.G. post. Nothing there.
"P" Patrol under Capt Anderson break off at X Rds to attack Guard House from Jetty.

0300 hrs   "Z" Patrol reach Square by CHURCH. Indefinite challenge by Sentry, not located, unanswered. No action taken by party. "J" Patrol under Lieut Gallagher in position by Church on the main road.

0310 hrs   Patrol of 5 Italians approach Town from NORTH on the main road. Fire opened by "J" patrol. 4 of Patrol killed, I escaped. "J" and "Z" Patrols advance towards enemy positions.

0315 hrs   Fire opened on both Patrols by 4x8m.m. LMGs, 2 guns on each Patrol. Both Patrols find wire obstacles blocking their road and well covered by these LMGs. Fire returned by Bren guns and PIATs. Capt Henshaw killed by grenade. Lieut Smith takes over Patrol. Pte Laverick, Spr Howard and Tpr Sanders wounded. 2x20mm. open fire in support of LMGs. Niether Patrol able to advance. No sign of action from "P" Patrol of folboat party. "P" Patrol were unable to get into position.

3. <u>NARRATIVE</u> (Contd)

0315 hrs   19 March (contd)
A barbed wire barrier and hire walls made it impossible for "P" Patrol to gain a position to bring fire on the enemy. Sgt Holmes was unable to land until after engagement had started as an enemy patrol guarded his landing beach. This prevented him from reaching his position in time to join in the attack.

0350 hrs   Signal given to withdraw.

0410 hrs   Capt Henshaw evacuated from jetty 311675.
Enemy 20mm opened fire on M.L.

0445 hrs   Main party evacuate from landing point.

0503 hrs   M.Ls open fire on OSSERO TOWN, replied to by 20mm.

0520 hrs   M/Ls cease fire.

0530 hrs   Folboat back on board.

1010 hrs   Disembark at ZARA.

4. <u>INTELLIGENCE.</u>

    (a) Intelligence report made to I.O.

    (b) Beach Intelligence from the point of landing.

        The coast to the jetty, 311675, is rocky and with fairly deep water close in. It should be possible to land from L.C.Ps. The jetty at 311675 is about 30 ft, of stone and, as far as could be ascertained, with sufficient water to take an M.L. alongside. There are two smaller jetties to the NORTH in the same Bay.

5. <u>CASUALTIES.</u>

    (a) Own Casualties.   1 killed.   Capt, Henshaw.

                         3 wounded.   Tpr Laverick.

                                   Spr Howard.

                                   Tpr Sanders.

    (b) Enemy Casualties. 9 killed.

                               2 wounded.

Field.

21 March, 45.

A McGonigal

Capt

L. Squadron.

H.Q.Patrol.	A. Patrol.
Major McGonigal.	Capt. Clark.
Capt. Witt.	Cpl. Bentley
SSM. Newland.	Cpl. Hawkins.
Cpl. Layzell.	Gnr. Cooper.
Cpl. Moran.	Mne. Heathcote.
Sgm. Wanless.	Tpr. Southwood.
Cpl. Bowles.	Tpr. Birrell.
Cpl. Webster.	Fus. McFaddenn.
Spr. Golding.	~~Pte. Scrivens.~~
Capt. Balsillie	Tpr. Hill.
S.G.M.S. Summers.	Tpr. Humphris.
B. Patrol.	C. Patrol.

Capt. Govier.
Sgt. McKenzie.
Cpl. Geal.
L/c. Rutter.
Pte. Jones.
R "Begley.
Mne. Hannaway.
Pte.Woodcock.
Tpr. O'Connell.
Tpr. Jenner.
Pte. Dignum.

Lieut. Lorimer.
Cpl. Hessell.
L/c. Ainsley.
Mne. Slee.
Tpr. Maynard.
Tpr. Elliott.
Gnr. Singleton.
Pte. Hough.
Pte. Hourahine ?.
L/Bdr. Marshall.
Gnr. Marshall.

D. Patrol.
Capt. Lodwick.
Sgt. Nixon.
Cpl. Stewart.
Gnr. Small.
Cfm. Wright.
Tpr. Chisholm.
Pte. Murray.
Pte. Powell.
Gnr. Smout.
Tpr. Nestor.
Tpr. Fox.
CFM. Wright

X. Patrol.
Capt. Stobie.
Sgt. Long.
Cpl. Clarke.
Cpl. Bagley.
Pte. Martin.
Mne. Waddell.
Gnr. Hall.
Gnr. Saunders.
Tpr. Smith.
Tpr. O'Neill.
Sgm. Cressey.
Sgm. Le Savage.

Remainder:-
Capt. Balsillie.
L/c. Geraghty.
Pte.Brighty.
Cpl. Martlew.

SOMS. Summers.
Gnr. Wrigg.
L/b. Greene.

To:- O.C., 'L' Sqdn
From:- I.O., 'L' Sqdn.

INTELLIGENCE REPORT.
EASTERN ISTRIA from 5 Apr 45 to 25 Apr 45.

I.   ENEMY MOVEMENTS.
     Movement of troops from SOUTH to NORTH appears to have started
     on about 1 April. These movements are confined to small bodies mainly
     under 200 strong and seem to originate in POLA. Local partisans
     report that POLA is being evacuated. It is more likely, however, that the
     garrison there is being thinned. Movement is effected on a [shunting]
     system. Small garrisons are thinned or completely evacuated to the
     NORTH. Where necessary, these are replenished by reinforcements
     from ARSIA, which in turn is furnished by reinforcements from
     POLA.
        Up to 24 April 45, routes used for this movement were as follows:-
     (i) DIGNANO (8896) – GIMINO (9216) – PISINO (9527) –
          CERRETO (0131) – MATTUGLIE (2541).
     (ii) DIGNANO – BARBANA (0108) – ALBONA (0910) – SAN
          DOMENICA (0816) – VALDARGA (1128) – AURANIA
          (1136) – MATTUGLIE.
     As a result of Partisan operations on the Eastern coast of ISTRIA,
     the VALDARGA – MATTUGLIE section of route (ii) is in little
     use, and VALDARGA has been reported evacuated. Up to 24 April,
     there was, however, spasmodic movement along the FELICIA (1024) –
     VALDARGA road, but the majority of movement appears to follow the
     minor road [P???NA] (0323) – GALLIGNANA (0125) to PISINO.
        A Partisan brigade is reported to be on its way to attack SAN
     DOMENICA, and a battalion of this brigade attacked a German
     column on 24 April, on the FELICIA – VALDARGA road. It may be
     presumed now that this road will be completely denied to the enemy.
     It would appear that the intentions of this Partisan brigade is to march
     on ALBONA and eventually attack ARSA, and this, coupled with the
     operations on [Futuae?] [a location in the EAST], will probably result
     in enemy troops being confined to the Western roads and proceeding
     NORTH in the TRIESTE direction.
        It is unlikely that the enemy will evacuate ARSA and ISTRIA
     SOUTH of ARSA without a struggle. Partisan opinion is that he will

attempt to retain the POLA – PISINO – TRIESTE triangle to the end.

II.   <u>ENEMY MORALE</u>.
Spasmodic desertions to the Partisans appears to be leaving a core of die-hard Fascists and Germans who retain good discipline. Troops around SAN DOMENICA have stated that they have nothing to lose by fighting to the last man.

III. RELATIONS BETWEEN THE PARTISANS AND CIVILIANS.
Civilians in Eastern ISTRIA do not appear whole-hearted in their support of the Partisans. The Partisans have lived off the country for long periods without producing concrete results. Small items such as vociferous civilian complaints about the misuse of their donkeys by the Partisans show that while outwardly submissive, many feel the presence of Partisans in their neighbourhood to be a burden. A large proportion of Istrians have been sailors, many working for years with the Cunard Line. They were disposed to be most friendly to British troops with whom they came in contact. This friendliness was openly discouraged by the Partisans. Incidents ranging from the Partisans forbidding civilians from accepting cigarettes from troops, to the arrest of a girl whom they considered over-friendly, illustrate Partisan insistence on aloofness vis-à-vis the British.

It was noticeable that in spite of political complications which resulted in the Partisans at one stage forbidding the civilians to help the British in any way, much help was given unofficially, local villagers furnished troops with eggs, and other food, although the Partisans had ordered that the British should be fed only through Partisan channels – local guides helped in reconnaissance entirely on a good will basis – donkeys were produced by villagers when the Partisans claimed that none were available. These and other examples show that the views of civilians with regard to the desirability of the presence of British troops by no means coincided with those of the Partisans. Expressions of regret on our evacuation appeared genuine.

<u>27 Apr 45.</u>   Capt., I.C., 'L' Sqdn S.B.S.

DISTRIBUTION:-

C.C., SBS.	1
L.F.A.	2
37 Mil Mission.	1
File	1
O.C., 'L' Sqdn	1

Bibliography and Sources

Published Sources

Almonds-Windmill, Lorna: *Gentleman Jim* (2001, Constable)

Asher, Michael: *The Regiment: The Real Story of the SAS* (2007, Viking), reissued as *The Regiment: The Definitive Story of the SAS* (2018, Penguin)

—— *Get Rommel* (2004, Weidenfeld & Nicolson)

Barry, Tom: *Guerrilla Days in Ireland* (1949, Irish Press Ltd)

Belfast Telegraph (various)

Benson-Gyles, Dick: *The Boy in the Mask: The Hidden World of Lawrence of Arabia* (2016, Lilliput)

Bradford, Roy and Dillon, Martin: *Rogue Warrior of the SAS* (1987, J. Murray)

Brittain, Vera: *Testament of Youth* (1933, Victor Gollancz Ltd)

Bryan, Gerald: *Be of Good Cheer* (2008, Wilton)

Byrne, J.V.: *The General Salutes a Soldier* (1986, Robert Hale Ltd)

Clongowes Wood College school annuals (various, including 1930–1938)

Cooper, Johnny: *One of the Originals: The Story of a Founder Member of the SAS* (1991, Pan Books Ltd)

Cowles, Virginia: *The Phantom Major: The Story of David Stirling and the SAS Regiment* (1958, Collins)

Daily Telegraph (various)

Davie, Michael (ed): *Diaries of Evelyn Waugh* (1976, Weidenfeld & Nicolson)

deZeng IV, H.L.: *Luftwaffe Airfields in Libya and Egypt between 1935 and 1945*

Dillon, Martin: *The Trigger Men* (2004, Mainstream Publishing)

Doherty, Richard: *In the Ranks of Death: The Irish in the Second World War* (2010, Pen & Sword)

Geraghty, Tony: *The Irish War* (1998, Harper Collins)

Halliday, Hugh A.: *Valour Reconsidered* (2006, Robin Brass Studio Inc

Hart, Sir Anthony: 'The Independent Bar of Northern Ireland – Past and Present' (2017, Wales & Chester Circuit lecture)

HMSO, *Combined Operations* (1942)

Hoe, Alan: *David Stirling: Founder of the SAS* (1992, Little, Brown)

Hunter, Robin: *True Stories of the SBS* (1998, Ebury Publishing)

Irish Times: various, including John O'Sullivan, 'Paddy Mayne, The bravehearted Irish Lion who joined the SAS' (2017) and Roisin Ingle, 'This idea that victims shouldn't speak … it's moral blackmail' (2011)

James, Malcolm [Malcolm Pleydell]: *Born of the Desert: With the SAS in North Africa* (1945, Collins)

Jellicoe, Nicholas C.: *George Jellicoe: SAS and SBS Commander* (2021, Pen & Sword)

Jones, Tim: *SAS: The First Secret Wars* (2005, Tauris)

—— *SAS Zero Hour: The Secret Origins of the Special Air Service* (2006, Naval Institute Press)

Ladd, James D.: *SBS: The Invisible Raiders* (1983, Arms & Armour Press)

Langley, Mike: *Anders Lassen VC, MC of the SAS* (1988, Hodder & Stoughton Ltd)

Lawyer, The: 'Ireland's Tribunal Millionaire' (February 1999)

Ledwidge, Francis ('Poet of the Blackbirds'): *Letter to Professor Chase* (1917, BEF Ypres)

Legrain & Brugeas: *The Regiment* (2019–21, Cinebook)

Lewes, John: *Jock Lewes, Co-founder of the SAS* (2000, Pen & Sword)

Lewis, Damien: *The Nazi Hunters: The Ultra-Secret SAS Unit and the Quest for Hitler's War Criminals* (2015, Quercus)

Lodwick, John: *The Filibusters. The Story of the Special Boat Service* (1947, Methuen & Co Ltd) reissued as *Raiders from the Sea: The Story of the Special Boat Service in WWII* (1990, The Naval Institute Press)

Macintyre, Ben: *SAS Rogue Heroes* (2016, Crown Publishing)

McHarg, Ian: *Litani River* (2011, SHN)

Macpherson, Sir Tommy: *Behind Enemy Lines* (2010, Mainstream Publishing)

Marrinan, Patrick: *Colonel Paddy* (1968, The Ulster Press)

—— *Paisley: Man of Wrath* (1973, Anvil)

Mather, Sir Carol: *When the Grass Stops Growing* (1997, Pen & Sword)

Messenger, Charles: *The Commandos 1940–1946* (1985)

Morgan, Mike: *Daggers Drawn* (2000, Spellmount)

Mortimer Gavin: *Stirling's Men* (2004, Orion)

—— *The SAS in World War II: An Illustrated History* (2011, Osprey)

—— *The Men Who Made the SAS: The History of the Long Range Desert Group* (2015, Constable)

—— *Kill Rommel! Operation Flipper 1941* (2014, Osprey)

—— *The Daring Dozen: 12 Special Forces Legends of World War II* (2012, Osprey)

—— 'The SAS and David Stirling's Leap of Faith' (30 July 2012)

—— *The SBS in World War II* (2013, Osprey)

O'Connor, Steven: *Irish Officers in the British Forces, 1922–45* (2014, Palgrave)

—— 'Why did the Irish volunteer as British officers in WWII?' (July 2014, *Irish Times*)

O'Dowd, Gearóid: *He Who Dared and Died: The Life and Death of an SAS Original, Sergeant Chris O'Dowd MM* (2011, Pen & Sword)

O'Neill, John: *Legendary Warrior of the SAS* (2015, Tommies Guides)

Parker, John: *S.B.S. The Inside Story of the Special Boat Service* (1997, Headline)

Pitt, Barrie: *Special Boat Squadron* (1983, Century Publishing)

Purdon, Corran: *List the Bugle: Reminiscences of an Irish Soldier* (1993, Greystone Books Ltd) (plus personal correspondence)

Ross, Hamish: *Paddy Mayne* (2003, Sutton Publishing)

SAS Regimental Association: *The SAS War Diary 1941–1945* (2011, Extraordinary Editions)

Stevens, Gordon: *The Originals: The Secret History of the Birth of the SAS* (2005, Ebury Press)

Stevens, Julie Anne: *Political Animals* (2011, OUP, in *Synge and Edwardian Ireland*)

Sutherland, David: *He Who Dares* (1999, The Naval Institute Press)

Taylor, Peter: *The Provos: The IRA and Sinn Fein* (1997, Bloomsbury)

Urwin, Margaret: *Counter-Gangs: A history of undercover military units in Northern Ireland 1971–1976* (2012, Spinwatch)

van der Bijl, Nicholas: *Commandos in Exile: The Story of 10 (Inter-Allied) Commando, 1942–1945* (2008, Pen & Sword)

Vick, Alan: *Snakes in the Eagle's Nest – A History of Ground Attacks on Air Bases* (RAND, a 1995 US Air Force report)

Waugh, Evelyn: *Officers and Gentlemen* (1955, Chapman & Hall)

Wynter, Brigadier H.W. DSO/Public Record Office: *Special Forces in the Desert War 1940–1943: The History of the Long Range Desert Group, June 1940 to March 1943* (2001, St Edmundsbury Press/Public Record Office)

'X', ex-Lance Corporal, QGM: *The SAS and LRDG Roll of Honour 1941–47 ('Deeds Show' Vol I; 'Utmost Devotion' Vol II; 'We Were Good Men' Vol III)* (2016, Cedar Group)

Online

Facebook groups: Special Air Service *WW11 Family and Friends Research Group. WW2 Middle East Commandos/Layforce Research Group*

www.britishnewspaperarchive.co.uk

www.combinedops.com: Graham Lappin: '11 (Scottish) Commando – The Black Hackle'

www.commandoveterans.org

www.findmypast.co.uk

www.forces.net: 'The SAS And Paddy Mayne – The Man Behind The Legend' (2020)

www.kingsinns.ie

www.tapatalk.com/groups/*parareunionclub*/general-f1

www.thequietmancunian.com: *Bill Fraser's War Diary* (2016)

https://voiceforarran.com

Wikipedia (various)

https://warfarehistorynetwork.com: Kelly Bell: 'Commando Paddy Mayne: Ireland's Wolf of the Desert'

www.ww2talk.com

Other

Hardiman Library Archive, NUI, Galway (thanks to Professor Kevin Boyle)

National Archives, Kew (various)

Orton, Alan: Rogues and Vagabonds and The Rhodes to Nowhere

Smith, Ian: The Happy Amateur (unpublished memoir, IWM)

Stirling, David, interview (Imperial War Museum)

Index

References to illustrations are in **bold**

Adair Arms Hotel, Ballymena, **36**
Addition, Operation, 77
Aircraft:
  Bristol Blenheim, 154
  Bristol Bombay, **138**, **153**
  Fairey Albacore, 154
  Messerschmidt Bf 109, **165**
Aircraft destroyed by SAS, 194–5
Airgraphs, 106–7, 131
Aiteniyé (Litani River), 89–90
Al Jaghbub oasis, **184**, 185–6, **186**
Almonds, Jim (writer), 109
Arran, Isle of, **46**, 47–64, **48, 49, 51, 52, 55**
Asher, Michael (writer), 99–100, 102
Auchinleck, General Sir Claude, 112, 158
Australian forces, 81–94, **90**

Ballygally, County Donegal, **10**
Ballymena Castle, **38**
Bardia, Libya, 77
Barry, Tom (soldier), 30–1
Beef Tribunal, 26
Bellamy, Corporal Robert, 214–16
Benina airfield raid, 194
Bennett, Parachutist Bob, 139–41, 167
Beret, SAS, 148
'The Black Prince' (AM's latter
  nickname), 263–4, **264**
Blakeney, Parachutist Jim, 247–9
Boccador, Sergeant Pierre-Charles, 208,
  213, 215, 218
Bolland, Parachutist Stanley, 170–1
Bonington, Charles, 113–17, 164–5
Boyle, Professor Kevin, 275
Browne, Albert Edward (UDA), 265–7
Bryan, Gerald, 62–4, **64**, 92, 114
Bully beef, **126**
Butler, Corporal H., 86

Cameronians (Scottish Rifles), 40–1
Capital punishment in Northern Ireland,
  265–7

Carson, Sir Edward, **6**
Carson, Lieutenant Colonel Robert
  'Jack', 14, 37
Charley, Colonel W. R. H., 241–3
Chetniks (pro-German Yugoslavian
  partisans), 227–8
Cheyne, Sergeant Jock, 170–1
Chiune Sugihara (Japanese diplomat),
  285
Churchill, Randolph, 58
Churchill, Winston, 42–4, 48–9, 223
Climate, desert, 150–2
Clongowes Wood College, **18**, 18–22
Combined Operations, 1940–1942
  (pamphlet), 258, **259**, 287–8
'Commando Order', Hitler's, 206–7
Commandos, formation of, 42–4
Conscription, 4–6, 33
Cooper, Parachutist Johnny, 164, 167,
  173
Cowan, Admiral Sir Walter, 55–7, **56**,
  68–9
Crete, 79
Croatia, 232–40
Crusader, Operation, 153–4
  see also Squatter, Operation
Cyprus, 78

D'Arcy, Guardsman M., 110–11
Davies, Parachutist Roy, 247–50
Davoren, Ambrose J. S. (uncle), 30
Davoren, Carmen (aunt), 30
Davoren, Margaret
  see McGonigal, Margaret (mother)
Davoren, May (aunt), 30
Davoren, Richard 'Birdie' (grandfather),
  14–17, **16**
Deeny, Sir Donnell, 264, 275–6
Defence Forces, Irish, 28
Dignac, Sergeant Andre, 213, 215–16
Diplock Courts (Northern Ireland),
  268–9, 271

Disenchantment by commandos, 76–8
Duffy, Parachutist Joe, 118, 137–9
DuVivier, Jeff, 155, 169–70

Eden, Captain (interpreter in
   Yugoslavia), 227–8
Exporter, Operation, 80–92

Famagusta, Cyprus, 78
Ferguson, Richard 'Dick' (QC), 264
Flipper, Operation, 154
'Forfar' raids, 207–9
Fraser, Lieutenant Bill, 44, 118, **118,**
   160–1
Fynn, Major Francis 'Ted,' 207–8

Galashiels, 44–7
Gallant, Steve, 284
Garland, Captain Eric, 89
Gazala airfields, Libya, 149–50, 244,
   251, 255–6
Glenearn, HMS, 68, 77
Glengyle, HMS, 77, 80–1, **81,** 84
Glenroy, HMS, 68
Gornall, Jim (No. 11 Commando), 94,
   247–8

Hailsham, Lord, 275
Hardtack, Operations, 213–18, **218**
Harran, Gordon (RUC), 265–7
Heliopolis airfield practice raid, 144–7
Hero, definition of, 284–6
Hiltforce, 220–2
Hilton-Jones, Captain Bryan, 220
Hitler, Adolf, 206
Holden, William (convicted killer), 266
Holmes, Sergeant, 233
Hore-Belisha, Leslie (SoS for War), 33

Irish War of Independence, 1–6

Jalo oasis, 192–3
Jellicoe, Lieutenant Colonel George, 196,
   212, 232
Jersey, raid on, 212–13

Kabrit training camp, Egypt, 122–33,
   125
Kafr Badda Bridge, Litani River, 86
Kauffman, Lance Corporal, 124–6
Keith, Private Doug, 133
Kershaw, Parachutist Dave, 166–7, 173
Keyes, Lieutenant Colonel Geoffrey, 82,
   94–6, **101,** 102, 198

'Kim's game', 128
King's Inns, Dublin, 12, 16, 23–6, **25**
Kipling, Rudyard (writer), 28
Knives, combat, **129**

'L' Detachment
   see Special Air Service Brigade, 'L'
      Detachment
Lamlash, Arran, 58–60, **62**
Landing Craft, Assault, **85**
Landladies, generosity of, on Arran,
   60–1
Landour Cottage, Lamlash (Arran),
   58–9, **59**
Lappin, Jimmy, 86
Lawrence, T. E., 111–12
Lawson, Piper Jimmy, **74,** 75
Lawton, Sir Frederick, 205
Laycock, Lieutenant Colonel Peter, 210,
   217–18
Laycock, Major General Robert, 58–9,
   76, 95, 112–13
Layforce, 76–7, 95–6
Layforce II, 210–11
Ledwidge, Francis (poet), 27–8
Legal system, Irish, 25–6
Lessing, Peter (war correspondent), 230
Lewes, Lieutenant John 'Jock,' 69,
   109–13, 123–4, 127–8, 133, **133, 161**
   and Operation Squatter, 174–6
   killed, 196
Lewes bomb, 127, 143
Lions rugby team, British and Irish,
   35–7, 73
Litani River, Syria, 79–91, **80, 83**
Lloyd Owen, Major General David,
   194–5
Lodwick, Captain John, 226, 232, 239
Long Range Desert Group (LRDG), 96,
   108, **149,** 184

MacDermott, Lord Chief Justice, 276
McElhone, Paddy (NI shooting victim),
   268
McGonigal, Major Sir Ambrose (AM),
   241–3
   birth, 1
   awarded Military Cross, 207, 217–18,
      222, **229**
   childhood, 9–10, **10, 11, 14,** 14–16, **17**
   schooldays, 18–20, **19, 20**
   joins Royal Ulster Rifles, 27, 32, 34
   selected for SBS, 201
   and Eoin's disappearance, 201–4

marries Patricia Taylor, 202–4, **203**
joins No. 12 Commando, 205
returns to Royal Ulster Rifles, **205,**
    241, **241**
and Fynn Force, 208–9
joins Layforce II, 210
and Sark raids, 212–18
and Tarbrush raids, 220–2
joins Special Boat Service, 223–5
in Yugoslavia, 226–9
in Croatia, 232–40
in Cairo, 242–3
record of service, **243**
called to Belfast Bar, 261
knighted, 263
nicknamed 'the Black Prince', 263–4,
    264
during Northern Ireland troubles,
    263–77
hands down death sentence, 265–7
views on torture, 271–3
son Eoin, 278–9
death, 274
McGonigal, Cattie (sister), 14, **14**
McGonigal, David (cousin), 29–30, 36
McGonigal, Dorrie (aunt), 30
McGonigal, Eoin (AM's son), 26, 278–9,
    280
McGonigal, Lieutenant Eoin (EM):
    birth, 1
    childhood, 9–10, **10, 11, 14,** 14–16,
        15
    schooldays, 18–22, **21**
    joins Royal Ulster Rifles, 27, 32, 34
    writes short stories, 39–40, 105, 132
    'Ian O'Donnell' pseudonym, 39–40
    serves with the Cameronians, **40,**
        40–1, **68**
    joins No. 11 (Scottish) Commando,
        41–2, **45**
    silver cigarette case, 54, 92, 279, **280**
    and plan to capture Rhodes, 67–77
    in Cyprus, 78
    in Litani River landing, 82–8
    disenchanted about Commandos,
        104–5
    joins 'L' Detachment, SAS Brigade,
        113–21
    in Kabrit, **123,** 123–32
    parachute training, **136, 137**
    and Heliopolis airfield practice raid,
        145–6
    and Operation Squatter, 149–57,
        182–3, 189–91

disappearance, 183, 188–90, 244–56,
    280
last photograph, **260**
prayer card, 288–9, **289**
McGonigal, Harold (cousin), 30
McGonigal, Ina (sister), 13
McGonigal, John (father), 1–8, **1, 4, 6**
McGonigal, Kathy (aunt), 30
McGonigal, Letty (sister), **17,** 37
McGonigal, Margaret (mother), 14–17,
    16, 203, 257–9
McGonigal, Michael (grandfather), 23
McGonigal, Peggy (sister), 13–14
McGonigal, Richard 'Dick' (brother),
    12–13, **12, 13,** 23, 33
McGonigal, Robert (cousin), 29
Machrie Bay, Arran, **61**
Maclean, Brigadier Fitzroy, 223
McPherson, Lieutenant Tommy, 49,
    69–70, **70**
McRitchie, Michael (NI journalist), 262,
    265–7
Malone Road, Belfast (brothers' teenage
    home), **9,** 9–10
Ma'ten Bagush, **186**
Mather, Lieutenant Colonel Carol, 129
Mayne, Lieutenant Colonel Robert Blair
    'Paddy', 35–6, **45,** 63–4, 92–103, **103,**
    187, 193–4, **195, 199**
    writes home, 60–2
    passionate about Ireland, 73–5
    joins 'L' Detachment, SAS Brigade,
        114–15
    and Operation Squatter, 166, 171–4
    agonises over loss of EM, 183, 188–9
    award of VC downgraded, 196–200,
        284
    investigates EM's disappearance,
        244–6
    post-war years, 278–9
Mine, Teller, **221**
More, Captain George, 82, **84,** 87–8
Morris, Dick, 232
Morris, Parachutist Billy, 247–8
Motor Torpedo Boat (MTB), 208, **211,**
    212

Napier, Lieutenant Charles, 99–101, **101**
Norney, Leo (NI victim), 269–70
Northern Ireland troubles, 263–77

O'Connor, Steven (writer), 31–2
'O'Donnell, Ian'
    see McGonigal, Lieutenant Eoin (EM)

Officers, No. 11 Commando, **97, 98**
Ogilby, Ann (NI victim), 269
Ossero Bridge, Croatia, 236–40, **237, 238**

Pantelleria island, 65–7
Parachute training, 109–11, 134–43, **135, 136, 137, 138, 140, 141, 142**
Patterson, Major Ian, 232
Pedder, Lieutenant Colonel Richard 'Dick', 44–8, **45**, 70–2, **72**, 89
Pigeons, homing, 208
Pleydell, Malcolm (SAS medical officer), 74–5
Poitín (illegal alcohol), 15
Purdon, Colonel Corran, 37–8

Quâsmiyeh Bridge, Litani River, 80, **82**
Queen's University, Belfast, 23, 35–6, 261

Rhodes island, 67
Riley, Sergeant Pat, 140, 170–1, 174–5, **175**
Rising Sun Inn, Warsash, **224**
Ritchie, General Sir Neil, 112
Robertson, Parachutist John, 249–50
Royal Irish Rifles, 34–5
   see also Royal Ulster Rifles
Royal Ulster Rifles, 34–41, **35**

Sark Island, 212–18, **212, 215**
SAS
   see Special Air Service Brigade, 'L' Detachment
Saunders, Hilary St George, 287–8
Seekings, Parachutist Reg, 134, 167
Sheean, Ordinary Seaman Teddy, 199
Sidi Haneish airfield, 194
Small Scale Raiding Force, 201, **220**, 223
Smith, Lieutenant Ian, 210, 219–25, 229–30
Smith, Molly (Paddy Taylor's mother), **202**
Smith, Philip (Paddy Taylor's grandfather), **202**, 202–3
Special Air Service Brigade, 'L' Detachment, **147, 185**, 192–5
   badge, 148, **148**, 185
   training, 108–22, 134–43
Special Boat Service/Squadron (SBS), 196, 223, 226–31, **231**
Special Raiding Squadron (SRS), 196, 223

Special Service Training Instructions, 44
Squatter, Operation, 145, 149–87
Stacpoole, Lieutenant Colonel Humphrey, 14
Starvation Order, 28
Stirling, Captain David, 59, 69, **125**, 139–41, **147, 161, 187**
   forms 'L' Detachment, SAS Brigade, 108–21
   and Operation Squatter, 149–64, 176–82
   and Benina airfield raid, 194
   captured, 196
   and EM's disappearance, 254–6
Storie, Corporal Jimmy, 127, 164
Suez Canal, 76
Sutherland, Lieutenant Colonel David, 232, 239
Syria, 79–91

Tait, Corporal Bob, 170, 177–9
Tarbrush, Operations, 220–2
Taylor, Patricia 'Paddy' (AM's wife), 201–2, **203**
Terrain, desert, **144, 168, 180**
Thomson, Captain F. C., 115, 150, 166
Tmimi airfield, Libya, 247–58
Toggle rope, **53**, 54, 214, 287
Torture in Northern Ireland, 271–3
Training, commando, 44–64, **53, 65, 66**
Trinity College, Dublin, 23

Victoria Cross (VC), 196–200, 284–5
Villa Punta, Lussino, Croatia, 233–6, **234**

Wadi Tamet airfield, 193
Wadis, **150, 151, 154, 173**
Warburton, Parachutist Ken, 118, 137–9
Ward, Gerry, 123
Wards Inquiry, 1936, 7–8
Waugh, Evelyn (writer), 56–8, 67, 72
Wavell, General Archibald, 76
Weapons, 128–9, **129, 130**
Welch, Sergeant Kenneth 'Joe', 158–60, 188–9
West, Flight Sergeant Charlie, 164–5
'Who Dares Wins' motto, 148
Willys jeep, **147, 185**, 192
Workman Clark Debenture case, 3
Workshop, Operation, 65–7

Yugoslavia, 223–9